Richard of Cornwall

The seal of Richard of Cornwall as the enthroned king of the Romans.

RICHARD OF CORNWALL

THE ENGLISH KING OF GERMANY

DARREN BAKER

AMBERLEY

First published 2022

Amberley Publishing
The Hill, Stroud
Gloucestershire, GL5 4EP

www.amberley-books.com

Copyright © Darren Baker, 2022

The right of Darren Baker to be identified as
the Author of this work has been asserted in
accordance with the Copyright, Designs and
Patents Act 1988.

ISBN 978 1 3981 1217 9 (hardback)
ISBN 978 1 3981 1218 6 (ebook)

British Library Cataloguing in Publication Data.
A catalogue record for this book is available
from the British Library.

1 2 3 4 5 6 7 8 9 10

Typesetting by SJmagic DESIGN SERVICES, India.
Printed in the UK.

CONTENTS

PREFACE

Two kings died in England in 1272. They were the king of England himself, Henry III, and his younger brother Richard, the earl of Cornwall. Richard was also the king of the Romans, an elective title he had pursued in the hope of becoming Holy Roman Emperor. It would have made him the only Englishman to occupy the imperial throne, but because it eluded him in the end, he is remembered today as neither king nor emperor, but simply as Richard of Cornwall.

At the time of his enthronement in 1257, Richard was one of the most famous men in Europe. A natural and widely travelled diplomat, he had successfully negotiated treaties from Scotland to the Holy Land, had earned the trust and favours of queen, pope, sultan, and emperor alike. Henry not only made use of his skills but encouraged and supported his brother's ambitions because they fit nicely into his own international strategy. They also provided Richard with an outlet for his overweening vanity.

Not that he appreciated any of it. Being completely dependent on Henry since they were children made him resentful and desperate to be his own man. At the age of sixteen, he sought marriage to a Spanish princess. Two years later it was to a Scottish princess. He eventually married a widow countess with six children, but in each case he went against his brother, who later had to bribe him into marrying his second wife. She was beautiful, French and twenty years younger. Richard survived her by a decade. His third wife, who was beautiful, German and forty years younger, outlived him, but just barely. Through it all, his womanising produced almost as many children outside of marriage as within.

The other great love of his life was money. Henry may have put him on the road to riches, but Richard exploited it to the hilt. As a tenacious landlord, mint operator, and crusade fundraiser, he amassed a fortune that made him the wealthiest man in England, if not in Europe. All he needed to dignify his newfound stature was a title with more allure to it than 'earl'. The untimely death of the king of the Romans gave him his chance. Had it not been for the tortured politics of the era, he might have gone on to attain the empire itself. Charlemagne, Otto the Great, Richard of Cornwall.

Few people besides himself and his brother mourned the missed opportunity. Richard and Henry had been raised to think of themselves on the world stage, but that was no longer the case for their countrymen. The loss of Normandy under their father King John had turned England into an inward-looking island kingdom. The brothers' attempt to revive the glory of their dynasty on the continent met fierce resistance back home and nearly cost them their respective thrones.

Richard got off lightly compared to Henry, but he was still savaged in song and record. His royal title was disparaged and his captors gleefully called him names to underscore his arrogance and treachery. Over the centuries, his reputation recovered mostly because Henry's never did. He came to be seen as the more intelligent and competent of the two, the one who would have freed England from all foreign influence had fate put him on the throne instead.

The first modern biography of Richard to appear in English takes this approach. With its terse style and list of landholdings and financial transactions, Noël Denholm-Young's *Richard of Cornwall* has remained iconic since it came out in 1947. He does not spare Richard his failings, but his contempt for Henry overshadows the entire book. In a bizarre conclusion, he blames him for the fact that England never had a Holy Roman Emperor.

The second biography is even more disdainful of Henry, but wholly laudatory of Richard. When *The King of Almayne* was released in 1966, the United Kingdom was moving towards closer integration with Europe. Author T.W.E. Roche used this development to take another look at Richard's similar achievement seven centuries before then. He could not foresee that fifty years after his book appeared, the UK would wrench itself completely away. Although his work is riddled with romantic flourishes and wild assumptions, Roche provides a full account of Richard's reign in Germany, something Denholm-Young did not cover in any detail.

This biography reflects a natural progression. Having figured prominently in my biographies of Henry III, Simon de Montfort, and their two wives named Eleanor, Richard of Cornwall was in need of a new interpretation as well. It differs from the two previous biographies of him in one crucial aspect. My portrait of Henry reveals a far more capable and accomplished ruler than most historians are willing to admit. The misguided imbalance long nurtured between the two brothers has been replaced here by a sibling rivalry that simmered for much of their long lives.

Richard's feat was a peculiar one. He was king for fifteen years, longer than his namesake uncle Richard the Lionheart, but he spent only a quarter of that time ruling in Germany, where the king of the Romans was based. The lack of wider recognition of his reign owes to many factors, not least the difficulty of understanding the man himself. Richard of Cornwall never comes across so clearly as other historic figures of his time. He was never the heroic type that Ranulf de Blondeville was, nor the anti-hero embodied by Ranulf's protégé Simon de Montfort.

The only thing for certain is that fate got it right, at least as far as Richard's enormous ego was concerned. For better or worse, vanity was everything to him. His brother Henry III may have been king of England, but there were lots of those. He was the only Englishman to be king of Germany. That gives him a unique place in the histories of both countries and makes his story worth retelling.

Producing this first biography of Richard of Cornwall in more than half a century went smoothly in part thanks to the online community that regularly discusses the medieval world. Other historians who have used it as their own proving ground include Sara Cockerill, Sharon Bennett Connolly, John Paul Davis, Erica Laine, David McKinlay, and David Pilling. There is also Rich Price, whose expertise in Latin has helped a lot of us better navigate the records of that age, and Kathryn Warner, who found the inspiration for her medieval undertakings in an historic novel about Richard.

In closing, I would like to mention two Michaels here. Michael Ray's years of scholarship have culminated in the first ever biography of Richard's son, Edmund of Cornwall. He has kindly shared it with me in advance of publication. On a sadder note, I must mention the passing of Michael Clanchy, who was already a legend in this field when I ventured into it. At our last meeting, in a bookshop in Oxford just before the Covid era began, he expressed his usual encouragement and excitement when I discussed the plans for this book. He was as true and rare a gentleman as any of us might hope to meet.

TIMELINE

1199   John, the youngest son of Henry II Plantagenet and Eleanor of Aquitaine, becomes king of England at the death of his brother Richard I

1200   Marriage of John and Isabella of Angoulême

1204   Loss of Normandy

1207   The future Henry III born at Winchester

1208   Probable birth year of Simon de Montfort

1209   Richard of Cornwall born at Devizes

1210   Joan, the future queen of Scots, born

1214   Richard in Poitou with his parents and sister Joan, battle of Bouvines, the future Louis IX and empress Isabella are born

1215   Magna Carta enacted and repudiated, civil war breaks out

1216   Richard's youngest sister Eleanor born, King John dies, Henry is crowned

1218   Isabella of Angoulême goes back to France

1221   Joan marries Alexander II of Scotland

1223   Eleanor of Provence born

1224   Eleanor Plantagenet marries William Marshal II

1225   Richard knighted by Henry, leads an expedition to Gascony, starts calling himself the count of Poitou

1227   Richard made earl of Cornwall, joins other earls in rebellion against Henry and his minister Hubert de Burgh, seeks a princess bride in Scotland

1229   Richard receives Wallingford and Berkhamsted

1230   Simon de Montfort arrives in England, Richard joins Henry's expedition to Brittany

1231   Richard marries Isabel de Clare, her brother William Marshal II dies, Simon acquires Leicester

1233   Richard joins and then abandons Richard Marshal's uprising, his manors are attacked by insurgents

1235 Isabella Plantagenet marries Emperor Frederick II, Richard's son Henry of Almain born

1236 Richard vows to go on crusade, Henry III marries Eleanor of Provence

1238 Henry arranges the secret marriage of his sister Eleanor Marshal to Simon de Montfort, Richard briefly rebels on account of it, their other sister Joan dies

1239 The future Edward I born, Henry banishes Simon over his abuse of trust

1240 Richard's wife Isabel dies, he leaves on crusade

1241 Richard leaves the Holy Land, spends several months at the court of Frederick II, his sister Empress Isabella dies

1242 Richard joins Henry's doomed invasion of Poitou, returns home in a sea storm, vows to build an abbey

1243 Richard marries Sanchia of Provence

1245 Henry commences the reconstruction of Westminster Abbey, Richard the construction of Hailes Abbey

1246 Richard bribed by the pope into doing an about-face on papal taxes

1247 Richard goes on a pilgrimage to France with his son Henry, undertakes the recoinage of the realm

1249   Son Edmund born to Richard and Sanchia

1250   Richard goes to Lyon to negotiate with the papal court, he refuses their offer of the kingdom of Sicily, Louis IX's crusade is destroyed in Egypt, Frederick dies

1251   Consecration of Hailes Abbey

1252   Richard again refuses the offer of Sicily

1253   Henry goes to Gascony, appoints Queen Eleanor regent and Richard as her adviser

1254   First parliament with elected representatives, the queen goes to Gascony, Richard becomes regent, start of the Sicilian business

1255   Richard leads the opposition to the Sicilian business

1256   The king of the Romans dies, Richard's candidacy to succeed him

1257   Richard of Cornwall elected king of the Romans, goes to Germany with his family, coronation in Aachen, his election disputed by Alfonso X of Castile

1258   Famine in England, Richard sends relief ships from Germany, the Provisions of Oxford are drawn up, the peace treaty between England, France and Germany is delayed

1259   Richard returns to England, Simon and Eleanor de Montfort obstruct the treaty, Henry goes to Paris to seal it with Louis

1260   Richard helps avert an uprising by Simon and Edward, he goes to Germany in the expectation of receiving the imperial crown, returns disappointed

1261   Richard helps Henry overthrow the Provisions of Oxford, the barons defect to the king, Simon goes into exile in France, Sanchia dies

1262   Henry goes to France, Richard goes to Germany, Welsh uprising, Henry returns to unrest

1263   Richard returns, Simon leads an uprising against the king, Richard supports the Montfortians with troops, Henry denounces Richard, he bribes him back to his side, Simon's government collapses

1264   Louis nullifies the Provisions of Oxford, civil war breaks out, Henry and Richard take Northampton but are captured with Edward at Lewes, Richard and his sons are imprisoned at Wallingford, then Kenilworth

1265   Edward escapes, defeats and kills Simon at Evesham, Richard freed by Simon the younger, promises to help his sister Eleanor, he opposes the disinheritance of the Montfortians but secretly participates in it

1266   War of the Disinherited, Richard withdraws, Henry of Almain dominant in government, the Dictum of Kenilworth

1267   Richard negotiates a peaceful end to the earl of Gloucester's occupation of London, Statute of Marlborough

1268   Richard and Edmund leave for Germany

1269   Richard marries Beatrix of Valkenburg, Henry of Almain marries Constance de Bearn, consecration of the new Westminster Abbey

1270   Louis leaves on crusade to Tunis and dies, Edward and the English crusaders winter on Sicily, Edmund joins them after presenting the holy blood relic to Hailes

1271   Henry of Almain is hacked to death in a church in Italy by Guy de Montfort, Edmund returns, Richard left incapacitated by a stroke

1272   Richard of Cornwall dies at Berkhamsted, Edmund succeeds him as earl of Cornwall, Henry III dies

1273   Rudolf of Habsburg is elected Richard's successor as king of the Romans

1277   Death of Beatrix of Valkenburg

1300   Edmund of Cornwall dies without issue, his wealth and Cornwall go to the crown

LIST OF ILLUSTRATIONS

12. Heraldic shields, Cotton MS Nero D I f. 171v.
13. Modern illustration of the shields by Rs-nourse.
14. Matthew Paris self-portrait, MS Royal 14 C VII f. 6r.
15. Matthew Paris itinerary, Cotton MS Nero D I, ff. 183v.
16. Pope Innocent IV, Royal 19 D I f. 148v.
17. Portrait of Alfonso X from the codex Tumbo 'A' de Santiago.
18. Rudolf of Habsburg, Kopialbuch des Stiftes St. Florian Cod. 101b.
19. Richard of Cornwall and Sanchia of Provence, Meissen Cathedral.
20. Trifels Castle, Arno Kohlem.
21. Wappentruhe von Cornwall, Sailko.
22. Simon de Montfort depicted in a stained-glass window of Chartres Cathedral.
23. Plaque remembering Snellings Mill in Lewes, author's collection.
24. Kenilworth Castle, author's collection.
25. Great Comet of 1264, Rosana de Montfort
26. Medieval English stained glass window depicting Beatrix of Valkenburg, Medieval Franciscan friars.
27. The murder of Henry of Almain in Viterbo, Nuova Cronica – ms. Chigiano L VIII 296 – Biblioteca Vaticana.
28. Ruins of Berkhamsted Castle, author's collection.
29. Ruins of cloisters at Hailes Abbey, John Paul Davis.
30. Area of shrine and high altar at Hailes Abbey, John Paul Davis.

MAPS

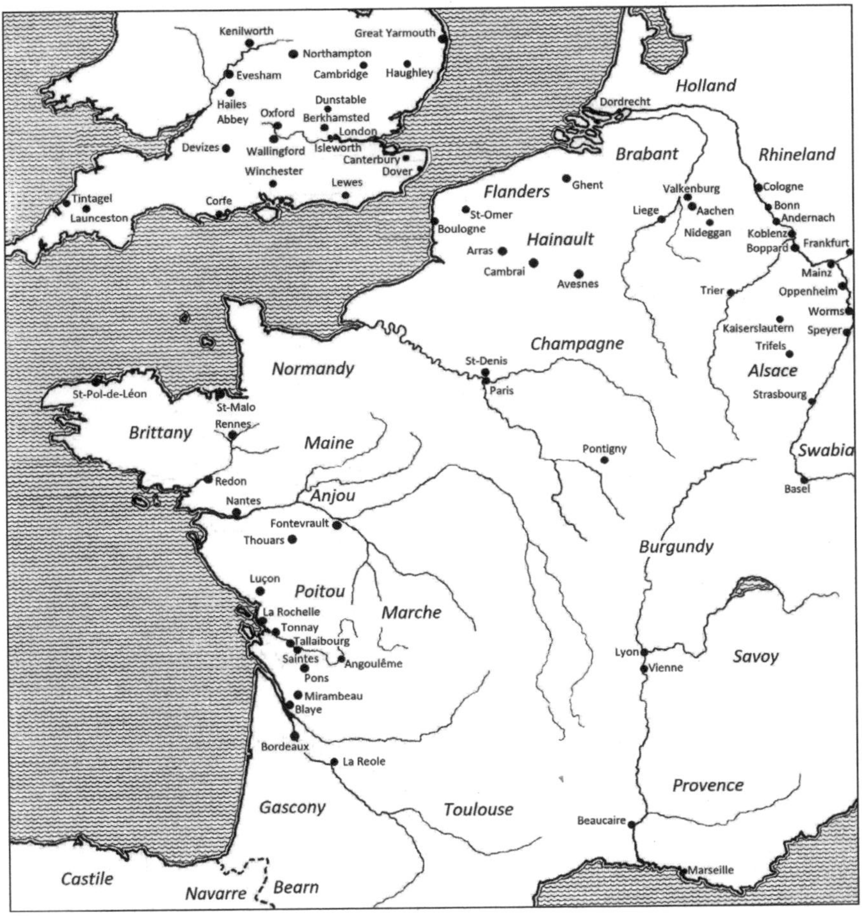

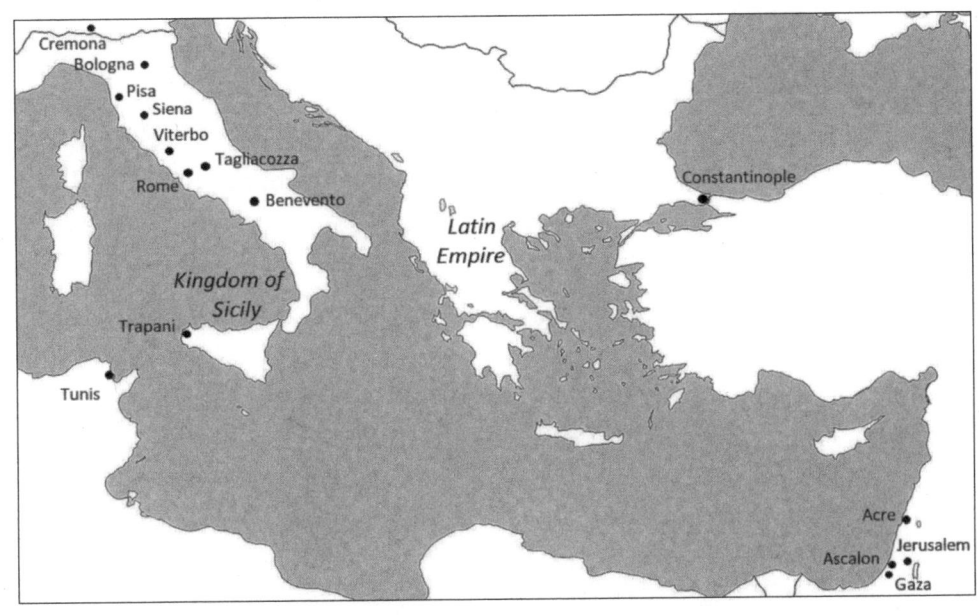

Kenilworth
Northampton
Great Yarmouth
Evesham
Cambridge
Haughley
Hailes Abbey
Oxford
Dunstable
Berkhamsted
London
Devizes
Wallingford
Isleworth
Winchester
Canterbury
Dover
Lewes
Corfe
Tintagel
Launceston
Holland
Dordrecht
Brabant
Rhineland
Flanders
Ghent
Valkenburg
Cologne
St-Omer
Liege
Aachen
Bonn
Andernach
Boulogne
Nideggan
Koblenz
Hainault
Boppard
Frankfurt
Arras
Mainz
Cambrai
Avesnes
Trier
Oppenheim
Worms
Kaiserslautern
Speyer
Champagne
Trifels
Normandy
St-Denis
Alsace
St-Pol-de-Léon
Paris
Strasbourg
St-Malo
Rennes
Maine
Pontigny
Swabia
Brittany
Basel
Redon
Anjou
Nantes
Burgundy
Fontevrault
Thouars
Luçon
Poitou
La Rochelle
Marche
Tonnay
Tallaibourg
Lyon
Savoy
Saintes
Angoulême
Vienne
Pons
Mirambeau
Blaye
Bordeaux
La Reole
Gascony
Toulouse
Provence
Beaucaire
Marseille
Castile
Navarre
Bearn

Cremona
Bologna
Pisa
Siena
Viterbo
Tagliacozza
Constantinople
Rome
Benevento
Latin Empire
Kingdom of Sicily
Trapani
Tunis
Acre
Jerusalem
Ascalon
Gaza

I

SECOND SON
1209–1234

Richard was born on Monday, 5 January 1209, most likely at Devizes, but Winchester, where his fifteen-month older brother Henry had been born, was also given as the location. As the second son of King John and Isabella of Angoulême, he was named after his uncle Richard the Lionheart. Henry had been named after their grandfather Henry II. Neither son would know any of the illustrious members of their father's family, not their aunts or uncles or grandmother Eleanor of Aquitaine. John, the youngest child, was already forty years old when Henry was born in 1207. All the children he produced during the years before he was crowned king in 1199 were out of wedlock. These illegitimate offspring included one son named Henry, another named Richard, and a daughter named Joan. The first daughter John welcomed with Isabella, in 1210, would also be Joan.[1]

Richard's mother Isabella was around twenty years old at the time of his birth. She was the heiress of Angoulême, a county in Poitou, which itself was part of the Aquitaine that John inherited from his brother Richard and mother Eleanor. As a girl, Isabella had been betrothed to her much older neighbour, Hugh IX Lusignan, the count of La Marche. Fearful the match would give Hugh too much power, John married her instead. Hugh complained about it to the king of France, Philip Augustus, who used it as an excuse to attack Normandy and John's other northern territories. By 1204, the conquest was over.

Winning back his Norman inheritance required money and discipline and to that end John put extraordinary pressure on his barons, clergymen and neighbours. In 1209, he marched against Scotland and imposed a treaty that called for a future marriage between King William's eldest daughter Margaret and John's son Henry, who was not quite two years old. Were Henry to die before the nuptials, his seven-month-old brother Richard would become the groom. William's second oldest daughter Isabelle served as Margaret's spare. Both girls, who were in their mid-teens, were taken into English care as surety for the agreement.

In 1212, John prepared to move against Welsh chieftain Llywelyn ap Iowerth, who was married to his natural daughter Joan. He called it off after learning that a cabal of his barons were planning to kill him. Another rumour spread that Queen Isabella had been raped and abducted from Marlborough Castle and the fortress put to the torch. The son with her at the time, three-year-old Richard, was reportedly murdered.[2]

John quelled the internal rumbling and in 1214 went to Poitou to launch his long-awaited campaign against the French. In June, he sent for Isabella to join him and to bring along five-year-old Richard and four-year-old Joan. The children were there for prospective marital alliances and one such match was arranged between Joan and the fully grown Hugh X Lusignan, the son of the man jilted by Isabella. The defeat of John's coalition at the battle of Bouvines on 27 July put an end to his dreams of re-conquest. He still needed the Lusignans if he hoped to hang on to Poitou, so he left Joan behind with Hugh's family and embarked for England with his wife, son, and a newborn daughter who was named Isabella after her mother. They reached Corfe in October.

The next two years saw a baronial uprising, Magna Carta, civil war and the birth of Eleanor, the last of John and Isabella's five children. In April 1215, Richard was sent to Corfe under the protection of Peter de Maulay, a loyal courtier who came from Poitou. Joining the boy there was Isabelle of Scotland, who was twelve years older, and his cousin Eleanor of Brittany, who was twenty-five years older. Together with his nursemaid Eva, they filled in as surrogate mothers to the six-year-old Richard. It was from Eva and other members of his household, including two trumpeters and a washerwoman, that Richard grew up speaking English as well as French.

His education was entrusted to a tutor named Roger d'Acastre, who instructed him in grammar, music, astronomy, Latin and other liberal arts. A long poem written in Latin at this time and dedicated to brothers Henry and Richard notes the 'pleasing appearance' of the boys. In September 1215, Richard and his tutor were relocated to Dover. War had broken out between the king and most of his baronage after he repudiated Magna Carta. He wanted his youngest son close to him while Henry remained with his mother at Bristol. The caring parent in John can be seen in the note of displeasure he penned to the custodian of Dover while he was in the field. 'You should also let us know how our son is. We are very surprised that you have told us nothing about him since our departure.'[3]

In the meantime, crown prince Louis of France accepted an invitation from the rebel barons to become their king and landed with an invasion force in the spring of 1216. For safety reasons, John sent Richard and his tutor back to Corfe. Having stalemated his opponents, John went on the offensive but caught dysentery and died in the evening of 18 October 1216. In his will, he implored his executors to safeguard the inheritances of his sons. Henry's was obvious, the kingdom itself, but Richard's was unspecified. Since London was in the enemy camp, John was buried at Worcester and nine-year-old Henry crowned at Gloucester. A proposal for Queen Isabella to take Richard to Ireland to ensure the safety of the new heir to the throne was politely ignored by the regency council.

Isabella took a leading role in the peace negotiations that brought the war to an end, but she was denied any share of her son's government. In 1218, she went to Poitou to check on the well-being of Joan and never came back. Richard was still at Corfe in May 1220 when Maulay brought him to Westminster to witness his brother's second, more ceremonial coronation. His studies came to an end three years later when he turned fourteen. Maulay was impressed with Roger's tutorial services and wrote a letter highly recommending him to the court.

In Poitou, Queen Isabella unexpectedly wed Hugh X Lusignan in place of her daughter Joan. The ten-year-old girl was sent home to marry Alexander II of Scotland and the plans for Henry or Richard to marry Alexander's sister Margaret were scrapped. She was wed instead to Hubert de Burgh, a courtier from Norfolk who had risen to dominate Henry's minority council. Her sister Isabelle was given in marriage to the much younger Roger Bigod, the heir to the earldom of Norfolk. In the spring of 1223, Richard fell gravely ill at Lambeth but was well enough by August to undertake a pilgrimage to the new shrine of Thomas Becket at Canterbury in the company of his brother-in-law King Alexander.[4]

Henry's minority lurched from one crisis to the next as the king and council sought to re-impose royal authority over the troubled land. In the summer of 1224, they invested the last remaining castle holding out against them despite the threats of the new king of France, Louis VIII, to overrun Poitou. The castle was destroyed and the garrison hanged, but as feared, Poitou was lost. The culprits were the new power couple in the region, Hugh and Isabella. Louis had put them on his payroll and told them that adjacent Gascony, the last Plantagenet territory on the continent, was theirs if Hugh could take it.

An English expeditionary force was put together to defend Gascony and, if possible, re-conquer Poitou. The leaders were two seasoned veterans, John's illegitimate half-brother William Longespee and Henry's own former tutor Philip d'Aubigny. Richard also went along, both as the emblem of loyalty and to gain experience for himself. Having just turned sixteen, he was knighted by his brother on 2 February 1225 together with ten other youths accompanying him as household knights. The fleet left Portsmouth one week before Easter.

On 2 May, Richard wrote to his brother to inform him that all of Gascony save the castle at La Réole had been pacified, but it took the next six months to take it. Hugh marched south to raise the siege of the castle but turned back when he saw English forces massed on the opposite bank of the river. Roger of Wendover reports that Richard and his men then laid an ambush for his stepfather, routed his men with lances in hand and trumpets blaring and pursued them for some distance.[5]

Richard next undertook an altogether different pursuit that raised alarm bells back at Westminster. He somehow conceived a marriage between himself and an unidentified princess of Leon, one of the Spanish kingdoms in the south. As the heir to the throne, Richard's future marriage was much too valuable to leave in his own hands. Longespee was recalled in October to discuss the matter. He arrived after some difficulty at sea and died six months later. The marriage plans were dropped.

The king himself had just overcome a serious illness. When word reached him that Louis had launched an attack on Toulouse, which was next door to Gascony, he grew worried and made plans to sail there. He was persuaded to stay his decision by a letter from his brother declaring that he, Richard, had everything under control, and also by a member of Henry's council who predicted that Louis would come to a bad end. This man was an astrologer who was perhaps inspired by a great conjunction of Jupiter and Saturn then visible in the pre-dawn sky. His prediction proved correct, for later that autumn Louis died of dysentery.

The son who succeeded him, twelve-year-old Louis IX, faced an immediate revolt by his barons. It was Henry's best chance to get Poitou back for his dynasty, and Richard, who had started calling himself the count of Poitou, went north to make it happen. After a promising start, negotiations failed when young Louis's mother, the regent Blanche of Castile, got involved. As the daughter of King John's older sister Eleanor, Blanche was Richard's cousin and the most formidable queen of her age. She used a mixture of inducements and threats to win over one disaffected French noble after another until they all caved. The collapse of the coalition left Richard little choice but to conclude a truce with her and return home in April 1227.[6]

He had been away for a little more than two years. What he looked like stepping off the plank, eighteen years old and fully grown, is impossible to say because no description of him has survived. In terms of ancestry, he was almost exclusively French. His mother and paternal grandmother came from Poitou and his paternal grandfather from neighbouring Anjou. The only British blood in him he owed to his great-great-grandmother, Matilda of Scotland.

Henry received his brother with joy and on 30 May conferred the title 'earl of Cornwall' on him at Westminster. Richard had already been granted the earldom prior to leaving for Gascony, but he held it temporarily because the king was a minor at the time. Since then, Henry, too, had passed into adulthood. The king did not make the grant permanent, however. Feeling unappreciated, Richard ejected one of his mother's former bodyguards, Walerand the German, from lands he held within the Cornish estates. Walerand complained about it to the king, who ordered Richard to give them back. Richard not only refused but fired back that he would only act in accordance with the judgement of his peers, not of his brother the king.

Wendover reports that Henry's all-powerful minister Hubert de Burgh advised the king to have Richard placed under house arrest until he cooled off. Suspecting something amiss, Richard fled in the night. He went to William Marshal, the earl of Pembroke and son of Henry's first regent. He and Richard had been brothers-in-law since Marshal married his eight-year-old sister Eleanor in 1224, a political match that would not be consummated until Eleanor reached her teens. Richard and William went to Ranulf de Blondeville, the earl of Chester and senior magnate of the realm, and together these three earls were joined by five others in collecting a large force of men and demanding an audience with the king. Backed by his own troops, Henry met them in August at Northampton to hear their grievances.

The current tension between the king and his earls went back to the Christmas court of 1224 and the crisis in Gascony. Funding an expeditionary force to save the province for the crown required a national tax, but the magnates approved it only after Henry agreed to reissue Magna Carta and the Forest Charter under his own seal. It was a defining moment in the history of the English monarchy. Never again would the barons stand up and offer to defend the lord king's rights unconditionally. He would have to give them something in return first.

Both charters were at the centre of the grievances of the earls. The king was reclaiming forests contrary to the Forest Charter and his sheriffs were exceeding their authority under Magna Carta. In the case of the forests, Henry refused to budge. He had his own grievance, namely that the earls had taken advantage of his need for the tax to appropriate certain royal woodlands. He was taking back what they should never have taken in the first place. As for the sheriffs, he agreed to summon a parliament to hear complaints about them. After receiving various gifts and favours, all the earls except one went home peacefully.

The holdout was Richard, who was still unsatisfied about his position. At Northampton, Henry granted him their mother's forfeited dower lands in England, which included Berkhamsted, but again it was only temporary and within weeks he took them back from him. Determined to show his brother, Richard went to Scotland in November 1227 to discuss marriage between himself and Margery, the youngest of King Alexander's sisters. Henry responded to his brother's latest show of defiance by following him as far north as Durham. Not wanting to provoke Henry, Alexander left the marriage negotiations to his mother Ermengarde, who met Richard at Kinghorn but found his demands for Margery's dowry unrealistic. Rebuffed, Richard slipped back into England quietly, but eventually joined the Christmas court at York.[7]

Across the Channel, unrest flared up again among the French nobles. One of them, the duke of Brittany, openly switched his allegiance to Henry. That gave the king the bargaining power he needed to offer Blanche a deal over his continental inheritance.

The various scenarios called for Henry to cede his claims to Normandy in return for the other confiscated territories, or to give his and Richard's middle sister Isabella to young king Louis in marriage in return for a generous dower (a lifetime endowment of lands for the bride provided by the groom's family). Blanche rejected all proposals out of hand and made war on the duke.

Henry and his council decided another expedition was in order. By 18 October 1229, a force of nearly six hundred knights and eight earls, including Richard, had assembled in Portsmouth. The troops never embarked, however, because not enough ships had been requisitioned for the fleet. Since they were at the end of the sailing season, that basically ruined everything. According to Wendover, Henry went berserk and accused Hubert, now the earl of Kent, of being in the pay of France. He might have killed him on the spot had Ranulf, the earl of Chester, not intervened.[8]

The expedition was postponed until spring. Henry made sure to keep Richard on board for it by granting him Wallingford on 1 November and returning Berkhamsted to him at the same time, but again only 'during pleasure'. The fleet left at the end of April 1230 and immediately ran into a problem. Henry and Richard's sister Isabella, who was going in the event a marital alliance presented itself, took ill at sea and the king ordered part of the fleet to divert to the island of Jersey. She quickly recovered and they made landfall in Brittany the next day. It was 3 May, just over five years to the date after Richard stepped ashore in Gascony. As on that earlier occasion, his former tutor Roger d'Acastre, now surely a father figure in his life, was with him.

The success of the expedition hinged on Isabella of Angoulême. It is not unlikely that Henry, a natural sentimentalist, thought a reunion between his mother and three of the five children she had not seen since abandoning them would induce her to abandon the French. But that was twelve years ago and she had nine more children in the meantime with her second husband. The Lusignans decided not to risk the hefty pension they were receiving from Blanche or the autonomy they enjoyed in Poitou. Without their support, Henry had no chance to re-conquer Anjou and Maine, let alone Normandy.

His prospects for success were further hampered by his senior advisers, who saw nothing in the expedition for them and therefore treated it as a holiday. Hubert was apathetic throughout, another indication he was working for the French. The only engagement was a ten-day siege conducted at Mirambeau. From there they went to Bordeaux, with Richard perhaps giving his brother a tour of the city, before heading back to Brittany to take stock of the situation. With money running low and disease plaguing the army and himself, the king went home. Richard, who had fallen ill as well, went with him.⁹

Together with Ranulf of Chester, William Marshal stayed behind to help defend Brittany. His brother-in-law Gilbert de Clare, the earl of Gloucester, died of dysentery just before crossing. It was up to the king to decide who got the wardship of Gilbert's eight-year-old son and heir, Richard. The boy's mother was Marshal's sister Isabel and the huge Clare estate edged up against his own in south Wales. Marshal expected to get the wardship and was incensed when Henry granted it to Hubert instead.

When Marshal came home in February, he found Richard of Cornwall also in a temper. On the 4th of that month, Henry had renewed the grant of their mother's English dower lands to his brother, but again only temporarily because the king still believed Isabella and Hugh would switch sides. Richard looked to marriage for the security he failed to get from Henry and set his sights on the widow Clare, whose dower entitled her to one-third of her late husband's estate. She was thirty years old, the mother of six, and described as *Isabel vis a bel* ('lovely face').

On 30 March 1231, Richard and Isabel were married by the abbot of Tewkesbury at Fawley. Henry, who was thirty kilometres away at Marlborough, was outraged. It was not just his wanting a say in his brother's marriage, as was his right as king, but in Isabel's too. One of the notorious practices of the past had been to force rich widows into marrying again, usually to a supporter of the regime. Magna Carta did away with that, but aristocratic widows were nevertheless required to ask the king for permission before they married according to their own wishes.[10]

One set of Marshal siblings, William and Isabel, was now married to one set of Plantagenet siblings, Richard and Eleanor, but it did not last. Barely a week after the wedding, William died, apparently from something he contracted at the feast. It was a disaster for Henry. William and Eleanor had no children and she showed no signs of being pregnant in the weeks following his death. Henry was desperate not to give the Pembroke earldom to William's brother Richard, who lived in Normandy and was a liegeman of the king of France. Worried where his loyalty lay, Henry put him off.

In the meantime, he tried to coax his brother Richard back to court by granting him the two custodies that were in the possession of William Marshal at the time of his death. They included the lands of William de Braose. In 1230, prior to the expedition leaving for Brittany, Braose had been caught in an indiscretion with Henry and Richard's half-sister Joan, the lady of Wales. Her husband Llywelyn had him hanged in front of a large crowd. Braose's death and those of Gilbert de Clare and William Marshal in the space of one year left a power vacuum in the region that Llywelyn was ready to exploit.

In committing the custodies to Richard, Henry expected him to defend these borderlands known as the Marches from Welsh incursions. In fact, quite quickly he began to suspect his brother of plotting with Richard Marshal to ease his way into Pembrokeshire. Henry moved to Gloucester in May and there he deprived his brother of the two custodies he had given him only three weeks earlier. He also cast Richard out of Wallingford.

Llywelyn struck that summer. Henry mustered his troops, but only to build a castle at Paincastle in North Wales to keep his Welsh brother-in-law in check. The king was there on 8 August 1231 when Richard Marshal showed up to do homage for Pembroke. Taking him at his word that he would be true and loyal, Henry granted him the earldom.

Two days later Richard of Cornwall arrived. Henry had reached out to him earlier by presenting him with two goshawks. Now he gave his brother what he wanted most, land that was his to pass on to his heirs. Richard's possession of Cornwall was made permanent, as too were Wallingford, Beckley, and Berkhamsted. He was finally an earl with an earldom to call his own.

As if placating these two earls were not enough, Henry received a third earl, Ranulf of Chester, three days later on 13 August. Ranulf had with him Simon de Montfort, a young knight from France whose namesake father led the Albigensian Crusade until he was killed in 1218. The elder Simon had inherited the earldom of Leicester through his English-born mother, but John confiscated it and gave it to the earl of Chester, who was the crusader's cousin. Ranulf was now prepared to give way to his younger relative. Henry agreed Simon could take possession of Leicester, but without the title of earl.[11]

Isabel and Richard's first child was born on 31 January 1232, ten months after their wedding. It was a boy they named John after his father. In May, the former king's body was moved to an elaborate new tomb at Worcester Cathedral with Henry and Eleanor in attendance. Hubert was also at the ceremony, if not standing as close to the king as he might have wished. After nearly a decade in power, his hold on the court was beginning to crumble.

Hubert's dominance had begun when he engineered the dismissal of Peter des Roches from Henry's minority council. Peter was among the loyal continental supporters of King John who settled in England after the loss of Normandy. In 1205, he was elected bishop of Winchester and later made Henry's guardian, just as Richard was entrusted to Peter's compatriot Peter de Maulay. Other foreigners were given castles, sheriffdoms, and heiresses as wives. Their good fortune created anger and jealously among the English elite, who tried to use Magna Carta to expel as many of them as possible.

The loyalty of these foreigners was instrumental in ensuring that the king who followed John was English (Henry) and not French (Louis), but peace had no sooner been re-established when they were targeted again, even while the barons and clergy who had supported Louis, including William Marshal II, were forgiven and reinstated. In 1223, Hubert made his move. Allied with Stephen Langton, the archbishop of Canterbury, he ousted the foreigners from their positions of power. Walking out the door at the time, Peter turned to Hubert and swore he would ruin him one day.

Roches reappeared in 1231 while Henry was building his castle in Wales. When the king complained of his empty treasury, Peter told him it was his own fault. He had allowed Hubert to use royal patronage to make himself and his family rich, not the king. The bishop hosted Christmas court that year at Winchester just so he could put on an outrageous display food, drink and precious ornaments for Henry to behold and to understand that they could all be his if someone else were in charge.

Hubert had manipulated anti-foreigner sentiment to check Peter the last time and now a similar opportunity arose. A Yorkshire knight named Robert Tweng had launched a campaign against foreign clergymen like Peter. At issue was the job security of the church. Typically, the patrons of cathedrals, abbeys, and other religious institutions had the right to decide who got to hop on the gravy train, but the papacy took advantage of Henry's minority to insinuate their own candidates as vicar, rector, dean, and in other salaried positions. They figured it was their reward for helping save the throne of England for the English.

The English patrons squeezed out by this policy included Tweng and his wife. With a group of horsemen, he went on a tear through the countryside, intimidating any 'Romans' they caught and seizing bags of money destined for them or their absentee brethren. Instead of cracking down on these perpetrators, Hubert aided and abetted them in the hope of driving out Peter and his circle. Although sympathetic to Tweng and other disenfranchised patrons of the church, Henry was deeply embarrassed by the lawlessness and in August 1232 he sacked Hubert after his role in it came to light. As the evidence against him mounted, Hubert ran for the sanctuary of church.

According to Wendover, Henry incited a mob of Londoners to bring back his former mentor dead or alive, but Ranulf again came to the rescue of his long-time nemesis. In fact, the sixty-year-old Ranulf was just then on his deathbed at Wallingford. It was Richard's castle, but Ranulf may have decided to end his days there because Wallingford had been his until he lost it in Hubert's purge of foreigners, whose cause he had always championed. Hearing Ranulf was close to death, Henry arrived from nearby

Reading to be with him, along with a host of magnates of the kingdom. The earl of Chester died on 26 October 1232, the last of the great Anglo-Norman barons.

After the embarrassing episode of sanctuary, Hubert was apprehended and brought to London for trial in front of four of his peers, including the earls of Cornwall and Pembroke. Henry dismissed calls to have him executed. 'I would rather be considered a simple and foolish king than a cruel and tyrannical one,' he reportedly said. On 10 November, Hubert was sentenced to the forfeiture of his ill-gotten gains and to house arrest indefinitely at Devizes.

By that time, Marshal was one of the leading members of court. Henry was eager to repair relations with him after their false start, even to the detriment of his sister Eleanor. As the widow of Marshal's brother William, Eleanor was entitled to one-third of his estate for her lifetime. Since she was only sixteen, Richard Marshal stood to lose a lot of money. Magna Carta stipulated that widows were supposed to receive their dower settlements within forty days, but it had been more than a year and nothing. Finally, Marshal offered her a flat £400 per year to be done with it, far less than a third of the value, but Eleanor accepted it at Henry's insistence.

Marshal's flouting of Magna Carta drew no comment because it was happening everywhere. As promised to Henry, the new regime of Peter des Roches had undertaken reforms to increase royal revenue. The prospects looked good with all the patronage coming in following Hubert's disgrace and Ranulf's death. But Peter squandered the chance. His priority was righting the wrongs of his own earlier disgrace by taking back what had been taken from him and the other foreigners. It required Henry overturning royal charters in contradiction to Magna Carta, but Peter did not see that as a problem. The only proper kingship in his mind was the way King John had done things. He encouraged his son to follow suit.

Henry took the bait. The ensuing reshuffle of wealth and power created a lot of anger and resentment and cries of too much foreign influence at court, but Marshal went along with it. He not only benefited from the king's new authoritarian policy but until recently he had been a Norman peer serving the king of France. He was as much a foreigner as Peter. The knights of his household, however, were English, all of them inherited from his brother, and he was obliged to stand by them. One of them was Gilbert Basset, who was also Richard's tenant. When Basset was evicted from a manor so that it could be given back to its original owner, Peter de Maulay, Marshal walked out of court.[12]

He went to see Richard of Cornwall, much the way Richard had gone to see Marshal's older brother William when he encountered similar trouble at court five years earlier. But Richard Marshal found Richard of Cornwall in a bind. On the one hand, Marshal was his brother-in-law and Basset his tenant, but on the other, Maulay had raised him and Henry was his brother. The tipping point for him proved to be the grievance he shared with Marshal, the lucrative wardship of Richard de Clare.

During his disgrace, Hubert was stripped of the wardship of the future earl of Gloucester. Logically the ten-year-old boy should have gone either to his uncle, Richard Marshal, or stepfather, Richard of Cornwall. Instead, he went to Peter des Roches. The grant could be justified as an attempt by the crown to reclaim patronage, but to both Richards it looked like Peter had adopted the guise of Hubert and was hoarding everything for himself.

Needing to make a statement, the two Richards joined forces in March 1233 to drive Llywelyn out of Radnor and other Braose lands.

Their aggression was calculated to provoke the king, who wanted it quiet in the Marches. By summer, Marshal and his adherents were in full defiance of royal authority. He called a meeting at the Basset ancestral home at High Wycombe to decide on their course of action, but practically nobody came. Henry had bought off most of the malcontents with favours, grants, sometimes with the properties he confiscated from the ringleaders. One such defector was Richard of Cornwall, who received the Basset family lands within his domains.

For Marshal, it was over and he agreed to make peace, but the Bassets were incensed by the traitors in their ranks. They made their own statement by launching a guerrilla campaign against them. They started out by seizing their castles, including Hay-on-Wye, which was in Richard's custody, and quickly moved on to burning their homes and crops. In this way, they dragged Marshal into their rebellion. Once committed, however, the earl of Pembroke went all out. He rejected all peace offers and entered into an alliance with the Welsh. Together they sacked Shrewsbury and beat off all of Henry's half-hearted attempts to bring them to heel.

Marshal had plenty of moral support from the English bishops, who despised their foreign colleague Peter des Roches. They were disciples of Stephen Langton, the deceased archbishop of Canterbury, and bitterly recalled how Peter stood by King John when he locked Langton out of his cathedral. Many a churchman was ruined by the interdict placed on England as a result of their quarrel. Spurred on by Langton, the bishops were also keen backers of Magna Carta, seeing it as their protection against both king and pope. As far as they were concerned, Peter's regime was the problem, not the insurgents.

Exasperated, Henry shrewdly moved the war to Ireland, which forced Marshal to go there to defend his family estates. He was wounded in an armed encounter on 1 April 1234 and died two weeks later from the botched treatment he received. The chroniclers recording these events were churchmen and so glorified Marshal as a martyr who tried to save England from being overrun by foreigners. Henry put on a show of remorse, got rid of Roches and his men, and made restitution. He later admitted he had been seduced by the 'plenitude of power' and promised to rule within the restrictions of Magna Carta.

Privately, he seethed. The windfall of patronage coming to the crown could have been used to cement his alliances on the continent. Instead, the money had been wasted on a senseless war. When the duke of Brittany failed to receive his subsidies, he defected back to France. Meanwhile, Henry was back to square one with his finances. Peter's reforms had been ambitious, but too radical and centralised to work in the short term.

The Marshals lost out too. Although Gilbert, the next brother in line, was allowed to succeed as the earl of Pembroke, their lands in Normandy were confiscated by the French monarchy. The Bassets, on the other hand, were quickly restored to favour. Over the next three decades, their family were Henry's most vociferous supporters, even as his relations with other barons and clergy ran aground.[13]

The Marshal rebellion was a turning point in Henry's reign. No more would he have any great ministers of state like Hubert or Peter. He would install a government run by able but lesser men who answered only to him. No more would he let the church decide who became the next bishops. He would insist on his own candidates the way his forebears had. And no more would he put up with the clannish behaviour of the English nobility. He would dilute their ranks with marriages that bound them closer to the court than to each other.

It all added up to the start of his personal rule, and the key to the success of it was his brother, the earl of Cornwall.

2

RISE AT COURT AND CRUSADE
1235–1241

Despite being targeted by the insurgents, Richard of Cornwall did nothing to suppress them. He left court and did not return until more than six months later. He was compensated for his losses out of the land seized from Hubert and members of the ousted Roches regime, but he was still angry about the destruction to his properties, and he was not alone. In early September 1234, friends and foes in the recent conflict, including the Marshals and their kinfolk, planned to hold a tournament in Northampton. Richard intended to join them, but Henry, worried it would end in a deadly brawl, banned it and another one planned for Cambridge.

Marshal's rebellion engendered personal vendettas and intrigues for years to come. Richard Siward, a swashbuckling knight married to Basset's sister, had twice plundered Richard of Cornwall's estates. Although Siward was pardoned and readmitted to the council, Richard eyed his chance to pay him back. He persuaded Henry to banish Siward in April 1236, a full two years after Marshal's death. When the king of Scotland interceded for Siward, Henry declared he would rather incur Siward's anger than his brother's. Henry eventually relented, but then had the hapless former insurgent imprisoned for a brief spell, this time at the instigation of a new cabal at court headed by Simon de Montfort.[1]

Some of Richard's lingering aggression could have sprung from home. He was married to the sister of his enemy. Wendover says that his wife Isabel warned her rebellious brother of a plot to seize and imprison him, which does not quite square with the official record but does indicate the divided loyalties of the families married to the ten-strong Marshal children. Adding to the strain in Richard's marriage to Isabel was the loss of both of their children. John died on 22 September 1232, less than eight months old, and their daughter Isabel, born on 9 September 1233, died on 6 October 1234, just over a year old.

In early 1235, Richard petitioned Pope Gregory IX for an annulment of his marriage on the grounds that he and Isabel's first husband Gilbert de Clare were distantly related. So serious was Richard about finding a new wife that the lucrative grant of Knaresborough made to him by Henry at this time neglected all mention of Isabel. The land was to be his and 'his heirs by his espoused wife', whoever she might be. The pope, however, advised him to 'lay aside all doubt and remain in lawful matrimony'. Indeed, when the letter from Rome arrived later that summer, Isabel was pregnant again. A boy was born to them on 1 November 1235 and baptised at Richard's manor of Haughley in Suffolk by the bishop of Hereford. He was called Henry after his uncle the king.[2]

In that same year, Richard's twenty-year-old sister Isabella was betrothed and married to Frederick II of the Holy Roman Empire. He was forty, already twice-married, and demanded a fortune for her dowry, but he seemed like a good bet as an ally against France. Both Richard and Henry accompanied her and her entourage to the coast in May 1235 for her departure for

Germany, where she became empress on 20 July. The siblings parted with a long, tearful embrace. Of the two brothers, only Richard would see their beloved sister again.

Henry was the last of the siblings still unmarried, though not for want of trying. A decade earlier, he was in competition with the emperor for the hand of a Bohemian princess, but she spurned both of them and entered a nunnery. He would have next married Margery, the Scottish princess Richard had pursued, had his council welcomed the idea, but as with the marriage of Isabella to the emperor, the king was supposed to marry for leverage against the French or at least to counter their moves.

It became the latter in 1234 when Louis IX married Margaret, the eldest daughter of the count and countess of Provence. Since Margaret's parents had no sons, Provence would go to the husband of one of their four daughters. Henry decided to put himself in the running for it by marrying their second eldest daughter Eleanor, which took place in Canterbury in January 1236.[3]

A fanciful story has come down through the ages that Richard of Cornwall was the unwitting matchmaker between Henry and Eleanor. The origins of it go back to the late sixteenth century and a short biography of Richard the Lionheart composed at that time. It describes how King Richard fell in love with Eleanor on a trip to Provence. Sometime after his return, he received an Arthurian-inspired romance from her called *Blandin of Cornwall*.

The problem with this account is the Lionheart died more than twenty years before Eleanor was born. Later historians assumed that Richard of Cornwall must have been her heroic inspiration, even though Eleanor was already Richard's sister-in-law by the time he made his first and only visit to Provence in 1240. These obstacles aside, it was too good a yarn not to take on a life of its own. And so it was reworked to have Richard of Cornwall receiving the poem, but, being otherwise occupied, he passes it along to his brother Henry. The king is smitten with the young damsel who wrote it and marries her for love, which, as the council made clear in the case of Margery, was out of the question.

Both Henry and Eleanor were romantics and tales of King Arthur were all the rage. Richard made his own contribution to this burgeoning knightly lore when he set about building a castle on a promontory jutting into the Atlantic Ocean one hundred kilometres up the coast from the tip of Cornwall. It served no strategic purpose and Richard did not even own the land until he swapped three manors for it in 1233. His reasons for wanting it had to do with Arthur and the castle at the heart of his legend.

As told by Geoffrey of Monmouth, Uther Pendragon, the king of Britain, lusts after Igerna, the wife of Gorlois, the duke of Cornwall. Gorlois commits Igerna to Tintagel Castle, his most secure stronghold, while he goes off to slug it out with Uther. Little does he realise that Merlin the wizard has altered Uther's appearance so that he looks like Gorlois when the lord of the castle shows up out of nowhere. Uther prowls the dark corridors of Tintagel until he finds the duke's unsuspecting wife. Thinking the lecherous man pounding the pavement is her husband, Igerna conceives little Arthur with him that night, right around the time her actual husband gets impaled in battle.

According to legend, Tintagel stood on the promontory where Richard undertook the building work. His father King John was well known for bedding the wives of his noblemen and Richard would prove every bit as lustful as John and Uther, but his erection of Tintagel was likely inspired by a group of monks. Four decades earlier, these monks claimed to have discovered the graves of Arthur and Guinevere within the confines of their religious house in Glastonbury. Their abbey there had been doing brisk business ever since. If Richard hoped to build on that success, it was one of the few times his commercial instincts led him astray. Tintagel never caught on and not even his brother played along. When Henry took his new bride to see Arthur and Guinevere's graves in the summer of 1236, he turned north instead of continuing west for the extra 150 kilometres it took to reach the spot of the deceitful conception.[4]

The marriage of his sister brought Richard of Cornwall to the emperor's attention. In early 1236, Frederick proposed to make war against France and so asked Henry to send Richard to him for that purpose. The marital alliance with the empire, which had cost an enormous dowry of £20,000, seemed to be paying dividends, but it soon emerged that the war Frederick really had in mind was against his rebellious city-states in northern Italy. He hoped to tap Richard's royal connections and accumulating wealth for what was going to be a long and bitter campaign.

Henry put Frederick off by saying the kingdom was unable to spare his brother. He was the heir to the throne and would be so for some time to come. The new queen, only twelve at her wedding, was not expected to produce an heir for several years.

Richard's status had nevertheless changed with Henry's marriage. Eleanor was accompanied to England by her uncle William of Savoy, the bishop-elect of Valence in France. The impressive and skilful William came from a family of power brokers with connections to all the courts of Europe that mattered. Henry asked him to stay on and work with the new men of his council to carry out long-awaited financial reforms.[5]

They did not disappoint, but the increased revenue came at the expense of the barons, who were already none too happy about a proposed tax to help pay for Henry's marriage and

Isabella's dowry. Added to these tensions was the arrival of a papal legate named Otto of Montferrat. Henry wanted Otto to tame the clergy much as William was taming the barons. The result, inevitably, was another outburst of anger towards foreigners, though William was no stranger to it. He was one of the absentee freeloaders targeted by Tweng and his horsemen back in 1232.

Richard held aloof through much of the controversy. His thoughts had turned to going overseas again. Back on 8 June 1236, he joined other nobles in taking the cross at a ceremony in Winchester. The latest crusade had been called by Pope Gregory because the ten-year truce between the sultanates and crusader states was set to expire in 1239. An adequate force was needed to defend Jerusalem when that happened. Given the expense it entailed, Richard immediately began raising funds by cutting down his trees and selling them.

Henry chipped in by asking the Jews of England to donate £2,000 towards his undertaking. The money did nothing to keep Richard on Henry's side for a contentious parliament that opened three days later on 20 January 1237. According to court gossip Matthew Paris, Richard denounced his brother in front of the assembly for plundering the kingdom to enrich foreigners and for daring nothing without first getting permission from the pope. The speech may have been contrived by Paris, a monk of St Albans Abbey who loathed foreigners and popes in equal measure and delighted in belittling Henry on that account.[6]

In September 1237, Richard accompanied his brother and the court to York to ratify a peace treaty with Scotland. The following month the council met at Woodstock to take up the marriage of Richard's fifteen-year-old stepson Richard de Clare. John de Lacy, the earl of Lincoln, wanted him for his daughter Maud and was willing to pay £3,333 for it. The other option was to offer the lad to one of the Lusignan daughters in Poitou. Richard counselled this approach, not just because the bride would be his half-sister, but his title 'count of Poitou' meant nothing until his mother Isabella and stepfather Hugh returned their allegiance to England. The council agreed but set a deadline of two months for the Lusignans to respond to the offer.

They never did and Lacy got the future earl of Gloucester for his daughter. Whatever disappointment Richard expressed about it was lost in the furore surrounding another marriage that had taken place in the meantime. On 7 January 1238, his sister Eleanor married Simon de Montfort in a secret ceremony. It caused a fair amount of outrage because Eleanor had taken a vow of perpetual widowhood in front of Edmund of Abingdon, the archbishop of Canterbury, back in 1234, when Edmund was striving to restore peace with the Marshals. Her oath to remain single and celibate forever ensured that her share of the Marshal estate would revert back to them when she died.

There was also the question of her status. Since Magna Carta prohibited the disparagement of widows and heiresses, the negotiations for her marriage to William Marshal involved years of discussion about whether the potential groom was worthy of a princess, and what, as the future brother-in-law of the king, he brought to the table. Simon failed on both accounts. He was a heavily indebted court favourite with a middling earldom that produced only half the income that Eleanor enjoyed.

And yet it was the king himself who gave the bride away. Henry had arranged the ceremony in his private chapel with his chaplain officiating. He did it because Eleanor greatly desired to become a mother and Simon had been his most loyal servant during that tumultuous decade. As he justified it later on, he learned that they were sleeping together and wished to avoid the scandal sure to come of it.

There was no scandal to speak of when word of the marriage got out. Henry had sought to mute the religious reaction by waiting until the person guaranteed to be aggrieved by her discarded vow, Archbishop Edmund, left on a trip to Rome. A few churchmen did get huffy over the news, but the legate was working for Henry by this point and raised no objections, and dispensation from the pope, which is to say buying an exemption, was easily obtainable.[7]

Henry had totally misread Richard, however, for whom the matter was personal. Eleanor was his sister too and he was still a brother-in-law of the Marshals. But his real grievance, in fact, was his own diminishing position in Henry's counsels. Simon and Lacy had joined William of Savoy to form an unofficial triumvirate around the king. They had eclipsed the influence of Richard and the council and now all three were reaping their rewards. William was given custody of the earldom of Richmond in the north, Simon got a wealthy princess for a bride, and two weeks after that Lacy got Richard de Clare as his son-in-law.

For his two previous revolts against Henry, in 1227 and 1233, Richard had help from William Marshal and Richard Marshal, neither of whom had benefitted from their defiance of the king. Gilbert Marshal would have been insane to throw in his lot with Richard, especially after Henry allowed him to marry Margery, the much-pursued Scottish princess, in 1235. But being small in size – not the man in the saddle his legendary father was – Gilbert felt he had something to prove. He joined ranks with Richard to demand that the king give an accounting of himself.[8]

Richard deftly moved to win the support of other magnates and cities like London and the Channel ports. The force of men and arms he gathered at Kingston, southwest of London, was of such magnitude that Henry sent four ranking barons to meet him and Gilbert on 25 January 1238. The talks got nowhere. When Otto attempted to negotiate, Richard told him to mind his own business. The legate went back to Henry and advised him to cave. He was seconded by Peter des Roches, who throughout his long career had never shied away from political blowback, but who was now too old and decrepit to endure one more.

On 23 February, there was enough unrest in London for Henry to relocate to the Tower, where the other barons took advantage of the disquiet to draft a power-sharing agreement with him. In full crisis mode, the king ordered his proctors to start making concessions to the malcontents as a way of buying time while Simon and Lacy went to work on Richard. They approached him with gifts and apologies, which were welcome, but it was not until Henry agreed to help fund his crusade that he stood down. The earl of Cornwall suddenly announced that he was satisfied and went home. Henry went back to Westminster and continued his personal rule as if nothing had happened.

For Matthew Paris, Richard's conduct was unforgivable. The irascible monk hoped the revolt would get rid of all the foreigners at court and he puts an impertinent speech into Richard's mouth to that effect:

> The king fattens all the relatives of his wife with lands, possessions, and money and allows the revenues bestowed by our pious ancestors to be seized as spoil and distributed amongst foreigners so that England is a vineyard and all who pass it gather the grapes.

By abandoning the noble cause he himself had started, Richard had 'protracted the miseries of the kingdom and clouded his fame'.

His abrupt turn may have been motivated by a different noble cause, the deteriorating condition of his sister Joan. The queen of Scotland had spent Christmas court with her siblings at Winchester, then embarked on a pilgrimage to Canterbury with the queen of England. On her way home, she fell gravely ill at Havering, outside of London. Henry and Richard came together to be with her, holding her in their arms when she died on 4 March 1238. 'With great grief', her brothers buried her at the church of Tarrant in Dorset, which was under the patronage of her newfound friend and sister-in-law Eleanor of Provence.[9]

Richard of Cornwall had done well for himself by his third rebellion. He was at last the dominant fixture at court. The triumvirate ceased to exist. At the end of March, Simon said goodbye to his pregnant wife and left for Rome to get her vow of chastity expunged. William of Savoy followed him a month later, and Lacy retreated from the scene because of illness. The total amount of money Richard received in gifts and subsidies included the enormous sum of £4,000 for his use on crusade.

The reconciliation did not immediately bring Richard back to court. He was at Berkhamsted on 26 May with his old tutor Roger d'Acastre, who sold his land in Cornwall to him for £66. Richard then went to Cornwall for his first visit there in nine years. While at Launceston in June, he settled a long-running dispute involving the abbey of Tewkesbury. Given his wife's special connection to the abbey, it is possible Isabel accompanied him on this visit. He may have taken her to see Tintagel and the walled garden he had built there to recall another local story of lust and betrayal. The chivalric romance of *Tristan and Isolde* has these two lovers, whose adulterous affair resembles that of

Lancelot and Guinevere, carry on their tryst at Tintagel, in a garden at the court of her husband, King Mark of Cornwall.

The current king and queen had their own garden to evoke Tristan and Isolde. It was near Woodstock and had been originally designed by Henry and Richard's grandfather Henry II so he could carry on with his mistress Rosamund without his wife Eleanor of Aquitaine poking around. Henry III and Eleanor of Provence were at Woodstock in early September 1238 when a crazed individual slipped into the palace to kill them, only he had not counted on the two of them having sex, if not conceiving their first child, that very night in her chamber. (Their first child Edward was born just over nine months later.) When the man found the king's bed empty, he created a racket that alerted the attendants. Found guilty of an offence against majesty, he was torn apart by horses in Coventry.

The assassination attempt was likely the talk of the feast of St Edward on 13 October in Westminster. The next day, Simon de Montfort arrived from his trip to Rome and hurried to Kenilworth, where his wife Eleanor was expecting their first child. Since it was now more than nine months since their secret wedding, Henry could rest easy that she was not pregnant when he gave her away in marriage. The king was back at Woodstock on 28 November when she gave birth and he made a day trip to Kenilworth to be at the baptism of the boy named after him.

It had been nearly two years since Richard took his crusader vow. In that time, Henry had grown uneasy about him and other nobles leaving the realm while the contentious financial reforms were still in progress. Gregory used that as an excuse to forbid Richard and other English crusaders from departing, but the pope's real reason was Emperor Frederick's aggression against his allies in northern Italy. The way Gregory saw it, Frederick would try to entice his brother-in-law Richard to visit him on his way to the Holy Land, then recruit him and his troops to make war on his behalf. Richard did in fact receive a letter from Frederick at this time, advising him to sail for the east from his imperial lands. 'It would not be agreeable to us if you were to make your journey without seeing us first,' the emperor wrote.[10]

The papal prohibition was issued on 25 February 1238, at the height of Richard's revolt. By the time it arrived six weeks later, Henry was of a completely different mindset about the crusade and was now keen for Richard to fulfil his vow. More disturbing to the pope, the king dispatched a hundred knights to fight for Frederick, probably as a gift for Empress Isabella's birth of a son named Henry. Compounding Gregory's dismay was word that the Latin Empire established by the Fourth Crusade at the start of the century was on the verge of collapse. Since Constantinople needed more help than Jerusalem, the pope wrote to Richard on 25 November 1238 with an offer to commute his vow. That way the money he had raised to go to the Holy Land could instead be used for Constantinople.

A month later, even before receiving a response, Gregory ordered that half of the money so far collected by Richard was to go to the Latin Empire, the other half to be held by the pope 'at our pleasure'. Henry tried to get Gregory to reconsider by confirming his brother's 'fervent desire to execute magnificently his vow'. While proctors for the brothers continued their petitions at the papal court, the main body of French crusaders assembled at Lyon in July 1239 and departed. Most of them reached Acre in September.[11]

On 12 November 1239, Richard and other English crusaders met at Northampton to reaffirm their vow to go to the Holy Land. Siward was there, as was Gilbert Marshal, who had been banished from court for his part in Richard's revolt. Henry had had enough of the Marshals and their treachery and ingratitude. When Gilbert and his brother Walter showed up for the previous Christmas court, the palace doorkeepers drove them away. Now Gilbert reaffirmed his vow but added he would go overseas only if he were restored to favour first. Richard told him to leave that to him.

Missing from their ranks was Simon de Montfort. In February, after a wait of nearly eight years, Henry invested Simon with the title 'earl of Leicester'. On 20 June 1239, Simon stood at the font with Richard and other godparents as Edward, the new heir to the throne born to the queen a couple of days earlier, was baptised in Westminster Abbey. All signs indicated that Simon was back and not about to let Richard's dominance at court go unchallenged.

Within weeks, however, he was in complete disgrace. In establishing himself in England at the start of the decade, Simon had loaded himself down with debt. Another crusader on the continent sued him for the money he owed him, and in one payment reorganisation Simon secretly named the king, his brother-in-law, as security for the money. When Henry learned of it, he went ballistic and ordered him to be thrown in the Tower, only to rescind the order after Richard intervened. Fearing the king's wrath, Simon and Eleanor fled to France in August 1239, so fast that they left their infant son behind.[12]

The crusaders at Northampton could not know it, but within days of their assembly Gregory reversed himself and restored their funding. The news may have been received by the time Christmas court met at Winchester, where Richard got Henry to invest his ward Baldwin de Redvers as the earl of Devon. He then left for Cornwall and was there when his wife Isabel, who was at Berkhamsted days away from giving birth to her tenth child overall, became jaundiced. On 17 January 1240, she died in her fortieth year along with Nicholas, the son she bore. Richard was inconsolable. He returned with all haste to bury his wife at Beaulieu Abbey, which had been founded by his father John, and not, as she wished, at Tewkesbury next to her first husband Gilbert de Clare. Richard gave money to the Templars and Jerusalem hospital for the benefit of her soul and established a chaplain at Wallingford to pray for her indefinitely.

In early April, Richard bade farewell at a parliament in Reading, then went to St Albans to solicit prayers for his expedition. He met up with his brother in London and got him to readmit Gilbert Marshal to favour, but Gilbert begged off the crusade for now, promising to join them the following year. The king and queen took Richard's four-year-old son Henry into their care, to be raised at Windsor with one-year-old Edward and the other royal children to follow, and together with Otto accompanied the crusaders to the coast. The men embarking on 10 June included Philip Basset, brother of Gilbert Basset, and William Longespee II, Richard's cousin and the son of the man who guided him on his first overseas campaign fifteen years earlier.[13]

The first stop was Paris, where Richard was royally received on 24 June by another cousin, Blanche of Castile, and her son King Louis, who provided them with a guide for the rest of their journey by land. Their first difficulty arose in the city of Vienne. The boats purchased by Richard to convey them down the River Rhône caught the eye of some locals. He turned down their offer to buy them at three times what he paid for them, saying only that he was no boat dealer. So they stole them. He and his men somehow managed their passage downriver, but when they reached Beaucaire, they found the boats waiting for them with a message from the culprits that they were sorry for the inconvenience. Richard responded by destroying the vessels, a sign that he had inherited the legendary Angevin temper of his forebears. The territory belonged to another one of his cousins, Count Raymond VII of Toulouse. Raymond expressed his shock and dismay over the offence given to the crusaders, but did nothing about it.

Another count came to meet them, Raymond Berenger V of Provence, the father of Queen Eleanor. He was at war with his neighbour Raymond of Toulouse and hoped to engage Richard on his side. More unwelcome visitors included a papal legate and the archbishop of Arles. These two prelates claimed to have the authority of the pope, who was still worried about Richard's connection to the emperor, to order him not to proceed any further. Now thoroughly antagonised, Richard got all his men except one on board ships at the port of Marseille. The lone exception was Robert Tweng, the former guerrilla leader who terrorised papal clerks and officials. Richard dispatched him to the imperial court to inform Frederick of the pope's latest 'cunning devices'.[14]

It had taken the crusaders three months to reach the Mediterranean overland, a distance of nearly one thousand kilometres, and another month at sea followed. On 8 October 1240, they disembarked at Acre. They were received with the greatest joy and acclamation, accompanied by chants, bells, harps, and dancers. The local prelates and chieftains greeted them in their official robes and led the crowds in crying out to heaven, 'Blessed is he who cometh in the name of the Lord.' The only thing missing from the celebration were the French crusaders who had preceded them there by a year. They were nowhere in sight.

Up until that point, the French part of the crusade had teetered on disaster. They had arrived to find the sultanates of Syria and Egypt in bitter conflict with each other, with four princes of the blood vying to recreate the empire of their ancestor Saladin.

Navigating that divide had allowed Frederick to diplomatically recover Jerusalem in 1229 during his own private crusade, but the military orders based in the Holy Land could no longer agree on which enemy to back. The Templars were for the Syrians, the Hospitallers for the Egyptians, and the crusader chieftains disagreed among themselves which strategy to undertake. Only part of their forces engaged the Egyptians at the battle of Gaza on 13 November 1239. They were outnumbered and routed, with hundreds of prisoners carried off to Cairo, including Simon de Montfort's older brother Amaury. One of the Muslim princes took advantage of their defeat to seize Jerusalem, the defence of which had been the whole point of the crusade.

Inasmuch as the reigning sultans feared each other more than they did the crusaders, each one approached Count Theobald IV of Champagne, the elected 'captain of the host', for a treaty of alliance. Richard knew him well. Back in 1227, England's best shot at regaining Poitou rested on Theobald and a cabal of French barons opposed to Blanche of Castile. As a relation (and rumoured lover) of the dowager queen, the count was charged with negotiating with her, but Richard, who had come up from Gascony, saw something suspicious about the way the talks were dragging out. As Theobald was returning from yet another visit to Blanche, Richard resolved to kidnap him but Theobald learned of the plot and fled. The rebellion was over after that.

When Theobald and the French crusaders arrived in Acre in 1239, the sultan of Damascus was Ayyub, but within a month he was expelled by his uncle Ismail. Ayyub yearned for revenge even after supplanting his own younger brother Abu Bakr as the sultan of Cairo. Ismail saw the crusader states as a buffer zone between him and his nephew and offered major land concessions for their support. Much to the dismay of the Hospitallers and comrades of the prisoners in Egypt, Theobald accepted the deal with the Syrians because it enabled the crusaders to reoccupy Jerusalem and adjoining areas that had not been under Christian control since 1187. Theobald made a quick pilgrimage to the holy city and left for home. According to Paris, some of his haste had to do with avoiding Richard, whose 'youth, inexperience and effeminacy' disgusted him.[15]

For Richard the contempt was mutual and he laid into Theobald when he learned that he had basically run for it, without fully implementing the treaty with Damascus. It was then that an envoy arrived from Cairo offering to release the prisoners in return for their own treaty. Richard led his forces south to Ascalon, near the border of Gaza, where Duke Hugh IV of Burgundy and the remaining French troops had set about rebuilding the castle constructed there by Richard's uncle, Richard the Lionheart. Hugh was for the rapprochement with Egypt, as were the Hospitallers and Frederick, who was still the titular king of Jerusalem. At the end of November, Richard dispatched a delegation to Cairo to work out a deal.

It took more than two months for them to reappear with a draft agreement. In that time, Richard kept his men busy working on Ascalon and otherwise assuming the role of undisputed leader of the crusade. Duke Hugh was relieved to relinquish command to him. His part in the crusade had been ignoble up until that point. He joined Amaury de Montfort in making the thrust into Gaza against the orders of Theobald, but the duke and others fled before the Egyptians blocked the escape route. Leaving the Holy Land while his surviving comrades were still captive was not an option. Hugh sent a letter to his cousin Beatrice de Montfort, Amaury's wife, with details of their plight and she showed the letter to Richard while he was in Paris.

Ratification of the treaty took another two months. With a truce in force, Richard had his men venture to the old battlefield with horses and carts to bring back the bones of the dead for interment at the cemetery in Ascalon. On 23 April 1241, several hundred French prisoners were freed after eighteen months of captivity. Richard assumed the expense of feeding and clothing them, as well as securing their journey homeward. Says Paris: 'When the French nobles were informed that the earl had, amongst his other acts of charity and kindness, performed such a pious action, he deservedly gained immortal praise and thanks from them.'[16]

Although the English crusaders engaged in no fighting while in the Holy Land, many never saw home again. Richard's steward John Fitz-John died there, as did his former guardian Peter de Maulay and Eudo Fitz-Roy, a natural son of King John and therefore another of Richard's half-brothers. Some died on the return voyage, like William de Forz, the earl of Albemarle, who had led a separate contingent overseas sometime after Richard left. Senior among Henry's earls, Forz could have contested Richard for the leadership, but he was old and only there to fulfil the vow he had made twenty years earlier to atone for his hell-raising during the king's minority.

The only other earl in the Holy Land at that time was Simon de Montfort. He was still in disgrace when he returned to England in the spring of 1240 to pick up his son and sell woods in Leicester to help finance his crusade. He found the king ready to forgive him for his presumption of the royal goodwill. Henry even dispatched a number of household knights to serve under him. Unlike Richard, Simon took up Frederick's offer to journey through Italy and he brought his wife Eleanor with him so she could meet her sister the empress again. Frederick put a palace in Brindisi at her disposal while Simon and his men headed east.[17]

On 3 May 1241, ten days after the release of the prisoners, Richard sailed for home. It was not his intention to meet Frederick or travel through Italy, but after two months the poor winds took him only as far as Sicily. Thoroughly fatigued, he made landfall at Trapani and sent word to the emperor of his arrival. Frederick was just then in the mood to receive him rapturously. Pope Gregory IX had summoned a council for the purpose of deposing the emperor, but the imperial fleet intercepted the papal flotilla on the day Richard left the Holy Land and all the prelates not killed or drowned in the mayhem were captured. The pope, defeated and broken, died three months later, although he was said to be almost a hundred years old at the time.

The procession that brought Richard to the emperor was festive but exhausting. The physically unprepossessing Frederick, who was fourteen years older, embraced the brother-in-law he had long desired to meet amidst the applause of his attendants. He stayed with his guest for the next couple of days while Richard underwent a cure of blood-letting, baths, and medical fomentations. Richard met his sister, whom he had not seen in six years. Because the empress was pregnant, protocol required imperial permission before the two were allowed to have a long and free discussion. For their entertainment, Frederick engaged two Saracen girls to dance about on two balls rolling underfoot while they sang, juggled, played instruments, and contorted their bodies to the wonder of the onlookers.

At Frederick's request, Richard went to Rome on 24 June to try to re-establish peace between the papacy and empire. Paris says that Richard was received with insults and contempt and his overtures were dismissed out of hand. Frederick knew the mission had no chance, but he wanted his brother-in-law to see for himself what he was dealing with at the papal court. After spending four months with the emperor, 'as a son with a father', Richard set off for home overland. It was slow-going with all the festivities that awaited him in every town. At Cremona, he was greeted by a band crammed into a howdah on top of an elephant.[18]

Richard arrived at Dover on 7 January 1242 to much the same fanfare. After an absence of eighteen months, the king 'rushed into his arms and received him with every mark of joy, fraternal blood arousing the affections on both sides'. London turned out to welcome him as if 'an angel' had appeared among them. Many familiar faces in the ranks of the nobility and clergy who greeted him were no longer there. John de Lacy, Gilbert Basset, and Gilbert Marshal were dead, the last two in horse-riding accidents. Edmund, the archbishop of Canterbury, had set off for Rome again to complain about his monks and died while still in France. Otto the legate was gone as well. He had left for the papal council and now numbered among Frederick's prisoners.

One new face at court was Peter of Savoy, a warrior-diplomat in the mould of his older brother William, who had died in Italy two years earlier after being poisoned. Henry had lured Peter to England with land and castles in the hope of cultivating his continental connections and outreach. He was expected to work hard for his rewards and had already undertaken his first assignment while Richard was visiting Frederick. Called a discreet and circumspect man, Peter of Savoy was prepared to defer to Richard, but a new mission took him abroad shortly before his arrival. It was a mission that Richard was expected to take very much to heart.

At a grand knighting ceremony in June 1241, the king of France invested his brother Alphonse with the county of Poitou. Louis could not yet know that Richard, who still called himself the count of Poitou, had just liberated hundreds of French crusaders and honourably buried their dead, but it would not have deterred

Louis in any case. Compounding the insult was the treatment meted out to Richard's mother Isabella. When she and her husband Hugh arrived to do homage to Alphonse as their new overlord, Blanche of Castile, who in the war against King John had tried to supplant Isabella as the queen of England, pretended not to notice her and kept her standing and waiting like a servant. Isabella and Hugh stormed off and renounced their allegiance.

After waiting almost twenty years for his mother and stepfather to finally come around, Henry dispatched Peter of Savoy to construct an international coalition against the Capetians. Louis learned of it and tried to capture Peter, but he made his escape and returned to England before Easter of 1242. It was then that Richard met the 'little Charlemagne' as Peter was later dubbed, and they fast became friends and associates.

In the meantime, Richard helped his brother lobby a parliament of nobles and clergy for the funds needed for the new campaign, but to no avail. They cited many reasons. They had been taxed enough, the Poitevins were not to be trusted, and the truce with France was still in force. The king's exhortation that they 'try the fortune of war against those who injure us' fell on deaf ears. The expedition set sail on 15 May with six earls but only 150 knights.[19]

3

GROWING WEALTH AND POWER
1242–1251

On paper it looked good. The kings of England and Aragon, the counts of Toulouse and Provence, and imperial vassals on the eastern border of France would put Louis in a vice while the rebellious Poitevin lords defied him. It could only succeed, however, if they all moved quickly and in the end no one did except Louis. He had a large feudal host in the field swallowing up castles even before the English landed and set up encampment in Poitou. Before leaving, Henry had promised Richard he would not deliberately break the truce with France and so found himself bogged down with initial negotiations that cost time. The campaign came down to contesting a single bridge at Taillebourg, and to their dismay Henry and his earls could see they had no chance of holding back the far bigger French army.

Richard was furious over the fiasco and denounced his stepfather for leading them into a trap. When Hugh just shrugged it off and blamed his wife, Richard removed his armour, picked up a staff, and made his way through the enemy line as a man of peace. The crusaders he saved in the Holy Land welcomed him with joy and respect and gladly conveyed him to the presence of their king. For Richard it had to be extremely humiliating. The last time he and Louis met, just two years earlier, he had been much feted and honoured. Now he was standing before him, a nervous and sweaty pilgrim humbly begging for a truce.

Louis reluctantly consented but only because Richard was his cousin, because he had liberated the French prisoners, and because it was a Sunday. And it was only for that day and night. In the morning, he was coming after them. Richard went back to camp with the news and the English forces quickly retired thirteen kilometres south to Saintes. They beat off the first attempt to encircle them on 22 July, but the situation grew hopeless as one Poitevin lord after another deserted them. Hugh Lusignan was not even among the last of them to crawl back to Louis. Completely cut off, the king and his earls ran for it. They got safely into Gascony, but the French were not about to stop there and prepared to invade. Only an epidemic checked their advance. Louis fell ill and went back to Paris, but a good many of his troops died, including several Richard had repatriated from Egypt.[1]

As the king, Henry had to take their defeat and flight on the chin, and one of his earls was ready to give it to him. It was Simon de Montfort, who had not sailed with the fleet but had arrived in Poitou directly from Burgundy. He had stayed behind in the Holy Land after Richard left, hoping in vain for Frederick to name him his regional governor. By mid-summer he had left with Duke Hugh and his brother Amaury, who died after they landed in Italy.

Simon answered Henry's summons to join the army and fought valiantly against the French troops in the vineyards outside Saintes, but then forgot himself and recommended that they lock up the king somewhere for his own good. As hostilities ceased and the earls began leaving for home, Simon was not among them. Having insulted Henry at the height of their flight, he had to worm his way back into favour for however long it took. When they all returned more than a year later, he and his wife Eleanor were still frozen out.

Richard was fed up with Henry himself. As a reward for securing the one-day truce with Louis, Henry agreed at Saintes to give his brother Gascony in compensation for losing Poitou. When they were out of harm's way, Henry reneged on the deal because he intended to give Gascony to Edward when he grew up. That had always been the case and Henry could claim that Richard had subjected him to extortion under the circumstances. As far as Richard was concerned, Henry could call it whatever he wanted, a promise was a promise. As to where the problem really lay, he was inclined to look over his brother's shoulder and see the meddlesome influence of the queen.

Eleanor of Provence was eight months pregnant when she boarded ship in England and gave birth to a daughter in Bordeaux just before the disaster unfolded. On the cusp of turning twenty years old, she was poised to dominate her husband's counsels and revive the dynamic sort of queenship England had not witnessed for a century. Richard had done very well for himself before she came along and would continue to do so as long as he steered clear of the patrimony that belonged to her children.

After a sharp exchange of words with his brother and sister-in-law, Richard agreed to take compensation in the form of money, £2,000 in cash plus £666 annually, and this was in addition to a prospective bride and the dowry Henry promised to go with her. She was Eleanor's sister Sanchia; prior to sailing Richard had empowered Peter of Savoy to finalise marriage arrangements between them. It was naturally a political move. With Henry and Richard married to two of the four daughters of the count of Provence, they stood at least half a chance of keeping the French from getting their hands on the province. The thirty-three-year-old Richard could well have met the sixteen-year-old Sanchia on his way to the Holy Land two years earlier and confirmed for himself the reports of her incomparable beauty.

In September 1242, Richard set off for Provence but turned back after learning that the French, who were keen to prevent the marriage, were waiting to ambush him. With his brother's blessing, he embarked for home on 18 October, leaving with his twenty-year-old stepson Richard de Clare and Walter Marshal, who had succeeded his brother Gilbert as earl of Pembroke. Their voyage was fraught with many dangers and tempests. Upon reaching England, Richard vowed to build an abbey as thanks for his deliverance.[2]

Two days before Richard left Gascony, Henry ordered his regents back home to put everything that the king owned at his brother's disposal: houses, castles, forests, parks, even his collection of falcons and hawks. After two years of service abroad, Richard was invited to relax. It was just as well he did not join the regency council headed by Walter de Gray, the archbishop of York. Henry was determined to renew the offensive in Poitou and got testy when his stream of orders for men and money failed to produce the desired effect. He dismissed one of the regents with a curt 'go and attend to the salvation of your soul.'

It took the surrender of the count of Toulouse to put an official end to the campaign. Henry agreed to a truce with France and sailed home with the queen and court in late September 1243.

They were followed a little over a month later by Sanchia and her mother Beatrice, who were treated to the splendour of thousands of candles lit in Canterbury churches. On 22 November 1243, Sanchia of Provence and Richard of Cornwall were married at Westminster Abbey in an elaborate ceremony that included, if Paris can be believed, a banquet for 30,000 guests. The newlyweds spent Christmas at Wallingford, where they entertained the king, queen, and most of the nobility. In the year he waited for his bride to arrive, Richard rebuilt Berkhamsted Castle, about fifty kilometres northwest of London, with a view to turning it into a magnificent residence for his young wife.

Like her sister before her, Sanchia found herself in a cloudier, greyer country populated by a people speaking an unfathomable language. The Occitan she grew up with was linguistically close enough to her husband's Anglo-Norman French for the two of them to communicate, but she would not have had a clue about the English he used with his staff and attendants. Generous and kind-hearted, she remained close to Eleanor throughout their time together in England and never aspired to become the 'second queen' that Paris feared lay in store for the kingdom in one of his usual diatribes against Henry and his diplomacy.[3]

Sanchia's first years in her new home were busy ones for her husband. Richard spent more than half his time at court and in the summer of 1244 he travelled north with the feudal host for a showdown with his former brother-in-law Alexander II of Scotland. Relations had soured in the six years following the death of Queen Joan. Remarried to the daughter of a prominent French nobleman and father at last to a son and heir, Alexander had his own army at the border to contest English claims of overlordship and other issues. Neither side wanted war and Richard was able to work out a treaty that finalised a future marriage between Alexander's namesake son and Henry's eldest daughter, Margaret. The peace thus achieved between both kingdoms lasted half a century.

Avoiding war was far less expensive than waging it, but the combined Poitevin and Scottish expeditions left Henry massively in debt. At a parliament convened in the dining hall of Westminster Abbey in late October, the king asked for a new tax. A committee of twelve, consisting of four bishops, four earls (Richard chief among them), two barons and two abbots was convened to discuss it with the clergy and laity. Most of them were unhappy with the crown's recent attempts to raise revenue through inquests or the recovery of rights and franchises usurped from Henry during his minority. The architects of this policy were the professional administrators of the king's council, men from obscure English backgrounds who answered only to him.

Acting in unison, the clergy and laity agreed to the tax only if Henry added four of their own to the council and invested them with the powers of oversight and restraint. They also wanted to revive the ministers of state like justiciar, with parliament alone able to appoint or dismiss them. Their proposal was more erosion of royal authority, far more radical than what Magna Carta intended. It never made it out of committee and the most Henry conceded was to revisit his current fiscal measures. When parliament reconvened early the following year, nothing had changed and no tax was forthcoming.[4]

Crown finances were fundamentally sound at this time. What Henry needed was stopgap funding and for that he had other sources available. He taxed the Jews, collected the income of lordships made vacant by the death of a baron or bishop, and he borrowed from his brother. Richard had grown immensely wealthy in the past decade, partly from farming out the tin mines of Cornwall, but mostly from the profits of the estates that he owned or were under his control. The wardships Henry granted him included the earldom of Devon. Some years ago, in April 1237,

Richard went to the Isle of Wight, which was part of the earldom, to search for treasure reportedly buried under any number of mounds there. Henry learned about the treasure hunt and wanted a piece of the action, but nothing further is known about it. If Richard found any chest laden with gold and pearls, he kept it to himself.

By the mid-1240s, his earnings had reached close to £6,000 a year, putting him far and away at the top of the richest earls in the land, ahead of the £3,500 enjoyed by his stepson Richard de Clare in Gloucester and Walter Marshal in Pembroke, and way ahead of his sister Eleanor's £930 and her husband Simon's £600. The earl and countess of Leicester had remained out of favour since their return to England. In desperation, they approached Sanchia's mother during her wedding celebrations to ask her to intercede for them personally. Beatrice of Provence worked her charm on her son-in-law the king with great success. Henry again started making gifts of deer and wine to Eleanor, he forgave both Montforts their debts, and he granted Simon the lucrative Umfraville wardship in the north. Richard desired the wardship for himself and was greatly displeased not to get it.

And he was still smarting over Henry cancelling the grant of Gascony to him. He thought his brother might make it up to him by granting him the earldom of Chester, which had lately come into crown hands, but the queen got it in the expectation that Chester would eventually go to the royal couple's second son Edmund, who was born in January 1245. Richard again saw his ambition thwarted by the queen and, rumour had it, made his feelings known about it at the worst possible moment.

His Welsh nephew David, son of his half-sister Joan, had succeeded his father Llywelyn after his death in 1240. He now led an uprising against English overlordship, forcing another showdown in Wales in August 1245. Always reluctant to go to war, Henry chose to build another castle for containment rather than launch a full-scale conquest. What fighting there was tended to be savage, and four of Richard's household were among the troops massacred in one ambush. A rumour nevertheless went around that Richard had actually favoured David on account of his dispute with the king and queen and that he had even offered him refuge at Tintagel.

Matthew Paris was always ready to believe the worst about the royals, but he discounted the rumour because Richard helped finance the campaign. Denied taxation by parliament, Henry had turned to his brother for a £2,000 loan. Richard gave it to him but demanded security for it. One of Richard's clerks went to the New Temple in London where the king's treasure was stored and there weighed and collected the value of enough gold bezants and bars to cover the loan.

Richard also had enough cash on hand to donate £1,000 for the relief of the Holy Land. The situation there had deteriorated since he left. The crusader states had decided to back Damascus against Cairo, figuring they would divide up Egypt between them. Ayyub got the jump on them and made an alliance with the fearsome Khorezmian horsemen, who captured and sacked Jerusalem in July 1244. A few months later they helped the Egyptians destroy a combined Christian and Syrian army near Gaza. In France, Louis vowed to go on crusade to reverse the setback. The new pope, Innocent IV, summoned the prelates of Christendom to a council at Lyon, but not to deal with Ayyub, rather Frederick.[5]

While Henry was encamped in Wales, Raymond Berenger V of Provence died. Since his two eldest daughters had married kings, it was not unreasonable to expect the husband of his next eldest daughter succeeding him as count. It was certainly part of the motivation behind Richard's marriage to Sanchia. Having made a name for himself across Europe and the Holy Land, Richard yearned for a title and position to go with his international reputation and standing. Raymond, however, was of a mind that all three of his older daughters had made illustrious matches. In the will he drew up in 1238, well before Sanchia's marriage, he left Provence to his youngest daughter, fifteen-year-old Beatrice, named after her mother.

The race was now on for her hand and Richard's ten-year-old son Henry was put forward as a candidate. Worried that all the interest might lead to her daughter's abduction, Beatrice of Provence named the pope as her guardian. This was excellent news for Innocent, who was determined to carry on his predecessor's work of deposing Frederick as emperor. In 1244, he fled Rome for Lyon, where the Alps stood between him and Frederick's armies. Should the emperor decide to come after him anyway, Innocent could call on the king of France for help. Like Henry, Louis tried hard not to take sides, but the opportunity here was obvious. He agreed to become the pope's protector in return for Beatrice's marriage to his youngest brother, nineteen-year-old Charles. In January 1246, the couple were married and Charles marched into Provence to take possession of it.

In England, the Plantagenet brothers were outraged and demanded redress from the pope. He agreed to 'induce' the Capetian brothers to respect their rights in Provence, but only because Innocent was wary of alienating England at this time. Although he had succeeded in deposing Frederick at the council of Lyon in 1245, the 'dragon' and his offspring were not giving up without a fight. Innocent needed money to complete his extermination of the Hohenstaufens and saw it in all the churches, abbeys and priories that made up Christendom. Rightly anticipating resistance to such an overtly political crusade against a Christian ruler, the pope and his people were counting on the cooperation of other Christian rulers to lean on their clergymen.[6]

Henry had nothing to gain from propping up Frederick. His sister the empress died in childbirth on 1 December 1241, only a few months after Richard's visit, and the emperor did not step up for his Poitevin campaign. Indeed, in all the time the king and emperor were bound by marital alliance, Frederick did nothing except write long letters bemoaning the vindictiveness of the pope. On a personal level, Henry was forever grateful to the papacy for saving his throne when English barons and churchmen attempted to depose his father John. But he was concerned for Isabella's children and the effect their father's deposition would have on their patrimony. Henry was, moreover, tenacious about who became the next bishops of his realm, and here Innocent IV, unlike Gregory IX before him, had failed him.

This issue started off peacefully enough when the pope confirmed Henry's choice of Boniface of Savoy, younger brother of William and Peter, as the archbishop of Canterbury. Henry finally got what he thought was an international prelate-statesman to advance his strategy at home and abroad, but Boniface's ultimate worth to him proved as ephemeral as Frederick's. Innocent then confirmed the remaining backlog of new bishops, three in all, but none of them was on the king's shortlist. A cabal of senior bishops had conspired to insinuate their own men into these positions and persuaded the guileless pope to approve them while they were attending his council in Lyon.

The parliament that convened at Westminster in March 1246 to consider the papal demand for money found the king, nobility and clergy in rare agreement. By their calculation, Rome was already enjoying ecclesiastical revenue in England to the tune of £40,000 annually, which was more than royal revenue at its peak. Various letters were drafted to explain the injustice of it all, but Innocent was prepared to use spiritual weapons to break open the vault if need be. The bishops acquiesced and were ready to assist the pontiff in placing England under interdict if the king continued to interfere with their collections for Rome. For Henry, it came down to support from the nobility.

The barons had long resisted attempts to purloin their patronage of churches and had recently run a hapless papal tax collector out of the country. They wrote their own letter to the pope pleading for 'a salutary remedy to the burdens, injuries, and oppressions repeatedly imposed and practised on the kingdom of England'. Topping the list of names in the letterhead was 'Richard of Cornwall'. To officials at the papal court, that was the weak link they needed. Richard was still owed money raised for his crusade, but the bishops had been slow in handing it over to him. Innocent now ordered them to make immediate amends and he empowered two proctors to pursue every claim in Richard's ledgers.

Their commission created a scandal, because much of the fundraising came in the form of a scam called redemptions. It worked like this: The friars who preached the crusade exhorted everyone to take the cross, even children, imbeciles, the elderly and the infirm. That made them crusaders, but since they had neither the money nor mental and physical fitness to proceed to the Holy Land, they were encouraged to redeem their vows, which is to say buy a redemption. In one infamous case, Richard's proctors sued the family of a deceased man whose executors disputed the claim that he had taken the cross. The proctors won and recovered £16 for the man's posthumous redemption, about £15,000 in modern terms.[7]

The papal mandate for the earl of Cornwall arrived just as parliament reconvened on 7 July 1246 at Winchester. The assembly was informed that, apart from granting some minor privileges, the pope refused to budge. The bishops were ordered to pay up. The king dug in as well and ordered them not to send a penny. His brother, however, reversed himself and now insisted that the tax collections go forward. With the united front of nobles and clergy no longer behind him, Henry finally concurred. Frederick called it a complete betrayal and denounced Richard for his 'effeminate connivance with the pope's party'. But Richard was nothing if not pragmatic. As with the emperor's deposition, he knew Innocent was going to get his way sooner or later. The trick was to cut the best possible deal with him.

In these years Richard and Henry were as close to each other as they had ever been. They spent Christmas court together with their sister wives. Richard gave his brother a huge tapestry which Henry had hung behind his throne on Christmas day. After two years of marriage, Sanchia was pregnant and on 10 July 1246, right around the time Richard switched sides at the Winchester parliament, she gave birth to a son named Richard. The king and queen and many nobles gathered at Wallingford for her purification the following month. The child died a short time afterwards and was buried at Hailes on 15 August.

Richard also lost two members of his staff at this time, his chancellor Nicholas Danne, a man very adept at keeping his coffers full, and Sir John Bretasche, the steward of Berkhamsted. By coincidence, both men got drunk on wine one night, fell off their horses, and broke their necks.[8]

With just fifteen months separating them, the relations between the Plantagenet brothers were underpinned by an understandable degree of resentment. Henry resented Richard for the price he put on his loyalty, and Richard resented Henry for being his lord and benefactor. There was also jealousy. As an aesthete and cosmopolitan, Henry envied the freedom of movement that took Richard to places like Paris, Rome and Jerusalem, and to meeting people like Frederick, with whom the king shared a passion for falconry. The source of Richard's envy was obvious. His brother sat on the throne and enjoyed all the power and trappings that went with it. The awareness of what might have been fuelled a sense of rivalry in Richard that never let up.

In July 1245, Henry undertook to rebuild Westminster Abbey into the glorious medieval wonder it is today. In that same month he gave Richard the land and manor of Hailes so he could build the new religious house he swore he would after he was nearly shipwrecked on his way home from Gascony. As the walls came down in the noisy environs of Westminster, they started going up in the serene Gloucestershire countryside. Richard also received gifts of timber and oak from Henry for the construction. On 17 June 1246, the two brothers were together at the dedication of Beaulieu Abbey, which had been founded by their father King John, and where Richard's first wife Isabel was buried. Richard took the opportunity of the dedication to poach thirteen monks from the abbey to populate his new spiritual dwelling in the woods.

For a patron saint, he could not ask for a better choice than St Edward the Confessor, whose feast day marking his death in 1066 was 5 January, Richard's birthday. Henry, however, got to him first. He named his firstborn son after Edward, he lavishly celebrated the saint's other feast day (translation of his relics) of 13 October, and he planned to build a shrine to Edward to form the centrepiece of the new Westminster Abbey. Richard could have settled for another popular Anglo-Saxon king, St Edmund, but Henry got to him first as well with both overt devotion and the naming of his second son after him.

It was just then that another Edmund became available. As one of the sops to England during the Council of Lyon, the pope fast-tracked the canonisation of Edmund of Abingdon, the archbishop of Canterbury who had died in France in 1240. According to Matthew Paris, Richard's English pride was hurt when he learned that Blanche and Louis attended the translation of the new saint's relics on 7 June 1247 in Pontigny and so he decided to co-opt him back from the French. Convinced Edmund's spirit had saved him from a 'severe and secret illness', he resolved to pay for one quarter of his new shrine. He got a chance to make a pilgrimage there when he set out on a diplomatic mission in late September. His son Henry, now eleven years old, went with him.[9]

The first stop was Paris and a meeting with Louis. It had been five years since they last met, at Saintes, when Richard stood before him as a lowly pilgrim seeking a truce. Louis was now making preparations to go on crusade, and as part of purging his conscience before setting out, he offered to do justice to anyone with a reasonable claim. Richard put forth his brother's claim to Normandy and other English territories seized by the French monarchy. Louis took up the matter with his advisers and came back with the response that King John had been deprived of them in a court of law and that was that. Again adopting the guise of a pilgrim, Richard and his son continued their journey to Pontigny, about 180 kilometres southeast of Paris. There they prayed at Edmund's shrine and offered up 'a most handsome collar, exceeding a man's hand in width, and ornamented with costly jewels, the like of which could not be found amongst the king's treasures'.

They arrived back in England on 28 October 1247, missing by fifteen days the most elaborate ceremony Henry had staged yet in honour of Edward the Confessor. He had received a crystal phial of holy blood from the patriarch of Jerusalem and carried it barefoot in front of throngs of onlookers from St Paul's Cathedral to Westminster Abbey, just over three kilometres. The festivities included the knighting of young nobles and on this occasion all eyes were on Henry and Richard's half-brother William de Valence.

He was part of the large brood of children Isabella of Angoulême had with Hugh Lusignan. She had died in June 1246 at the abbey of Fontevrault, where she had gone to live out her life as a nun following the debacle of their uprising against Louis.

Henry was anxious to maintain close contacts with his much younger siblings. From their lordships in Poitou, they could keep an eye on the security of Gascony on their southern border. Hoping to establish some of them in England, he found a husband for his half-sister Alice in John de Warenne, the young earl of Surrey, and a wife for William de Valence in Joan Munchesney. She was one of the heiresses to the Pembroke estate following the deaths of Walter Marshal and his brother Anselm within a month of each other in late 1245. Had Joan not been the first cousin of Richard's son Henry, she might have become his bride, for earlier in February 1247 the king had promised his brother 'the first best marriage' for the prince.

In setting up his foreign relations in this fashion, Henry was seeking to bind the baronial clans closer to the crown. He also wanted to strengthen his position among the clergy, and for that he had another half-brother, Aymer de Valence. The death of the bishop of Winchester who had succeeded Peter des Roches allowed Henry to manipulate the election so that Aymer became the next bishop despite his relative youth. Together with Richard, these two Lusignans, William and Aymer, gave Henry three brothers in control of major lordships throughout the kingdom, much like Louis had with his three brothers in France.

Related to them or not, Richard was wary of his half-siblings becoming rivals for his brother's favours. He made it clear to Henry that his own position at the head of the patronage queue was to remain unassailable. That condition did not necessarily apply to their sister Eleanor de Montfort, however. She claimed dower lands from the Pembroke estate that were now in William de Valence's possession, and neither she nor her husband Simon was happy about it.[10]

The only English currency in circulation at this time was the silver penny. It took 240 of them to make a pound (£), which was only a unit of account. When travelling about at home or abroad, Richard and his retinue paid their way with pennies stuffed into sacks and saddlebags, or they hauled around chests and barrels full of them for longer journeys. The current penny had been issued by his grandfather Henry II in 1179, thirty years before Richard was born. It was now in a sorry state, both from wear and tear or the shaving and clipping of coins for their silver content. The debasement of the currency was having a detrimental effect on the economy despite the booming trade in wool. In France, Louis ordered any English coins found not worth their weight in silver to be confiscated and melted down.

Meeting at Oxford in April 1247, parliament agreed that a recoinage was necessary and Henry assigned the task to his brother. Richard was the obvious choice because he had the cash to purchase bulk quantities of silver ingot for the royal mints in London and Canterbury. His commission was to run for seven years, later extended to twelve. He set to work in August, prior to his trip to France, by engaging an expert from Brussels. On 11 March 1248, the silver content of the new coins was tested in London with Richard and Henry present. They were minted with the image of the crowned king 'Henricus III' on the obverse side and a 'long cross' on the reverse. The intention was to replace only coins that had been tampered with or were in poor condition, but the new coin proved a hit, requiring the opening of seventeen temporary mints throughout the kingdom to accommodate the exchange of money. Over 138,000,000 pennies worth £577,000 were minted in the first three years.

Richard not only made the recoinage a success, but himself richer in the bargain. The owners of old coins had to bear the exchange charges, which worked out to six pennies on the pound for the king as his customary profit and ten pennies for the mint. Richard's agreement gave him half of Henry's profit for the twelve years of his commission and his own old money was exempted from the charges. He did not have to suffer the roughly seven per cent loss on the pound that everyone else did. In addition, he was entitled to all the fines imposed for exchange infringements. Matthew Paris was not too far off the mark estimating that Richard made a total profit of £20,000 off the enterprise. Forever obsessed with money, the monk was bitterly critical of him as a result.[11]

The king himself did not make a profit for several years, not until the loans Richard had made to purchase the silver and other supplies were paid off. In the end, Henry's share was a respectable £7,000. Perhaps in gratitude for the success Richard had made of the recoinage, Henry summoned parliament in 1249 to meet on 5 January, the first time ever on that day. Although they were officially gathered for the feast of St Edward, it was of course a milestone for Richard, his fortieth birthday. He came to London from Wallingford along with a great many nobles who had spent Christmas of 1248 there as his guests.

Throughout the previous year Henry had had no success pushing a tax through parliament. The standoff had become more of the same routine. The barons and clergy wanted to revive the great offices of states and to appoint the ministers to fill them, but Henry saw that as too much of a curtailment of his power in exchange for the money he needed. When parliament met next in April 1249, it was expected that the king would finally make concessions, but Richard never showed up. He had suddenly left for a distant part of Cornwall 'as if on business', says Paris with much disapproval. The business was actually a ruse, for Richard had lent Henry £3,333 the previous month to stay afloat. This allowed the king to go before parliament and tell them again that there would be no reforms in return for a tax. Since Richard was considered the chief among the barons, his absence left his peers stymied and confused. Thanks to him, parliament again failed to bring the king's personal rule to an end.[12]

Christmas of 1249 was spent at Berkhamsted, where Sanchia was expecting their second child. On 26 December, she gave birth to a son they named after their patron saint Edmund. They soon got a chance to give their thanks for a safe delivery by making a pilgrimage to his shrine. In March 1250, the king, queen and various nobles vowed to go on crusade in front of a packed great hall at Westminster. Henry aimed to fund it with ten per cent of English church revenues and asked his brother to arrange it at the papal court in Lyon. Richard took Sanchia and his son Henry with him, as well as a large retinue to bedazzle the French. They consisted of 'forty knights, equipped with new accoutrements and mounted on beautiful horses with new harnesses glittering with gold'.

They stopped in Paris where, together with Peter of Savoy, Richard renewed the truce with France. It had been almost two years since Louis, his three brothers and their wives left on crusade, leaving Blanche of Castile, now in her sixties, to rule again as regent. She received Richard with the greatest joy and respect. Given the twenty-year age difference between these two first cousins, she considered him a 'particularly beloved son'. Blanche had been firmly opposed to her sons going on crusade and was relieved to learn of their spectacular success after landing in Egypt in June 1249. She could not know it, none of them could know it, but their crusade was just then on the verge of annihilation. On 6 April 1250, Louis surrendered his army and went into captivity with the rest of the survivors.

On that same day Richard arrived in Lyon. According to his own account, all the cardinals except one came out to welcome him. They took him to meet Pope Innocent IV, who rose from his chair, saluted Richard, embraced him, and invited him to dine. They sat together, the pope and earl, with other notables like Richard de Clare, now the earl of Gloucester, sitting nearby. To the discomfort of the English bishops who were also in Lyon on official business, the pope granted what Richard had come there for. Henry could have a tenth of all church revenues for three years to finance his crusade.

Richard and his family continued to St Edmund's shrine at Pontigny, then went back by way of St Denis near Paris so he could purchase Deerhurst Priory just north of Gloucester, which was owned by the French abbey. After he returned to England on 3 May, Richard had the monks living at Deerhurst expelled and all the outbuildings of the priory destroyed. He planned to build a castle on the site overlooking the River Severn. He did not fear the opposition of the neighbours because the pope had given the plan his personal approval. It may not have been enough, however, because Richard never went through with it and the priory survived until 1540.[13]

Another noble who met up with Richard's party in Paris was Simon de Montfort. He had come up from Gascony, where he had been serving as the king's viceroy for the past eighteen months. Simon and Eleanor had planned to join Louis's crusade, but the duchy had again become unstable and Henry turned to Simon, who had grown up in the region, to restore order there. His first year had been successful, but the Gascon nobility chafed against his tough way of doing business. When Simon reached Paris, he wrote Henry a frank letter indicating that more trouble lay ahead. He crossed the Channel with Richard's party to discuss the situation with him and the council.

While in England, Simon joined Richard and other nobles in mediating a dispute that had broken out between London and the abbot of Westminster. To help promote a new fair granted to the abbot, Henry ordered the closure of all shops and stalls in London while the fair was in progress. The Londoners were naturally aggrieved by the king's favouritism (and by the lousy weather that forced them to trek through the rain and mud around the abbey to do their shopping). Fed up with the griping of the mayor and aldermen, Henry took direct control of the city, but he relented after pressure from Richard and the rest of the council. The favoured fair, however, remained.

On 25 July 1250, news of the disaster in Egypt reached London. A week later Richard was at the exchequer, located next to Westminster Hall, when a messenger arrived with a letter for him describing the events. In it he read how the advance guard of Louis's army made it across the River Nile, but then failed to wait for the rest of the troops to cross before launching an attack against Mansourah. They were trapped within the walls of the city and cut to pieces, among them Richard's cousin William Longespee II.

The Egyptians then counterattacked and nearly drove the rest of the crusaders into the river. Louis's pride would not allow him to retreat until it was too late. Hemmed in and captured, he was forced to pay £100,000 to ransom himself and the survivors.

Louis stayed behind in the Holy Land while his brothers Alphonse and Charles sailed home to deal with the repercussions. They blamed the calamity on the pope and warned him to make peace with Frederick or run the risk of being evicted from Lyon. Innocent was worried enough by the threat to ask Henry for asylum in England, even in Gascony, despite the full-scale war that greeted Simon on his return there. In the end Frederick died on 13 December 1250 and the pope left Lyon the following April after six years of exile. Other political tensions prevented his return to Rome for another two years.[14]

Parliament in February 1251 was another contentious affair, but it had nothing to do with taxes. Henry of Bath, the senior royal justice, stood accused of taking bribes. The king ordered his arrest for high treason but allowed him bail on the surety of twenty-four knights so he could answer the charges before an assembly of his peers. Paris claims that it was Bath's wife Alina who pushed him into corruption. She was a Basset, the sister of Fulk, the bishop of London, and Philip, who became a close friend and ally of Richard when they crusaded together. They did not have to push Richard too hard to intervene on Bath's behalf because the specific case in question arose from the circuit court, called an eyre, that the judge undertook the previous summer. All fines collected from the eyre went towards paying off the king's debts to Richard.

Henry was unmoved by his brother's entreaties and Bath only made things worse by showing up in strength to answer the charges. When the king saw all the knights, family, friends and in-laws in his train before parliament, he declared that the judge was acting in a seditious manner. Richard and Bishop Fulk were able to assuage the royal wrath and Bath was eventually granted a pardon in return for a fine of £1,333. He still had to stand trial on individual charges, which ran on for years, but he was back in service within two years, albeit at only two-thirds of his former annual salary of £100.[15]

In late October, Henry and Eleanor were guests of Richard and Sanchia at Wallingford. On 5 November 1251, they came to Hailes for the dedication of the abbey that Richard built there. Thirteen bishops were in attendance, as were most of the prelates and nobles of the kingdom. It being a Sunday, the clergy were careful to consume fish instead of meat at the banquet afterwards. As a favour to Richard, Henry granted twenty marks a year to keep four candles burning all year round at the shrine of St Edmund in Pontigny. Paris got the story of the dedication and ceremony from Richard himself, and when he asked him how much the construction cost, Richard replied 10,000 marks (£6,700). He then added, 'Would that it had pleased God that I expended all that I have spent on the castle of Wallingford in as wise and salutary a manner.'

From Gloucestershire the court proceeded north in stages to York. King Alexander II of Scotland had died suddenly in 1249, leaving the throne to his underage son. Henry wanted to go ahead with the marriage of his eleven-year-old daughter Margaret to ten-year-old Alexander III before he left on crusade. Henry knighted the young king on Christmas day, the wedding was held the following morning, and the rest of the six-day celebration was given over to entertainment and feasting. The quantity of food supplied by the English side alone was staggering, with requisitions for, but not limited to, 70 boar, 125 swans,

400 rabbits, 1,000 deer, 7,000 chickens, 10,000 haddock and 68,500 loaves of bread.

The nobles in attendance included the earls of Gloucester, Norfolk, Leicester and Derby, but nowhere is the earl of Cornwall mentioned. If Richard missed his niece's wedding, as seems likely, his vanity probably could not suffer the occasion. His presence would be overshadowed not just by two kings, but by his twelve-year-old nephew Edward. The youth made his public debut on the international stage in York, wearing a tabard with the three leopards of the royal arms emblazoned in gold. It was a reminder to all that he was the heir to the throne, the position Richard had enjoyed for nearly twenty-three years. Richard's resentment was compounded by the grudge he still nursed over Gascony, which had been formally granted to Edward in September 1249. Sensitive to his brother's feelings on the issue, Henry made numerous gifts of deer, boar, fish and timber to him in the years that followed.

The king himself was then at his wit's end over Gascony, where the situation had become critical. Simon de Montfort was at the wedding in York only because he had returned to England to again ask for more money. He had begun building castles to put down the insurgency there and expected Henry to pay for them. In Henry's mind, it should never have come to this. Much to Simon's dismay, the king decided to send a commission there to see whether the complaints of the Gascons against his viceroy were true or not. How different it all might have been had Henry made good the grant of the duchy to his brother is hard to guess, but it is equally hard to imagine the Gascons ever calling Richard of Cornwall 'the exterminating earl' the way they did Simon.[16]

4

SICILY AND THE REGENCY
1252–1255

'The buffalo is an animal similar to the ox, well adapted for carrying or drawing burdens, a great enemy to the crocodile, fond of water, and provided with large horns to defend himself.' Such is Matthew Paris's description of the strange creatures, seen for the first time in England, that were sent to Richard in early 1252. Frustratingly Paris fails to add who sent the herd of water buffalo or what Richard did with them. Henry had received a polar bear the year before from the king of Norway and kept it at the Tower of London, where it was sometimes seen fishing in the Thames at the end of a tether, but what became of it also remains a mystery.[1]

One possibility for the buffalo is that they came from Richard's fourteen-year-old nephew Henry Hohenstaufen. He was a 'handsome and agreeable youth' based in Sicily, where the proximity to Africa enabled the trade in animals from that continent to flourish. In sending the buffalos, young Henry may have wanted to imitate his father Frederick, who after marrying his mother Isabella had sent a gift of three leopards to his new brother-in-law, the king of England. The boy certainly wanted to forge closer ties to his English family. Since Frederick's death, relations had not improved between the papacy and the emperor's heirs, who included Henry and his older half-brothers Conrad and Manfred. In January 1252, just before the buffalo arrived, Conrad imposed his rule over the kingdom of Sicily, with young Henry acting as his lieutenant on the island.

Now in a position of strength, Conrad attempted to negotiate, but as he was unwilling to cede any of his ancestral rights, Pope Innocent looked for another prince to install on the throne of the kingdom. In a letter written in August 1252, he asked Henry III to persuade his brother Richard of Cornwall to accept the crown. Innocent had already tried with Richard during their meeting in Lyon in 1250, but Frederick was still alive then and so nothing came of it. The pope renewed his offer now because he believed Richard 'possessed an unquenchable thirst for wealth and world dignity'. And yet, as Paris continues:

The majority of people, however, did not believe that the earl would on any account listen to the pope's promises, because he [Richard] was not well or strong in bodily health, nor brave or skilful in war; again, because it would appear dishonourable to supplant his nephew Henry; and lastly, because it is not the act of a wise man to give certainties in exchange for uncertainties. But the pope considered all these defects to be endurable, and not even inconveniences.

In November that year, a papal official, Albert of Parma, arrived in England to take up the matter with Richard personally. The earl of Cornwall was open to the offer because, now forty-three years old, he might not ever get another chance at such world dignity. He seems to have overcome the quandary of disinheriting his nephew, whom he almost certainly met during his sojourn in Sicily, but as with the money he loaned out to his brother the king, he demanded sufficient security. He wanted Innocent to give up hostages from among his family members to attest to his good faith and to hand over various fortresses along the frontier with the kingdom of Sicily; and he wanted the papal court to provide a certain amount of money for the expedition against Conrad.

His conditions were harsh, but as Richard pointed out, 'the pope is giving me what he is not strong enough himself to obtain.' He told Albert to tell Innocent that unless he agreed, then he might as well be offering him the moon. Innocent found neither Richard's conditions nor his attitude conducive to a productive partnership. 'We shall not enter into any treaty with him,' he huffed, 'or have anything more to do with him.'[2]

Following Albert's visit, Henry sent Innocent a polite thank-you note on behalf of his brother. He must have been disappointed by the outcome. Back in April 1252, the king made a solemn oath to leave on crusade on 24 June 1256. Should Richard be ruling Sicily by then, it would make it easier for Henry to get an army to the Holy Land. Henry had also begun to rethink the entire range of his foreign policy. For the last quarter of a century, all his efforts to recover Normandy and other Plantagenet lands in France had come to nothing. He was not about to let up the pressure, not with the Capetians reeling from their humiliation in Egypt, but if the papacy succeeded in carving up Frederick's former empire he saw no reason why England should not profit from it.

Henry himself was in no position just then to take advantage of these developments. The situation in Gascony had spiralled completely out of control. The fact-finding mission he sent there earlier in the year found that the Gascons were rebelling because Simon de Montfort had been ruthless in his quest for order, but also that the Gascons were a treacherous lot and so deserved their rough treatment. Exasperated, Henry ordered both sides to make their case before him and his council at a parliament specially convened in the dining hall of Westminster Abbey in May 1252. After a stormy affair, particularly the exchanges between the king and his viceroy, Richard and the other magnates of the realm threw their support behind Simon, but Henry could not be so sure he was completely innocent. He ordered him and the Gascons to go back and observe a truce, but when that failed to happen, he blamed Simon for sabotaging the peace process and dismissed him outright in August 1252.

It was already too late to win back the trust of the Gascons. Back in May, as the charges were flying back and forth in Westminster Abbey, the Spanish kingdom of Castile got a new king in Alfonso X. He asserted he had a better claim to Gascony than Henry through his own lineage back to Eleanor of Aquitaine, the original duchess. He began wooing the Gascons away from their allegiance to England. Even with Simon gone, the duchy was likely lost unless Henry went there in person to crush the revolt.

In May 1253, he summoned parliament to provide the money for the expedition. He was entitled to an aid (tax) for the knighting of his eldest son, but it brought in only £6,000, barely a tenth of the money that had sent Richard to Gascony in 1225. For the rest, Henry turned to his usual sources like Ireland, the Jews, and of course his brother. Richard lent him £6,000 in three instalments, secured in part with the king's jewels and gold treasure.[3]

Richard was not expected to join the expedition. He had long since abdicated his title of count of Poitou, and the grant of Gascony to Edward had been reaffirmed the previous year. Eleanor of Provence, who was pregnant with what would be her fifth and last child, would also stay behind to rule the kingdom in her husband's absence. She was given possession of his great seal on 22 June. Henry's choice of his wife as regent was a practical one. Should 'the lot of humanity' befall him in Gascony, he wanted the queen in a position to safeguard Edward's succession and minority until the boy came of age.

While appointing her as sole regent, Henry stipulated that she was to govern the realm 'with the counsel of Richard, earl of Cornwall'. To ensure there was no confusion about who was in charge, Richard surrendered his seal to Eleanor. She was to keep both his seal and the great seal locked up until Henry returned. All acts of state would be sealed by the chancellor using the privy seal.

Henry carefully demarcated certain powers. Like the queen, Richard could command the removal of sheriffs who 'exceeded or fell short of their offices'. In the case of church offices, only Richard and the chancellor were allowed to confer any benefice that fell vacant. This too was a practical move. For all her queenly status, Eleanor was a foreigner in a land where grumblings about foreigners siphoning off local revenue were as pervasive as ever. It may also reflect a quarrel over a church appointment the year before between the king and queen themselves, with Eleanor coming out on top.

Eager to secure Richard's engagement and cooperation, Henry made sure he received his rewards up front. He authorised his brother to take an aid from his tenants for the knighting of his own eldest son (not actually performed for another four years) and to Sanchia he promised various wardships. If £500 of land came to the crown while the king was away, Eleanor was to use it to satisfy the arrears of her sister's dowry. As for the care and maintenance of the regent herself, Richard was to make sure £200 of similar patronage went to her needs.[4]

The expedition left on 6 August. Because of Eleanor's pregnancy, the regency government remained based at Westminster or Windsor, the latter because it was the home of royal children and wards. Richard's son Henry, now eighteen, had been raised there, and Sanchia probably moved to Windsor at this time with three-year-old Edmund because a three-storey tower was being built and roofed with lead at Berkhamsted. The letters and mandates issued by the chancery, which travelled with the court, were attested by Eleanor and Richard jointly or Eleanor alone, sometimes by a member of the council. Most touched on the same sorts of business that Henry had been dealing with in his thirty-seven years on the throne up to that point.

An example was a warning to the people of Great Yarmouth, who were feuding with rival port towns. They were not to disturb the peace of the kingdom, because otherwise 'the king will betake himself to their bodies, wives and their little ones so that they shall feel it forever.' Then there was the death of a certain Gilbert de Cunnynggesholm, who left behind a pregnant widow. His manor was supposed to go to his unborn child, but his brother was not convinced his sister-in-law, the widow, was pregnant and so he squatted on the premises. The pregnant regent and her chief counsellor ordered the sheriff of Lincolnshire to have a few 'good matrons examine the widow by words and belly' and if she was indeed expecting, he was to evict the presumptuous brother.

As well as running the realm, Eleanor and Richard had to attend to Henry's needs overseas. When his offensive stalled in October, the king asked Simon de Montfort, who had remained behind in France after his recall, to put aside their differences and rejoin him. Still angry and resentful, Simon had to be reminded by friends that he, like Richard, owed everything to Henry. Simon did not see it that way, but he went and, like Richard, received his rewards up front. The queen and two councillors signed off on the payments made to him and Eleanor de Montfort in December. Interestingly, apart from the enormous sum of £8,700 dispatched to Henry on 30 October, Richard did not authorise a single payment made by the government until the following year.

Eleanor did not relinquish control of the regency at any time before or after her daughter Katherine arrived on 25 November. Her last three deliveries had been difficult ones and she suffered several miscarriages in the eight intervening years, but here, Paris says, 'She rose well from childbed.' She even authorised a writ on the day of the birth itself, in the presence of Henry of Bath, the corrupt judge since restored to favour and serving on the council. Her purification feast coincided with the feast of St Edward on 5 January 1254. On that day Richard turned forty-five.[5]

Doubtless discussion during the feast was dominated by events in Gascony. To avoid war with Castile, Henry had proposed an alliance with Alfonso by marrying Edward to his half-sister. Alfonso not only took his time with the offer but began mobilising his forces. Unsure of his intentions, Henry asked his wife and brother to convene parliament to hear the envoys he was sending home to give a full account of the situation. Following a summons dispatched on 27 December, the first ever issued by a queen of England, parliament met at Westminster on 27 January 1254.

It was a notable assembly, not least because Eleanor of Provence, as the regent, was the first woman known to have attended parliament. According to Paris, it was Richard who led the call to arms. 'Being more powerful, and more bound to do so than the rest of you, I will effectively assist my lord and brother by furnishing him with three hundred soldiers to fight for him at my own expense for a year.' Other lords then chimed in their support, but when the king's envoys arrived on 4 February to make their appeal for assistance, the tone had completely changed. The Dunstable annalist records that:

> All those assembled refused this help, unless a definite assurance
> was given that Magna Carta and the Charter of the Forest would
> be fully observed, that the sheriffs would be commanded to execute
> this by letters patent of the lord king, and that the church would be
> fully reformed in respect of its liberties.[6]

Prior to the arrival of the envoys, Richard had drafted a letter to his brother to report on the proceedings. It became part of a more detailed letter sent by him and Eleanor together from Windsor on 14 February after parliament had adjourned. They informed Henry that the earls and barons would muster in London on 3 May to go to his aid should the king of Castile persist in his designs. The prelates promised to send either a strong military force or money, in either case 'as much as it lay in their power'. The hope of a tax, however, hinged on the publication and enforcement of Magna Carta, which the king had confirmed at the parliament preceding his departure. Richard's original draft closed with a resounding declaration, not included in the official letter, that speaks much about his relationship with Henry.

> I, Richard, your brother, the earl of Cornwall, will not be wanting
> to you, but will come to you with a force for your advantage and
> my own honour, if, as you announce to me, the king of Castile
> should oppose you in Gascony, provided that you and your heirs
> are well disposed with the help of God to me forever.[7]

On 11 February 1254, three days before sending their letter to the king, Eleanor and Richard attested letters ordering all the sheriffs to have two local knights elected for the purpose of coming to

Westminster after Easter to discuss what money their respective counties might provide towards a new expedition. This, too, was an historic occasion. For the first time ever, parliament was to be convened on the basis of a democratic mandate. For no particular reason, historians have long credited Richard of Cornwall with this landmark constitutional innovation, but one of the surviving letters to the sheriffs bears the name of the queen only, and the overall attestation of letters indicates that Eleanor of Provence was the driving force of government at this time.

Henry's response on 24 March was styled as a proclamation to be read out loud. The threat from Castile was real. Those unable to serve abroad should provide money and he ordered Eleanor and Richard to lean on the sheriffs to ensure full observance of Magna Carta. Parliament was supposed to meet on 26 April, but Paris claims it got off to a late start because of the tardy arrival of Richard and some other nobles, by as many as three weeks. This is clearly wrong. Richard was at Windsor with the queen two days before the opening of the assembly and everyone had gone home by 9 May. At some point, all talk about the tax was dropped because there was no longer any need for it. Simon de Montfort showed up all the way from the continent with news of a peace treaty with Castile (and to pick up the last of the money Henry owed him).

It was the outcome everyone had hoped for as far back as the January parliament, which put the realm on a war footing. At that time plans were put into motion for the queen to cross over with Edward in the expectation that Alfonso would eventually agree to the marriage alliance. During the Easter parliament Eleanor went about putting together ships, supplies, reinforcements and several barrels of the king's treasure to take with her. She also collected money, including £2,666 borrowed from her brother-in-law, again secured against the king's dwindling gold treasure.

Richard accompanied her to the coast where, on 29 May 1254, Eleanor and Edward embarked at Portsmouth for the voyage to Gascony.[8]

Richard of Cornwall had not been the first choice to become the new regent. Walter de Gray, the archbishop of York, was nominated to succeed Eleanor, probably as a matter of formality since he had served as regent during Henry's previous time abroad. But he was quite old now and begged off on account of age and illness. If some of the council had a problem with Richard becoming regent, fearing he would look after his own interests first and foremost, then like any good ruler in transition his initial concern was the peace of the realm.

In the week of the queen's departure, the feud between the port towns had erupted in violence when the men of Winchelsea attacked and destroyed a ship built by Great Yarmouth for Edward's crossing. Richard immediately ordered representatives from all the ports to meet him at a special parliament in Oxford to thrash out their differences. Back at Windsor on 5 June, he prohibited a tournament from taking place at Wylton. These medieval war games were notorious for their personal brawls and riots and banning them had been a regular feature of Henry's reign. In July, at the parliament he summoned to Oxford, Richard acted on complaints about the sheriff of Yorkshire and his bailiffs. He sacked the lot of them and set up a commission to investigate their 'rapines, extortions, trespasses and injuries'.

He cracked down on ordinary criminals as well. While in Northampton on 13 July, Richard ordered the sheriff of Cambridgeshire to arrest Cecily the widow and William the cook on the charge of receiving stolen goods and to convey the two of them to the gaol in London for further questioning. They turned out to be part of a bigger racket involving dozens of suspects across several counties. More arrest warrants were issued for people like Gervase the baker, John the miller, and Walter the one-handed. In Walter's case, the sheriff was advised to proceed cautiously.[9]

Richard was not about to set aside his pursuit of riches during his regency, however. Trees always being a profitable windfall, he had a swath of them felled in Sundon Park, which had come to him in the dowry of his first wife Isabel. He seized wagons in and around nearby Dunstable to haul the wood away and in doing so caused great disruption in the trade of the town. Then there were his infamous crusade redemptions. He was determined to collect every last cent and had his Italian agent Berard de Nympha actively comb the countryside for people who had taken the cross but stayed home. Worried by the grace granted to eight avowed crusaders during the January parliament, he took advantage of his Oxford assembly to order all the sheriffs to confiscate the property of any debtor who appeared on Nympha's list.

The big money was still in the fines paid for infringements of the currency exchange. In 1253, St Albans Abbey, the home of Matthew Paris, was fined £100 over a technicality related to the exchange. One of their monks took on the role of legal counsel and went to great lengths to prove the injustice of it. He succeeded in having the transgression expunged from the record during the Easter parliament, but not before he had secretly paid the fine to Richard. London also disputed the exchange infringements imputed to them, but they needed the regent to confirm their newly elected mayor and sheriffs and so agreed to pay Richard £400 to have all his claims remitted.[10]

Unconstrained as Eleanor had been by her pregnancy and emergency parliaments, Richard went further afield as regent, travelling as far as Worcester in the west country, but he, too, made Windsor and Westminster his base of operations. Mostly it was the same routine work, such as authorising payments for renovations and upkeeps. His brother would be pleased by the repairs he had done on the thatched roof of Henry's chapel in Oxford and his concern that the buildings of Clarendon Palace should look 'as they were before the king's voyage to Gascony'.

The royal children were not neglected. The adage about the highborn growing up with silver spoons in their mouths is embodied in the twenty-four such spoons that Richard had made for the children at a cost of about a thousand pounds in today's money. He ordered a thousand gallons of wine to be sent to Windsor for their consumption – diluted with water to enjoy in soft-drink form. At Henry's request, he made sure the feast of St Edward on 13 October was celebrated in lavish style at Westminster. New linen, towels and napkins were made and the victuals included 30 oxen, 100 deer and 126 boar and pigs. The allocations just for bread, flour, fish and salt from London cost nearly £32.[11]

But where he really did his brother and sister-in-law a favour was to send Sanchia to Paris for a meeting of the two royal families. With Edward married and installed as the lord of Gascony, Henry and Eleanor proceeded homeward overland. They made pilgrimages to Fontevrault, where Henry had their mother Isabella of Angoulême reinterred inside the chapel under a glorious effigy, and to St Edmund at Pontigny. Louis and Margaret, back from their crusade after an absence of six years, invited the couple to spend a week with them in Paris. Since Margaret and Eleanor's mother and youngest sister were to be there as well, plans were made for Sanchia to join them so that all four sisters could be together for the first time in twenty years.

It was important for Richard that his wife arrived in such style and magnificence that the French would be overawed by her stately and illustrious retinue. He chose only the best knights mounted on the best horses to accompany her, everyone clad in the finest apparel. Sanchia's presence in Paris in December 1254 made the splendour of the occasion that much more memorable after she and her younger sister Beatrice later achieved queenly status like their two elder sisters. Doubtless there was discussion, however, about Richard's absence.

He was regent, of course, and even though it was not under an official mandate, it could be argued that there were too few magnates just then in the kingdom besides him. The archbishop of Canterbury had sailed with the queen, as had the earl of Gloucester, who was the only noble close in rank to Richard. The earl of Norfolk was known for eschewing duties at court and the idea of entrusting the kingdom to Simon after the debacle of Gascony was out of the question. Still, the king was on his way home. The chancellor or council alone could have easily managed affairs until his expected return in a fortnight or so.

The most likely reason Richard stayed away was vanity and wounded pride. The two other times he met Louis in Paris he had been the centre of attention. Now it would be Henry, as turned out to be the case. Richard would be lucky to get any attention at all with the cream of the French nobility and clergy also in attendance. At the banquets he would be seated next to the other counts, notably Louis's brothers Alphonse, who now enjoyed his title of count of Poitou, and Charles, who was the count of Provence that Richard should have been. Mixing with those two would only feed the undercurrent of superiority sure to be present at the gathering.[12]

Christmas being Henry's favourite time of the year, the king aimed to get back in time to celebrate it in England. Richard moved to Canterbury on 15 December in expectation of his arrival, but poor winds kept the court stranded near the coast for eight days. They celebrated Christmas in Boulogne, Richard in Dover. The king and queen landed two days later and were received with joy by the nobles and prelates assembled to greet them. On 29 December, the day marking the murder of Thomas Becket, Henry threw a magnificent banquet in Canterbury. All in all, it had been a successful expedition and Henry topped it off by bringing home an elephant given him by Louis. As another animal seen in England for the first time, the beast made a far bigger splash than Richard's entire herd of buffalo, which by that point seems to have disappeared. The elephant died two years later.[13]

Securing Gascony and establishing friendship with Castile and France were achievements that lasted well beyond Henry's reign, but he did not stop there. Sicily suddenly hove into view again, or more precisely Albert of Parma did. After being rebuffed by Richard earlier, Albert had offered Sicily to Henry on behalf of his younger son Edmund, but that entailed the king making war on his nephew Henry Hohenstaufen and Henry refused to 'thirst after his own blood'.

That was in early 1253. Henry Hohenstaufen died later that year, still a teenager, and Innocent told Albert to ask about Edmund again. The pope knew Henry was in Gascony at the time trying to suppress a rebellion, but he was desperate. Albert had also approached Charles of Anjou, who wanted Sicily, but he was forced to reject the offer at the insistence of the French regency council (minus Blanche of Castile, who had died the year before) and Louis, who was still in the Holy Land. Henry and Albert quickly came to terms and Innocent ratified their agreement on 14 May 1254.

Conrad was already ill of a fever and died a week later. Innocent now had second thoughts. Edmund would become king of Sicily for nothing, and it would have to be for nothing. As Albert found out to his horror when he met Henry in Gascony, the king was broke. Albert refused to confirm the grant to Edmund and Innocent acted like it never happened. Not until November, when Frederick's illegitimate son Manfred became a threat, did the pope tell Henry he could still have 'the thing' if he came for it. On 2 December, Manfred crushed papal forces near Foggia. Five days later, as Henry was rapturously received in Paris, Innocent died. The new pope, Alexander IV, was determined to succeed with Manfred.

For Henry, it was a missed opportunity. Gascony had cost him nearly all his gold and saddled him with enormous debts. He was counting on his wife's Savoyard relatives to manage the grunt work of eliminating Manfred and putting Edmund on the throne of Sicily. Not only would he recoup his losses from that wealthy kingdom, but it would revive the honour and prestige lost by the Plantagenets to the Capetians under his father.

Sicily would also resolve the dilemma he now faced with Edmund. His younger son had suddenly found himself as much a 'Lackland' as King John had been; in establishing the marital alliance with Alfonso, Henry had to make Edward a great lord worthy of a princess of Castile. He had to endow him with property valued at £10,000 a year, nearly twice what Richard held. Besides Gascony, Edward's new lands included the earldom of Chester, which was originally meant for Edmund. Henry did not expect Richard to be any less sore about not getting Chester, let alone Gascony, so he made sure that the grant of these lands to Edward did not come with their respective titles. The heir to the throne was neither the duke of Aquitaine (Gascony) nor the earl of Chester. Until he became king, he was simply Lord Edward.[14]

As much as Richard might admire Henry for his boldness, he had to think he was completely mad. Sicily was not going to come free under any conditions and he knew his brother's poverty better than anyone. Back on 1 September 1254, Henry wrote to the exchequer to say that he was unable to leave Gascony because of the debts he owed to local merchants. The treasurer was asked to procure a loan from Richard of £2,667, specifically mentioning that Henry needed the money in order to make a pilgrimage to Pontigny and that he, the king, was directing his prayers towards him, his brother, to that effect. During his regency, Richard sent him cash injections totalling £5,782.

Back home and impoverished, Henry made two new covenants with Richard. For the first, Henry received £3,333 pledged against his 'old treasure'. If the November 1256 deadline for repayment was missed, the jewels and ornaments were Richard's. For the second covenant, his brother lent him another £3,333, this one pledged with a novel form of security, England's Jews. In the previous decade, they had absorbed punishing taxation of more than £50,000. Now a schedule was created for them to pay back the new loan from Richard plus £2,000 outstanding from other loans. Richard seems to have left court immediately afterwards, for just two days later, on 26 February 1255, Henry sent two of his clerks to Wallingford to pick up the money from him in person or from whomever had the keys to the vault there.[15]

Richard's dealings with the Jewish community went back at least twenty years. In February 1235, Henry gave permission to the Jews who had settled at Berkhamsted to remain there indefinitely. Exactly seven years later Richard, just home from his crusade, moved them to Wallingford, which was to become the administrative centre of his estates. Long before the move he had befriended one of them, Abraham of Berkhamsted. Paris recounts that Abraham had a beautiful wife named Floria. When she tried to stop him from defiling an image of the Virgin Mary and baby Jesus he kept in his privy for the call of nature, he smothered her.

Abraham was thrown in the Tower of London, where other Jews came forward to accuse him of coin clipping and other crimes. They offered Richard £666 to withdraw his protection, but he stood by his friend. In February 1250, Abraham paid Henry £466 for his freedom and the king's protection. Now, five years later, the new financial arrangement between the king and his brother included the transfer of Abraham and all his possessions from Henry to Richard for £333. The debts owed to Abraham, whom Paris described as 'moderately rich', amounted to £1,800 and were to be collected on Richard's behalf.

According to the Dunstable annalist, Richard engaged in a disreputable transaction with another Abraham, this one from Norwich, who produced a charter to show that two manors in Bedfordshire had been used as security for loans that were now in default. At Richard's instigation, the occupants were allegedly evicted and those who resisted were imprisoned or harassed in some way. It is an obscure case that appears in none of the official records but may have some connection to a personal quarrel between Richard and the lords of the manors, William de Beauchamp and his wife Ida. During his regency, the Beauchamps had refused to answer litigation brought against them and Richard responded by depriving them of their barony.[16]

In the autumn of 1255, Richard became involved in the affair of the Jews of Lincoln who were accused of killing a Christian boy named Hugh as part of a mock crucifixion ritual. Henry was on his way home from attending a delicate matter with the Scottish minority council when the boy's mother pleaded with him to intervene. By the time the king arrived in Lincoln, one of the detained Jews had confessed to the murder in return for his life. Henry negated the agreement and ordered the man's execution. The other detainees, some ninety-one in all, were sent to London for trial, where eighteen were hanged for refusing to submit to judgement by an all-Christian jury.

Richard was in Lincoln at the time investigating the report of miracles attributed to Robert Grosseteste, the local bishop who died in 1253. Richard would have seen the shrine erected to little Hugh next to the bishop's tomb. Given his presence in the city and his pre-eminence on the council, Richard must have been consulted on the matter. Later events suggest he would have urged Henry to take the harder line, and not just because he was to profit from the possessions of the Jews who were executed. But as their community provided the security for the money he had lent to the king, his stance eventually softened, and in the spring of the following year he coordinated efforts with the friars to get the remaining incarcerated Jews freed.[17]

There was a special guest at parliament in October 1255. He was the bishop of Bologna and he was there to place a ring on the finger of nine-year-old Edmund Plantagenet, proclaiming him, in the eyes of the papacy, the king of Sicily. It was not surprising news. Back in March, the new pope Alexander IV had lost control of the situation with Manfred in southern Italy and so revived the 'Sicilian business' with Henry, who was eager as ever to pursue it. The difference, however, was in the terms. Disabusing Henry of the notion that he was going to get the kingdom for free, he now demanded money (£90,000 as opposed to the £25,000 the king was to receive from Innocent) and troops, everything according to deadlines and subject to ecclesiastical penalties for the failure to comply.

It was a gamble of unbelievable proportions, but Henry did not feel he could act otherwise. There was still the problem of Edmund's endowment, and the chance of success, while diminishing by the day, was indeed real. He would suffer lasting ignominy if Sicily went instead to the Capetians for his want of faith and courage at that moment. Then there was his vow to crusade in the Holy Land, now less than a year away. The number of men and amount of money needed for that venture far surpassed the demands of Sicily, and there was absolutely no chance of success there. Louis's defeat and imprisonment had been bad enough, but it inspired the Egyptians, now led by the Mamluk warrior class, to wipe out the crusader states once and for all. Alfonso encouraged Henry to crusade with him in North Africa instead, but Alexander saw Manfred as the greater threat to Christendom. He commuted Henry's vow to fight against the Hohenstaufen prince and ordered the crusade tax redirected for that purpose.

Henry was nevertheless going to need a lot more money and only parliament could provide it. He could reasonably expect his leading men to provide it even if he again offered no concessions on his personal rule. Over the last decade he had carefully crafted a nobility tied to the crown through marriages to his relatives or the queen's. The earls of Derby, Devon, Gloucester, Lincoln, Surrey and Warwick had all been roped in at the altar and they were a mostly young and ambitious lot, keen on tournaments and knightly endeavour. The trouble was, they were not the ones who counted anymore.

When King John needed a tax, he consulted only his leading men and got it. Magna Carta changed all that. The charter of liberties empowered knights, freeholders, peasants and urban dwellers to defend their rights and privileges against encroachment by the sheriffs and other crown officials. Unlike his father, Henry had to appeal to the wider realm for a tax, and these lower orders were unwilling to part with their money unless their local grievances were addressed.

Henry had unwittingly aggravated the situation by going easy on his barons. Where his father harassed them endlessly, he gave them free rein, but they took advantage of it to play the petty potentate over their lordships. They even defied his own officials when the occasion suited them. Knowing them too well, he refused to share power with them at the top. Their answer was to deny him taxation, which is to say they refused to lobby for it with the people who had to pay it. In this standoff, now almost two decades old, he had been able to get by from other sources of revenue, such as the Jews, the church, and his brother.

Having turned down Sicily for himself, Richard was not going to bankroll it for his nephew. If Paris can be believed, he even vilified Henry in front of parliament after Edmund received his ring. The king should never have agreed to undertake the project without consulting him or the other magnates first. He also took aim at the bishop of Hereford and at Robert Walerand, a rising star at court, for carrying through the transaction in Rome.

The rebuke certainly stung. When parliament adjourned ('without effecting anything'), Henry convened a council meeting at Windsor on 21 November 1255 to obtain assent in some form or other for Sicily. Apart from the earl of Warwick and three of his Lusignan brothers, all were native Englishmen with no stake in the venture. They included top judges like Henry Bracton (author of the famous law treatise) and bishops like Walter Cantilupe of Worcester, soon to be one of Henry's most determined opponents. All said yes.

The only other earl there besides Warwick was Gloucester. The message from Richard was clear. Henry would have to manage it without his help. He could understand his brother's desire to revive the fortunes of the Plantagenet dynasty, which was his dynasty too, but Henry was the king. It was his affair. Richard had his own family to worry about, more so now that his eldest son had turned twenty years old. It was time for him to start thinking about a legacy no longer attached to his older brother.[18]

5

A KINGDOM BECKONS
1256–1258

The kingdom of Sicily, established by a family of Norman adventurers in the early twelfth century, had been a prize in the making since the end of that century. In 1191, Frederick's father was crowned Holy Roman Emperor Henry VI following the death of his father Frederick I (Barbarossa) during the Third Crusade. Henry was married to Constance, the heiress to the kingdom, but Sicily fell under the rule of Tancred, an illegitimate prince of the Norman line. When Richard the Lionheart passed through Sicily on his way to the Third Crusade, he insulted the emperor by making an alliance with Tancred. Forced to make his way home from the crusade overland, Richard was captured and held to a ransom of £100,000, which the emperor then used to conquer the kingdom. It was English money that brought Sicily and southern Italy into the imperial fold.

The papacy was disturbed by this development, for it now put the empire on its northern and southern borders. The untimely deaths of both Henry VI and Constance left their only child

Frederick II a ward of Pope Innocent III, who sought to rectify the situation. Frederick was crowned king of Sicily, then king of the Romans (Germany), and finally Holy Roman Emperor, but under condition that the two subordinate thrones were never united under one ruler. Frederick preferred Sicily, where he was born, and left Germany to his eldest son, but discord led to the prince's banishment and early death in prison. The emperor also infuriated successive popes by failing to make good his crusade vow. He only left for the Holy Land after obtaining the title of king of Jerusalem through his second wife, the mother of Conrad.

Innocent IV made good his deposition of the Hohenstaufens by having a new king of Germany elected in 1246 in place of Conrad. After nine months of struggle, this so-called 'anti-king' was dead. Richard made the shortlist of candidates to succeed him because, in the pope's mind, he was a man of 'great cunning who abounded in money'. When the offer came, however, Richard refused it on account of knowing he would have to fight for it. The odds of victory there, he said, were 'too dubious'. It was 1247 and he busied himself that year instead with the recoinage.

Eventually, William of Holland was elected king of the Romans and by 1252 he had driven Conrad out of Germany. That freed him to aid his brother-in-law John d'Avesnes in the latter's war against his own mother Margaret, the countess of Flanders. Margaret had disinherited John and another son from her first marriage in favour of the three sons she had from her second marriage. In a grossly unfair arbitration, Louis awarded Flanders to the second crop of children and the smaller county of Hainault to John. War broke out in the family and John had the early advantage until Margaret called in help from Charles of Anjou. To help counter this growing influence of the Capetians in their region, John d'Avesnes and William of Holland turned to England.

For ten years Henry III waited in vain for his alliance with Frederick to pay off in his own struggle with France. Where the emperor had always shied away from confrontation with the Capetians, John and William proved more than willing to take them on. But Henry did not meet their overtures with only France in mind. Conrad had left behind an infant son in Germany named Conradin who, assuming Manfred was defeated someday, might easily upset Edmund's claim to Sicily. So long as William of Holland was the king of Germany, the aspirations of Conradin and his family were kept in check. Then on 28 January 1256, while Henry was visiting Richard at Wallingford, William was killed during a skirmish in Friesland and the crown of Germany was vacant again.

John d'Avesnes rushed to England with the news and on 5 February he was put on retainer at £200 annually. His task was to work for the election of a king who was friendly to England's interests in a land long wracked by division. The papal-imperial dispute had created two dynastic rivals in Germany, one centred around Saxony in the east, the other around Swabia in the west. During Frederick's reign, they took their fight south into Italy, where their local adherents became known as Guelfs and Ghibellines. Broadly speaking, Guelfs supported the papacy, Ghibellines the Hohenstaufens. Whoever hoped to succeed William of Holland as king of the Romans had to navigate this conflict.[1]

The king was chosen by seven electors. Six of them were German and one was the Czech king of Bohemia. An early candidate from outside Germany was King Alfonso of Castile. His grandfather Philip of Swabia, the brother of Emperor Henry VI, had been king of the Romans between the death of the emperor in 1197 and his own assassination a decade later. That made Alfonso a Hohenstaufen but not a wholehearted Ghibelline the way his cousin Manfred was and Conradin was sure to be. In 1255, Pope Alexander actively promoted Alfonso over Conradin for the lordship of the Hohenstaufen heartland of Swabia, whose inhabitants had resolutely refused to accept William of Holland.

It was not Alexander who put the king of Castile in the running as a candidate. On 17 March 1256, a delegation arrived from Pisa to proclaim Alfonso as the new king of the Romans. All he had to do in return was restore Pisa's trading interests in Sicily and Africa and provide an army of 500 knights to protect them and their Ghibelline allies. He humbly accepted their investiture despite knowing that Pisa had no legal right to confer the title. He treated it as a launch pad to lobby the real electors for their votes.

In that same month Henry's proctor in Rome advised the papal court to send a legate to Germany to make sure no king was elected there who might impair the Sicilian business. Alexander declined to act, obviously aggrieved that Henry was busying himself with German matters instead of doing more for Sicily. In May, the king's council met at Windsor. It was probably then that Richard of Cornwall threw his hat in the ring. On 12 June, Richard de Clare and Robert Walerand were dispatched to make the rounds of the German princes. John d'Avesnes and his kinsman Nicholas, the bishop of Cambrai, were empowered to negotiate on his behalf with the individual electors.[2]

Unlike the king of Castile, Richard had the advantage of no personal connection to the dynastic politics of Germany, nor did he already have a kingdom to run. Equally important was his wealth. With no land in Germany, he could finance everything he needed from his own resources. The only thing expected of him was to sit on his throne and let the Germans go on ruling their principalities as before. William of Holland had taken the role of king too seriously and consequently ended up running afoul of his principal supporter among the electors, Konrad of Hochstaden, the archbishop of Cologne. Prior to William's death, the prelate had been implicated in a plot to assassinate him.

In July, the archbishop-elector travelled to Prague for discussions with fellow elector King Ottokar II. Konrad had intended to replace William with Ottokar, who was interested in acquiring a second throne. From Prague, Konrad went to visit another archbishop-elector, Gerhard of Mainz. None of these three electors had declared for any candidate when, on 26 November, John d'Avesnes reached an agreement with a fourth elector, Duke Ludwig of Bavaria. In return for £8,000, Ludwig would vote for Richard. The money was presented as the dowry for a future marriage between the duke and an English princess, which was never going to happen. Ludwig was just then a pariah for going berserk earlier in the year and chopping off his wife's head after suspecting her of an affair.

The following month Richard secured the votes of archbishop-electors Konrad and Gerhard for £5,333 each. Konrad acted on behalf of Gerhard because the archbishop of Mainz was just then a prisoner of the duke of Brunswick. Indeed, most of the money Gerhard was to receive would go towards his ransom. Although much would be made of it later, buying the election in this manner was nothing unusual. By the end of the century the price of a single vote would go as high as £25,000. What was different in Richard's case was the evidence. Since he had proctors do his campaigning for him, all the negotiations and amounts were put down in writing.

On 28 December 1256, during Christmas court, parliament gathered in St Stephens Chapel at Westminster Palace. While a thunderstorm raged outside, a delegation from Germany informed them that Richard of Cornwall had been elected king of the Romans, adding that 'no one has ever been elected to that dignity so spontaneously, so unanimously, and with such few obstacles.' Of course, none of it was true. Apparently, Henry had put the delegates up to the deception as a means of winning support for Sicily. If Germany could be so easily had, so too could that other kingdom. Richard went along with the charade by hesitating whether or not to accept the crown. Henry then chimed in, as if on cue, with a warning not to let 'pusillanimity appear by refusing to accept this honour, which is granted and offered to you both by heaven and man'. After more encouragement, Richard made a solemn acceptance speech.

> I, trusting in God's mercy, incompetent and unworthy as I am, willingly take on myself this burden and honour, offered to me, as I hope, by heaven, that I may not be called timid and pusillanimous. As for me, before I leave this chapel, may I be consumed by infernal fire, and die a sudden death, if I do so from ambition or avarice, or for any other purpose than to ameliorate the condition of that kingdom, which may God give me power to do, and to govern with all justice, moderation, and honour, these who have spontaneously chosen me as their lord.[3]

Satisfied with Richard's commitment, the delegates returned to Germany with Richard de Clare and councillor John Mansel to monitor the election, which was held in Frankfurt. On 13 January 1257, Duke Ludwig and Archbishop Konrad, still acting for the imprisoned Gerhard, arrived outside the city walls but could not gain entrance because the other German electors, having declared for Alfonso, were inside and refused to participate. Konrad, whose right it was to crown the new king, proclaimed Richard king of the Romans and left to prepare for his coronation in the imperial city of Aachen.

On 27 January at Windsor, Henry informed the bishop of Hereford that Richard had been elected and that he would be making the trip with him to Germany. It was another case of Henry's wishful thinking. There was no way Richard was going to allow him to steal his thunder on this occasion. The king spent a week at St Albans in early March, where Matthew Paris was his companion throughout his stay, and the chronicler says that Henry talked endlessly of his brother. Apart from the political considerations, he was excited by the extra dignity conferred on England by Richard's election. They would be three Plantagenet kings enthroned at the same time – Henry, Richard and Edmund – much like the Magi. When Konrad arrived later that month, Henry permitted him to solicit funds for the rebuilding of Cologne Cathedral, where the shrine of the Magi was located.[4]

The only word from Ottokar in all this comes from a letter written by Richard to the archbishop of Messina on 30 January 1257. Addressing himself as 'Richard by the grace of the Romans, elected King of the same, ever Augustus', he claimed that envoys from Ottokar arrived in England to see what he might do for the king of Bohemia to obtain his vote. Told that the election was over, the envoys gave Ottokar's 'consent' to the outcome and a promise that the Czech king would provide him with the service of 16,000 soldiers, presumably to deal with the other faction, should resistance continue.

The archbishop of Messina arrived shortly afterwards. Henry had summoned parliament to meet on 18 March and the prelate was there to further 'the business' on behalf of the pope. The venue was the chapter house at Westminster Abbey, newly built by Henry and with such exquisite features that he boasted it was 'the house of houses'. Richard de Clare and John Mansel had returned from Germany with Konrad and other distinguished guests so that they might do homage to their new king.

According to Paris, Richard gave the archbishop £333 for his travel expenses and a mitre ornamented with gold and precious stones. The prelate fitted the object on his head and exclaimed, 'Earl Richard has enriched me and my church with a handsome gift; and as he has placed a mitre on my head, so will I impose on his head the crown of the German or Roman kingdom. He has mitred me, and I will crown him.' Paris, who views all foreign churchmen as useless spongers, added bitterly, 'I have thought it worthwhile to insert this speech of the archbishop's in this book, that posterity may learn how cunningly foreigners found means of circumventing the simplicity of the English.'

On 9 April, Richard carried out his first act as king-elect. At his instance, Henry exempted the citizens of Aachen from paying tolls in England 'for the life of king Richard'. To watch over his affairs back home, Richard appointed brothers Fulk and Philip Basset as his trustees. When the affairs concerned the Jewish community, brothers Cresse and Hagin of London were to act as his attorneys. Richard and his entourage proceeded to Yarmouth for their departure. They had to wait some days for the winds to prove favourable. It was just as well, for the bridges and hurdles ordered for his ships were not there. Richard told his men to go to the nearby royal forest and chop down thirty-six oak trees for the wood they needed to build them, all without licence. The fines could have been huge for such an infraction, but Henry accepted that the fault lay with the sheriff of Essex for failing to deliver the material in time.[5]

Richard embarked on 27 April with his wife Sanchia, his twenty-one-year-old son Henry, and his and Sanchia's seven-year-old son Edmund. They were accompanied by Roger de Meuland, whose election as bishop of Coventry in mid-February had been vigorously promoted by Richard. In the official records, Roger is referred to as 'the king's nephew', which suggests he was Richard's son, but a couple of cryptic entries by Paris in his chronicle seem to rule this out. Richard nevertheless had at least one illegitimate child before he was married, a certain Philip of Cornwall who was raised for a career in the church. His sole identification comes from a papal indult in 1248 allowing him to become a pluralist. Since Philip was more than likely an adult by then, he was born before 1230, when Richard was twenty-one. If Roger was born in those years, too, that would make him thirty at the time of his consecration, which was the minimum age for a bishop. Roger died in 1295, having outlived Richard by twenty-three years.

The senior ranking nobleman in the king-elect's entourage was his brother-in-law John de Warenne, the earl of Surrey, whose wife Alice, Richard's half-sister, had died the previous year in childbirth. Another baron making the trip, Hugh Despenser, later became one of Richard's bitterest enemies. In all, forty-seven barons, knights and officials made the journey with him and his family in a fleet of about fifty ships. They landed in Holland on 1 May and spent two days there resting up before commencing their journey to Aachen, which they reached on 11 May.

It had been almost twenty-two years to the day since crowds in Germany rapturously greeted the arrival of his sister Isabella as their new empress. Doubtless some of those same onlookers now caught a glimpse of the man who would be their next emperor. In a letter home afterwards, Richard said he and his suite were welcomed 'magnificently and honourably amidst the greatest joyousness and jubilation, glad and rejoicing, without any obstacle or difficulty whatsoever intervening'. He noted that not a single king or emperor had entered Aachen in the last two centuries without there being some kind of commotion or disturbance. He had broken the cycle. In her own modest letter home, the only one of hers known to survive, Sanchia wrote that the city received them 'cheerfully and with the highest joy and honour'.

The coronation took place on 17 May 1257. Since Archbishop Konrad had been excommunicated for his role in trying to kill the previous king, Archbishop Gerhard, now free from prison, did the honours. Sitting on the throne of Charlemagne, Richard of Cornwall was anointed with the chrism of the holy unction and crowned king of the Romans. He was forty-eight years old, just a year shy of his father King John when he died under wretched circumstances. Sanchia, whose 'inestimable beauty greatly adorned the ceremony', was then crowned, making her the third sister out of four raised to queenly dignity.

The next day Richard knighted his son Henry in an equally splendid ceremony. From that point onward the young man was known as Henry of Almain to reflect his status as a prince of *Allemagne* (Germany). The banquets for both occasions left the Germans speechless. They must have cost the new king a fortune if they were indeed attended, as he claimed, by twelve bishops and archbishops, thirty dukes and counts, and three thousand knights.[6]

For his court, Richard relied on the people already in place. Bishop Nicholas of Cambrai was appointed chancellor and John d'Avesnes seneschal. Other officials were also local, taken over from William of Holland or, in the case of Richard's chamberlain Philip of Falkenstein, from the Hohenstaufens. There was no thought of anyone in his English entourage staying on in an official capacity. Some, like Roger de Meuland, left after the coronation. On 21 June, Roger received a papal mandate to assist Berard de Nympha in the collection of crusade legacies and redemptions still owed to Richard. They were to pursue even those debtors who were 'in distant parts or otherwise dead'.

The mandate does not identify Richard as king of the Romans, just earl of Cornwall. Papal confirmation of his election was not in the foreseeable future because his German opponents refused to budge. Before sailing, Richard was probably aware that the chief among them had held a new election in Frankfurt on 1 April. He was Archbishop Arnold of Trier, 'a powerful and warlike man' who claimed to have the proxies of the two electors in his camp as well as Ottokar's. He cast all four votes for Alfonso of Castile and proclaimed him king. Shortly after, Archbishop Arnold set out to capture an imperial castle on Alfonso's behalf but was beaten off by Archbishop Gerhard in the week before Richard's arrival.[7]

Five days after his coronation, Richard proceeded to Cologne, where he remained for nearly a month as the guest of Konrad. There he commenced his policy of rewarding those who backed him 'so long as they be of good behaviour' and making life miserable for those who did not. On 16 June, he left Sanchia in Cologne to cultivate her position as queen of the Romans while he undertook a progress along the course of the River Rhine. He was stopped 122 kilometres south at Boppard, a hilltop castle with a longstanding pledge to admit only a king elected unanimously.

For this first opportunity to exercise his power, Richard continued twenty-five kilometres upstream to the island castle of Pfalzgrafenstein while his marshal battered away at Boppard's walls. He set up court there, waiting for assistance from his allies in Cologne and Mainz, should it come to that. In many cases the supplicants ushered into his presence would not have known any French, but there were still enough similarities between medieval English and German to facilitate some level of comprehension between the new king and his subjects. The German delegation at the Christmas parliament even chalked up Richard's ability to speak English as another thing in his favour.[8]

This would have been a hindrance to Alfonso, but no deterrence to his quest. According to English chronicler Thomas Wykes, he paid £40,000 for his votes, twice as much as Richard had. On 15 August 1257, while the siege of Boppard was still going on, a German delegation from the archbishop-elector of Trier arrived at Burgos with news of his election. Following protocol, Alfonso took three days to accept their offer of the crown, then made the same type of speech that Richard did. He was not acting out of ambition, avarice or selfishness, he assured everybody. He only wanted to work for peace, justice and freedom in the world. He was nevertheless advised to appear in Germany at the head of an army as soon as possible, to halt the other king's advancement.

Since problems at home prevented his departure, Alfonso relied on diplomatic support to enforce his claim. He had backing from Louis, who did not like the idea of a Plantagenet king positioned on his flank. Pope Alexander was likeminded in that regard. The whole point of the war against the Hohenstaufens had been to keep Germany and Sicily from being ruled by one family. Diplomacy was an expensive option just the same. Despite an economic crisis in the kingdom he already ruled, Alfonso pushed through an austerity programme and 'double tax' at a *cortes* (parliament) the following year to defray the costs of his pursuit.

He even expected his nominal ally the king of England to come to his aid. In a subtle jab back at him, Henry said he was certain that had Alfonso been duly elected first, Richard would never have consented to his own election. He promised to look into the matter and relations between the two monarchs continued peacefully, but Richard was contemptuous of Alfonso's threats to settle their dispute through a force of arms. 'Let him come with all his strength and do his worst,' he boasted. 'I will meet him before he reaches the boundaries of my kingdom.'[9]

Richard had every reason to feel confident. Towards the end of summer Boppard had been starved out. He treated the garrison leniently, happy that he was to receive the tolls paid to them by the traffic passing through that bend in the river. On 26 August, he entered the 'Golden City' of Mainz, where he was Gerhard's guest. Sanchia journeyed from Cologne to be present at his first *diet* (parliament), which convened there on 8 September. He received the homage of Frankfurt and other cities and he in turn confirmed their privileges. He also began conferring or confirming privileges for towns and abbeys, or else taking them under imperial protection.

He brought his progress to an end on 26 September, just south of Oppenheim. He almost certainly did not get as far as the Alps as he claimed in a letter to the bishop of Lincoln, which begins with 'Out of innate goodness to you...' He might have liked to continue on to Worms, which still held out for Alfonso, but neither Ottokar nor his army had shown up in support and Richard had run short of money. He sent instructions home to begin selling off some of his woods, probably conveyed by his son Henry of Almain, who returned to England at this time with the remaining members of his entourage save for eight knights.[10]

Winter in Cologne was given over to the diplomatic front. There was still the conflict over Flanders. In September 1256, Louis issued a second arbitral award that was even more biased than his first one. It was at that point that John threw himself into final negotiations for Richard's election. The new king, however, could not afford to alienate Louis and had the Avesnes brothers reconfirm the award in November 1257. John was already then in a state of declining health and died the following month on Christmas Eve, not quite forty years old.

When Richard left England earlier that year, the weather had been awful for some time. Paris noted that from February up until Richard's departure storms had rendered the land 'like a muddy marsh'. The excessive rains continued well into autumn and ruined the harvest. As bread became scarce and prices skyrocketed, famine set in to such a degree that in London fifteen thousand people reportedly died, many of them from the countryside who had come there in search of food. Learning of the distress, Richard dispatched fifty ships laden with more corn, wheat and bread than any three English counties combined were able to produce then. Other ships from Holland and Germany continued to arrive well into summer.[11]

His brother's humane intervention was a godsend to Henry, who had been plagued by tragedy and misfortune since Richard left. On 3 May 1257, his youngest daughter Katherine, born during the queen's regency, died from an unknown disorder, leaving her parents bedridden with grief. After nearly a decade of peace, Wales was again in revolt. The new chieftain was Llywelyn's namesake grandson, described as 'a very handsome man, bold in warfare'. Henry and Edward's campaign to put down his uprising, undertaken while Richard was marching triumphantly through the Rhineland, ended in apathy and retreat.

And there was still the Sicilian business. By now, Manfred and the Ghibellines controlled not just the kingdom of Sicily itself but large areas north of the papal states. The £40,000 that had been collected for Henry's crusade had been wasted by the pope and his Guelf allies. Despairing of continuing the struggle under these circumstances, Henry and his proctors offered alternatives such as Edmund marrying Manfred's daughter and receiving Sicily as her dowry. In his feverish mind, Alexander refused to countenance any change in their agreement and sacked his own agent in England when he expressed sympathy for Henry's plight. He sent a new agent with new deadlines and was insistent as ever that it was pay up or face excommunication.[12]

The pope did play one positive role by promoting peace between England and France. In June 1257, Henry sent a delegation to Paris to open negotiations with Louis. One of the envoys, Bishop Walter of Worcester, was instructed to journey afterwards to Richard to inform him of the outcome of those talks. Richard welcomed the development because a peace treaty between the Plantagenets and Capetians was vital towards cutting off Louis's support for Alfonso.

The sticking point remained Normandy and other territories confiscated by the French fifty years earlier. Throughout the negotiations, the English envoys had insisted on their return, but Louis was equally adamant that his peers would never allow it. Alexander proposed a compromise to both break the impasse and get the business back on track. In return for Henry surrendering his claims, Louis would compensate him by funding an army of one thousand knights to fight for England for one year. Louis would also cede certain outlying territories close to Gascony and Henry would do homage for all of them as the duke of Aquitaine.[13]

Parliament met in April 1258 with Wales, Sicily, famine, and freedom of the church on the agenda. At its conclusion, Henry agreed to take the barons into partnership to carry out much-needed reforms in return for their promise to lobby the wider realm for a new tax, meaning an end to the king's twenty-four years of personal rule. On 2 May, he established a committee of twenty-four, half named by him, half by the barons, to prepare the way for a special parliament the following month. Six days later, Henry empowered Simon de Montfort, Peter of Savoy, Hugh Bigod (brother of Roger, the earl of Norfolk) and two of his Lusignan half-brothers, Guy and Geoffrey, to go to Paris to work out the final arrangements of the peace treaty.

Since envoys typically needed twelve days to get from London to Paris, they arrived around 20 May, when the French parliament was meeting. There they met Richard's envoy, Arnold of Wetzlar, who was another holdover from William of Holland. Arnold was there to act as Richard's proctor because, in addition to Henry renouncing his rights to Normandy, the treaty called for King John's other two living children, Richard and Eleanor, to do the same. All parties agreed to keep the contents of the treaty secret until 25 November 1258, when the kings of England, France and Germany would meet at Cambrai to publish and ratify it together.[14]

The English envoys hurried back for the special parliament that convened in Oxford on 11 June. The wide range of enactments included the formation of a council of fifteen with executive authority over grants and appointments. Parliament would no longer meet at the king's summons, rather at fixed intervals, thus making it an institution of state. Teams of knights were charged with investigating abuses by sheriffs and crown officials in each county, and the office of justiciar was revived to provide everyone with one-off, unencumbered justice, something similar to Louis's own reforms, which were meant to facilitate the collection of his crusade tax. The newly appointed justiciar, Hugh Bigod, was to set off through the countryside to receive complaints (*querala*) and issue judgements on the spot.

Beneath the sincerity and good faith of these Provisions of Oxford, as they were called, ran an undercurrent of intrigue and vindictiveness. Behind the scenes of the parliament that preceded it in April, seven nobles conspired to oust Henry and Richard's four Lusignan half-brothers. The brash and arrogant manner of the brothers, no less than their good fortune and access to the king, had stirred up envy and resentment at court. Aymer de Valence was especially hated for his high-handed behaviour as the bishop-elect of Winchester, and it was a brawl on 1 April between his men and those of one of the seven nobles, John Fitz-Geoffrey, that led to the formation of the secret confederation against them.

The nominal leaders were Richard's brother-in-law Simon de Montfort and stepson Richard de Clare. Simon had a long-standing personal quarrel with William de Valence, who held certain lands that he felt should have gone to his wife Eleanor as her Marshal dower. Simon enlisted his good friend (and no relation) Peter de Montfort to join the plotters. Clare had worked closely with the Lusignans and rode with them on the tournament circuit, but William called him and Simon traitors over their lacklustre response during the Welsh campaign. In Clare's case, it had to do with his disappearance from the front so that he could meet the queen, who was arranging the marriage of his daughter to an esteemed Franco-Italian nobleman.

Eleanor of Provence had never warmed to her four Lusignan brothers-in-law. They were not just competitors for her husband's favours, but they physically clashed with her Savoyard relatives over patronage. Her unease over their presence at court grew to alarm after they started exerting undue influence over her son Edward, now nineteen years old. Having lured Clare away from their orbit, she could not enter the conspiracy for fear of alienating her husband and son, so her uncle Peter of Savoy did it for her. She remained behind the scenes but in close contact with John du Plessis, the earl of Warwick, and John Mansel, both members of her husband's half of the reform committee.[15]

Little did Guy and Geoffrey Lusignan realise that their fellow envoys Simon de Montfort and Peter of Savoy were plotting their destruction while they were all together in Paris. Hugh Bigod and his brother Roger made up the last two members of the confederation, having joined in support of their brother-in-law Fitz-Geoffrey. On 22 June, they struck. With Henry's permission to proceed with reforms without fear of his indignation, four members of the committee, Plessis and Mansel for the king and the Bigod brothers for the barons, were delegated to choose the fifteen councillors to run the realm. They did not name a single Lusignan to it. When parliament next demanded that all aliens surrender the castles they held, the brothers knew they had been targeted. They refused to take an oath to observe and protect the Provisions of Oxford and tried to get Henry and Edward to do the same. Henry held fast, but Edward sided with his uncles and fled with them to organise resistance.

The Lusignans were not completely without supporters. Two members of the committee who stood by them were their brother-in-law John de Warenne and nephew Henry of Almain. Warenne fled with them, but Almain stayed behind. The king and barons took off in pursuit and tracked them down to Aymer's castle in Winchester. After a brief standoff, the brothers agreed to take the oath, but it was too late. They were expelled from the realm in July.

Edward and Warenne remained defiant and only with great difficulty were they persuaded to take the oath. Henry of Almain insisted he had to consult his father before doing so. He was given forty days to do so. The bishop of Exeter was then preparing to travel to see Richard in Germany and may have been the one to convey to him the news of what was going on in England.[16]

While these events were taking place, Richard was reducing the last holdouts for Alfonso. He sent the bishop of Lübeck to work on the archbishop of Trier, authorising him to pay out up to £8,000 if necessary. The king himself proceeded up the Rhine again and forced Worms to capitulate on 25 July 1258. He went back there on 19 October before setting off for Cambrai and the meeting of three kings.

Trouble was already afoot. Having sent word ahead of his intention to continue to England, Richard received a cautionary letter from Henry enjoining him to take the oath to the Provisions of Oxford and provide certain sureties. It seemed that the new king's council had become almighty and was now calling the shots. They even grounded the king and sent a delegation to ratify the peace treaty in his place. When informed of this surprising turn of events, Louis refused to attend. He found the whole idea of dealing with underlings and not principals on such an important matter degrading. And so Richard was the only king to show up at Cambrai. He decided to continue on to England anyway because something had clearly gone wrong there.[17]

6

COOL HOMECOMINGS
1259–1260

Richard, king of Germany, subdued his enemies, and enticed and attached them to his cause with such prudence, that the people of the noble cities of Italy offered him the right hand of friendship. The threats of his enemies, namely, the French, Spanish, the people of Trier and the neighbouring countries, were also silenced, although they had sought to injure him.

They did not come harder to please than Matthew Paris, but he was impressed by what Richard had managed to accomplish in his first year as an enthroned monarch. Even imperial exaltation looked within reach. With Alfonso still a no-show and Henry in more difficulty than usual, Richard had become the pope's last line of defence against Manfred and the Ghibellines. There was a strong anglophile faction of cardinals at the papal court encouraging Alexander to end his vacillation and summon Richard to Rome to be crowned emperor. The peace treaty with France should have certainly sealed it.[1]

The stumbling block to the treaty went back six months to the very beginning of the reform programme. On 5 May 1258, three days after the committee of twenty-four was named, Henry gave the committee power to settle Simon and Eleanor de Montfort's claims for land. Three days after that, Simon was dispatched to Paris to finalise the articles of peace. As per the agreement, Arnold of Wetzlar renounced Richard's rights to any lands in France save those that belonged to his mother Isabella of Angoulême. Richard ratified the instrument on 20 June 1258, two days before Henry took the fateful decision to continue with reforms. Simon did not renounce for Eleanor.

Busy promulgating the Provisions of Oxford, the committee never addressed the Montfort claims. Simon was appointed to the council that superseded the committee along with several close associates, but his position did not become dominant until Clare fell victim to an epidemic that struck Winchester just after the Lusignans were banished. Henry was wary of Simon's motives, but he was feeling especially penitent that summer. The truest expression of his piety was feeding the poor and the famine sweeping through the land made him realise that, like Louis after his failed crusade, he needed to put his house in order. He expressed his gratitude to the barons for shouldering the burden with him.[2]

In the beginning, things worked smoothly. The council was under the king's lordship and therefore accommodated his wishes, but Simon was simply biding his time. It was not just about his unsatisfied claims for land or even his fraught relationship with Henry, now in its third decade. He was fifty years old when the reform period started. His father, brother and cousin had all achieved far more fame and influence at a similar point in their lives. He had had his chance with Gascony but that ended in disgrace. He was not about to let another chance slip away and so set out to make the council the supreme authority of the realm, preferably with himself at the head of it. With the personality and prestige to pull it off, he won many adherents from among churchmen who yearned for freedom from the king and pope, and from knights and freeholders who wanted more protections from royal officials.

He made his move in October 1258, when the first parliament summoned and controlled by the council convened. On the 18th, letters were dispatched throughout the land reaffirming the king's support for reforms, with the added feature that anyone who opposed them would be considered an enemy of the people. Simon had advocated such militancy back at Oxford when he warned the Lusignans to give up their resistance or face execution. Even though Henry had signed off on their expulsion, Simon now used the threat of the Lusignans to raise suspicions about the king's forthcoming trip abroad. Henry might decide he had had enough of reforms and return with an armed force led by his outlawed brothers. The council decided to forbid the king from attending his cherished project.

Having engineered the baronial usurpation of royal authority and prestige, Simon next got himself named to the delegation that went to France instead of Henry. Going with him were Bishop Walter of Worcester and the new bishop of Lincoln, two churchmen who were wholly devoted to him, as was Louis's chief negotiator of the peace treaty, the archbishop of Rouen. It turned out to be the first instance of Simon's overreach, however. Louis had encountered a lot of resistance from his own council over the concessions he was making in the treaty and refused to ratify it under such flippant circumstances. It was a stark reminder to Simon that there would always be a huge difference between an earl and a king.[3]

That was the issue now facing Richard. To the council in England, he was the earl of Cornwall, a peer like the rest of them, and like them he was required to take the oath to the Provisions of Oxford. Paris says he exploded when he heard that. 'I am the son of the late king and brother of the present one. I have no peer.' He celebrated his fiftieth birthday on 5 January 1259. In addition to his family, he had only a small entourage with him of eight English knights and two German counts, each of whom was accompanied by three knights.

By the middle of January they reached the coast. An embassy consisting of Bishop Walter, Peter of Savoy, and John Mansel, men long familiar to Richard, arrived to discuss the council's concerns. He offered them assurances that he would take the oath upon landing in England if Henry asked him to, but to be compelled to do so outside the kingdom was an affront to his dignity. The hardliners on the council nevertheless insisted the danger he posed was real and they made decapitation the penalty for anyone who tried to ferry him over. Not until 23 January did they relent, although Richard was warned not to make any attempt to smuggle his half-brothers into the country. Five days later, he and his party landed at Dover.

They were less than twenty in number, hardly an invasion force, but access to Dover Castle was denied to them just the same. They were joyously received by Henry and Archbishop Boniface, who rode with them to Canterbury and the feast that awaited them. The next day in the chapter house, with his stepson the earl of Gloucester officiating, Richard swore on his soul to preserve and protect the Provisions of Oxford.

Hear all of you, that I here swear upon the holy Gospels, that I, Richard, earl of Cornwall, will faithfully and diligently join with you in reforming the kingdom of England, heretofore too often disturbed by evil counsellors; and I will also effectively aid you in expelling the enemies and disturbers of the kingdom from it. And this oath I will inviolably observe, on pain of losing all the lands which I hold in England.

On 2 February, he and Sanchia were escorted to London by Henry and Eleanor of Provence. The crowds were enthusiastic to see the two kings, both brothers, in the company of the two queens, both sisters. Wherever they went, there was standing room only. One week later parliament opened, and the next day, on 10 February 1259, Richard and his son Henry of Almain solemnly renounced their rights to Normandy, Anjou, Maine and Poitou in front of the three French envoys sent there for the occasion. Two weeks later Henry announced that he had done the same. The only ones missing were Edward and Eleanor de Montfort.[4]

In all the time preceding and following Richard's arrival in England, Simon de Montfort had lingered on the continent. His absence worried reformers, because Richard de Clare was back. As the second richest earl in the realm, Clare wanted to go slow on reforms and at the Oxford parliament he had surreptitiously represented both king and barons in the discussions. He surely would have checked Simon's ambitions, had he not been incapacitated in Winchester the previous summer. Whatever it was that killed his brother and left the earl himself bald, disfigured and scabby, he had fully recovered from it and was ready to reassert control over the baronage.

Parliament that February had reforms of the nobility on the agenda. Clare, who had the most to lose under such scrutiny, wished to delay the legislation. At that moment Simon reappeared on the scene and castigated him in front of the others. They all had a duty to set an example, he declared, but Clare more so because of his wealth and status. Rather than making sure he did so, Simon left again for France, but his performance moved the other nobles to round on Clare as well. He was sufficiently unnerved by the rebuke to order his steward to bring his estates management in line with the reform programme.

Simon's dramatic intervention and departure was more than just championing the people, however. Just as Henry and Richard hoped to profit from the renunciation of their father's patrimony, so too did their sister. Eleanor refused to renounce her rights until her grievances over her Marshal dower, now going back a quarter of a century, were settled. Her husband was handling that for her. If Henry and Richard wanted the treaty, they would have to talk to him first.

Henry was furious and in time came to believe that the clause of renunciation by family members was Simon's work. He had planted a trump card to play later on. His obstruction of the treaty was not just extortion, but treasonous given his role as one of the negotiators. There was no help for it now. On 10 March, Henry appointed a commission to deal with him.

One of the commissioners was Clare, who was still smarting over Simon's outburst in parliament. In his mind, he was a hypocrite for calling him a backslider on reform while at the same time demanding money and land for his cooperation. During the talks in France, Clare hurled insults at him and the two earls got into a slugging match in front of their French hosts. Simon still refused to yield or come home. The way he saw it, the reform movement was about giving justice to everyone, the Montfort family included.

The cancellation of the three-kings summit at Cambrai had been a rude awakening for Henry and there was another sharp poke in the ribs coinciding with Richard's arrival. It was a letter from the pope responding to events in England. To the council's demand for a new set of conditions before they considered a tax for Sicily, Alexander said there was no need for any. Since the king was in default for lack of full payment, he put Edmund's throne back on the market.

In his own letter to the pope, Henry asked him to send a legate to guide both the peace and reform process. Unofficially, he wanted to have papal authority on hand not just to keep the rebellious clergy in line, but to quash his oath to the Provisions if it ever came to that. But it was a measure of the pope's anger over the whole business that he rejected his request. He figured the king had got himself into this mess, he could stew in it for a while.[5]

Sometime after the no-show in Cambrai, Richard wrote his own letter to Alexander. The treaty may have been stalled by the Montforts, but peace between England, France and Germany was inevitable. The same was true with the imperial coronation. It was only Alfonso's continued pretensions that prevented the pope from summoning Richard to Rome. And it was outrageous. Richard had been elected king of the Romans over two years ago, and the king of Castile, who had yet to step inside Germany, still persisted in his delusions. Richard had had enough. Showing remarkable candour and grasp of history, he set out to expose his opponent for the fraud that he was:

Richard, by the grace of God King of the Romans, ever Augustus, seeks justice and beseeches the grace and favour of his most holy mother church of Rome. The canonical election which preceded the proper and solemn coronation, the oaths given and the homage received from the loyal subjects of the empire and from vassals, the rightful and full possession of the cities and castles pertaining to the imperial crown, are proof enough that entitlement to these certainly requires no other formal recommendation, as this well shows. For our sovereign rule benefits all, is burdensome to none, and prefers rather to be loved than feared. And so, with few fawning flatterers about it, it will prevail against countless others. Furthermore, it ardently pursues the profit of each and everyone and the security and growth of the empire. For a ruler is called Augustus not because he always increases the empire's borders but because he always strives to do so. What I have written, I have written.

Having established himself as the lawful and rightful ruler, Richard next refers to himself in the third person. He calls Alfonso a 'dead lion', apparently meant as a weak pun on the Spaniard's other title as king of Leon, and his contempt is evident in the suggestion that Alfonso should not have simply refused the offer, but actually 'spat it out'.

Surely I am hearing what I can scarce believe? Whilst the commonly accepted understanding of the title rejects it and common sense argues against it, it appears that the illustrious king of Castile is adding the glory of this title to his many styles, calling himself king of the Romans, of Castile, Leon and the other names of that country. On what grounds can this be justified? For before there was any mention of his nomination as emperor, he knew or could have known that the lord king Richard had been elected and solemnly crowned as king of the Romans. This prince, owing so great a debt of honour to his kinsman, ought to have spat out the offer when first asked and stepped back when invited. God forbid, then, that he should now suddenly creep up and seek self-aggrandisement.

If he is magnificent, where is the magnificence in his puffing himself up in name only? He tries to take another's title and calls himself king of the Romans, but really he resembles a dead lion or even a painted picture of one. If he is wise, where is the wisdom in trying to claim a higher rank and contending for what he cannot have? It is the mark of a wise man that he understands the measure of his power and does not exceed it.

Richard then takes a personal swipe at Alfonso by comparing him to Caesar in a most unflattering way. He closes with some classical references, perhaps overly eager to prove his learning in the face of Alfonso's reputation as one of the most learned men of his time.

I hear though that some people are suggesting that it was revealed to [Alfonso] in a dream that he is to be the future emperor. Well, I will grant you that Gaius Caesar, when in his youth, used to dream of committing incest in his mother's bed. Overcome by its carnal shamefulness, he referred the dream to astrologers, who one and all told him that the entire world would come under his dominion; upon this was built the foundation of this great man's hope of seizing imperial power.

But dreams and night-time fantasies fade away and we read that many dreams were illusions, for we know that Alexander was deceived by Apollo's oracle. But why am I wasting time on such things? We have no opportunity to overcome this infamous king of Castile by conquest, as he does not attack us with arms and fighting-men but with letters and the representations of his minions. Nor ought we fret over this, for as Antony said to Tiberius, 'Tiberius, my friend, do not be worried if someone speaks ill of you. It is enough that he cannot harm you.' Socrates, too, answered someone asking how he might gain good repute by saying, 'Do your best and say little.' Now this blustering bragging will assuredly be put to a stop, indeed it will, for king Richard seeks justice and beseeches the grace and favour of the most holy church of Rome.

Ironically, Henry's troubles had already convinced the pope that Emperor Richard was his best option to roll back Manfred, who had had himself crowned king of Sicily in Palermo in August 1258. On 30 April 1259, Alexander wrote to congratulate Richard on his royal coronation, nearly two years late, and accredited a proctor to Germany to prepare the way for his promotion. It was not an official summons, just an understanding that if Richard came to Rome, he would find the holy father not averse to placing Frederick's imperial crown on his head.

Richard received this news from Arnold of Wetzlar, who arrived in June at the head of a papal delegation. He was then lying low, avoiding a pestilence in London that had claimed the life of his good friend Fulk Basset, the bishop. He informed the delegation that he was willing to come to Rome and that they should convey these tidings to the princes of Germany to sound them out, but he would not undertake the journey until he had made complete preparations for it. He told them that he refused to submit himself 'without due consideration to the wheel of fortune'.[6]

In the meantime the envoys to France returned with a proposal for another attempt to bring the three kings together, this time at Abbeville near the Channel coast. Parliament decided that the peace treaty had remained in limbo long enough and plans were made for Henry and Richard to cross over together. Simon was unable to block the move because he was still in France, but he knew his obstructionism could hold up the treaty forever if he wanted. Henry and the council had attempted to mollify the Montforts by giving them the land they desired, even though the legality of this was in question, but the couple replied that it was only half their grievance.

The other half was money. They calculated that the money Eleanor was owed for the shortcomings in her Marshal dower over the last twenty-six years was £24,258. It was a ridiculous amount, more than all of royal revenue for one year. But as a negotiator of the treaty, Simon knew that Louis was obliged to pay Henry the cost of one thousand knights in the field for one year of service. Later valued at £33,500, the treaty stipulated that the money was to be used with the 'advice of the good men of the realm'. Simon had had that clause inserted to make sure the council decided how the money was spent, not the king.

By now his defiance had alienated all but his hardcore supporters. His long friendship and alliance with Peter of Savoy came to an end when he refused to stand surety for the money owed to Peter's relatives. Simon could not understand why these foreign scroungers were getting their money and not he. He came home for parliament in October 1259, but he was politically isolated. When a group of disaffected knights demanded the full implementation of reforms, they protested their grievances to Edward and Clare, not to Simon. The result was new enactments, collectively known as the Provisions of Westminster, which took aim at great landowners like Richard. Complaints against their bailiffs and managers had always been adjudicated by the landowners themselves. Now plaintiffs could go to the council or king's court and receive judgement there.[7]

On 20 October, while parliament was still in progress, Richard dispatched the abbot of Abingdon overseas as his envoy. Nine days later Henry authorised him, as the earl of

Cornwall, to tax his demesne boroughs and manors because he was 'going to the court of Rome'. After parliament adjourned, Richard remained in London in preparation for first going to Abbeville with Henry. Their sister and her husband, however, would not relent. They proposed to cross over as well, to take up the matter of her renunciation with Louis personally. Rather than risk another embarrassing defunct summit of three kings, Richard decided to go back to Cornwall and concentrate on amassing his wealth.

It was his sixth and last visit to the county by which he is remembered. His first visit in 1229 would have informed Richard of the remoteness and separateness of his earldom from the rest of England. Medieval Cornwall was described then as 'not only the ends of the earth, but the very end of the ends thereof'. The people spoke Cornish, the same family group as Welsh, and had an extreme aversion to external authority. In 1233, six years after Richard became earl, all the inhabitants fled to the woods when they learned that royal justices had arrived. They had to be coaxed out with assurances that only those accused of murder might better stay hidden.

He spent Christmas in Launceston and celebrated his fifty-first birthday there. If there was enough of his romantic side left in him, he may have taken a quick trip to Tintagel thirty-two kilometres away to visit the castle he had rebuilt a quarter of a century earlier to underpin his legacy with Arthurian lore and profit from it at the same time. Richard was now both a king and the lord of Cornwall, as Arthur's father Uther and his adversary Gorlois had been on that fateful night. Like Uther, Richard was similarly lustbound. In his own time he was called a 'great lecher towards all women of whatever profession or condition'. He had other illegitimate children besides Philip of Cornwall and (possibly) Bishop Roger de Meuland. He is said to have had a mistress in Cornwall, Joan de Vautort, and sired at least two children with her, named naturally Richard and Joan. A Walter of Cornwall was his as well.[8]

In late January 1260, Richard was informed that the council had received several complaints about his bailiffs at Wallingford. He was instructed to correct their abuses before the king's court got involved. The citation was ignored as events spiralled out of control in London. Simon de Montfort was again at the centre of it. Back in France, Eleanor finally renounced her rights to her father's lands after Louis agreed to withhold £10,000 of the treaty money as surety for her claims. Still dissatisfied, Simon left court without taking leave of Henry. When Henry ordered the council not to convene parliament until his return, Simon demanded they forget him. The king was no longer supreme. The Provisions of Oxford dictated that parliament shall meet, and meet it shall.

When the council showed their willingness to oblige the king, Simon and his followers began recruiting mercenaries abroad and called in support from Edward. Now twenty years old, the heir to the throne chafed under the tutelage imposed on him by the council and his parents. In an audacious stroke of underhandedness, Simon even invited the Lusignans to return to England, hoping to blame it on Henry and unite the barons against a common enemy. Henry found out about it and on 18 April wrote to Richard to guard the coast of Cornwall to prevent their brothers from landing. 'We want you to be absolutely clear that you cannot offend us worse than by admitting them, coming in this fashion, into our realm,' he warned him.

Richard was then in London, meeting with city officials who were worried about riots breaking out in their streets. Clare had arrived with a warlike retinue to use force if necessary to keep the Montfortians from holding parliament. Already at odds with Edward over the ownership of Bristol Castle, Clare became his arch-enemy after he spread a rumour that Edward, with Simon's encouragement, was seeking to depose his father. Under Richard's guidance, both sides were expelled outside the city walls pending the king's arrival. Henry entered London on 30 April with three hundred mercenaries (paid for with treaty money) ready to stamp out opposition.

Despite boasting he would give the mercenaries a welcome they would never forget, Simon was nowhere in sight. Henry focused his anger on Edward and refused to have anything to do with him until Richard convinced him to let the lad have his day in court. In front of parliament convened at St Paul's, Edward declared he had meant no disobedience or rebellion but insisted that only a king could judge him. Together, the kings of England and Germany absolved him of his conduct, and Richard moved to his house in Westminster to make the final preparations for going abroad.

One of Henry's last acts before crossing the Channel homeward had been to issue a safe-conduct to Walter de Rogate, a papal nuncio on his way to England to see Richard. His mission was to remind the king of Germany that it had been a year since the pope issued his summons for him to come to Rome and there was still no sign of him. On 30 May, Henry asked Louis for £3,333 under the treaty so that he might repay Richard the money he still owed him. It was an extraordinary request unimaginable in any other age. Here was the ruler of England asking the ruler of France for money so that the ruler of Germany might advance his continental ambitions.

Richard undertook to reconcile Edward and Clare prior to leaving. In what would become standard for him, he waited until the last minute to issue his arbitral award, and then it was only to invalidate all the ill will that existed between his nephew and stepson up until that point and to validate all their agreements. On 17 June 1260, he took a ship down the Thames to Gravesend, where Sanchia and their modest retinue were waiting for him. Henry of Almain, now a trusted member of his cousin Edward's household, was staying behind. Another mark of Henry's affection for Richard was his request that his brother let him know about his situation, to tell him 'how he crossed the sea and how the affairs of his realm are'.[9]

At the outset, Richard showed no indication of being rushed to Rome. He stopped in Cambrai to invest Countess Margaret of Flanders with her imperial lands and lingered there for ten days. He found Archbishop Konrad secure in his authority over Cologne and surrounding parts of the Rhineland, but such was Konrad's quarrelsome rule that he dared not leave to accompany the king when he headed south at the end of July. With his chief opponent Archbishop Arnold of Trier recently dead, Richard stopped in Koblenz to work for the election of a new archbishop friendly to him. After leaving Germany, he had been deserted by Archbishop Gerhard of Mainz, the prelate who crowned him, but he, too, was dead. His successor Werner of Eppstein was easily won over. On 12 August, the king reached Worms.

To ensure his passage across the Alps, Richard alienated imperial land to Peter of Savoy that guarded the Great St Bernard Pass. With his usual aplomb, he wrote to the people of Bologna to expect his arrival any day. The Italian city was then part of a Guelf alliance arrayed for battle against Ghibelline forces. Although greater in number, they were crushed at Montaperti near Sienna on 4 September 1260. With Manfred in effective control of northern Italy, the way to Rome for Richard now passed through hostile territory.

Even before word of this latest misfortune reached the papal court, Alexander had decided not to crown Richard emperor. Back in November 1259, as Richard busied himself with preparations for his trip to Rome, Manuel of Castile arrived at the court to lobby on behalf of his brother Alfonso, who was still determined to claim the imperial dignity despite making no effort to do so in person. In late August, Alexander sent a papal nuncio to Richard with news that he was again unable to choose between the two candidates.

Learning of both the Guelf defeat and papal equivocation at the same time sealed it for Richard. On 16 September, he held a diet at Worms to tie up the loose ends of his realm. The next day he left by the same route he came, going down the Rhine past Mainz, Boppard, Cologne, then west to Liège, Cambrai and finally reaching Dover on 24 October. Lacking the means to carry his family and retinue further, he borrowed horses and harnesses from the local prior, who was indignant not to get them back for a full week.

His surprising return and apparent poverty led to much speculation about what had happened to him on the continent. The *Flores* chronicler offered three scenarios. First there was Manfred, who supposedly intercepted his advance party, robbed them of all Richard's treasure, and warned him that his life would be in danger should he dare cross the Alps. The second scenario has the Germans talking him out of making the crossing with the winter season soon upon them. Finally, there was the pope, who wanted to conduct secret business in England under the cover of Richard's return. As *quid pro quo*, the pope would then crown him emperor.[10]

Richard reached London on 29 October, one day before Henry's son-in-law Alexander III arrived from the north on a planned state visit. The long-awaited meeting of three kings was suddenly made possible by Richard's unexpected appearance. Witnessing the kings of England, Germany, and Scotland enjoying a family reunion was not quite the same awe-inspiring concept of the kings of England, Germany, and France bringing peace to the world, but it was a much-needed boost for Henry. Simon de Montfort was still out to undercut his authority and Edward was abetting him. When parliament opened with the feast of St Edward on 13 October, Edward knighted his older Montfort cousins in a ceremony separate from the one Henry traditionally performed.

At the feast itself, Simon did not perform his duty as the steward of England, an office he held as the earl of Leicester. A quarter of a century earlier, he fought off an attempt by Roger Bigod to claim the honour at the coronation feast of the queen. Now he loathed the idea of standing behind Henry in full view of everyone, waiting for the king to summon him with a wash basin and napkin after the meal. Simon deputised Henry of Almain to undertake the role for him. The king pointed out that it was not his prerogative to appoint a deputy, but concurred at the urging of Edward, Clare, and Hugh Bigod.

Before Richard's departure for Germany, Henry intended to put Simon on trial again, this time for sedition. They were well into the preliminary phase of it when an attack by Llywelyn in July forced Henry to postpone it until the October parliament. Clare then got the trial effectively cancelled after Simon agreed to changes in reform legislation that gutted protections for the common people. The radical who famously upbraided Clare on this same subject eighteen months earlier now had new priorities, none more important than maintaining tight control of the king.[11]

Edward and Henry of Almain planned to lead an entourage of new knights to the continent for a pre-arranged tournament.

They did not leave until 8 November, giving Richard and his son time to catch up on each other's affairs. At Berkhamsted, Sanchia retired to bed and did not join her husband for the Christmas court at Windsor. Richard's niece, Queen Margaret of Scotland, was there. She was expecting her first child and wanted to have the birth with her mother at her side. The Scots had sensed that was the whole point of the trip and wanted assurances the heir to their throne would not be born in England, but Alexander returned alone.

The political discussion of the court was dominated by the death of Henry and Richard's half-brother Aymer de Valence, the most controversial of the Lusignans. He had been consecrated bishop of Winchester by the pope and was on his way to England to resume his position when he died suddenly in Paris on 4 December. He was only in his early thirties and his return had been dreaded by the queen as well as many reformers, but no foul play was suspected. Henry mourned his passing but saw it as an opportunity to reinstate the Lusignans and the other courtiers expelled during the first wrong turn of the reform movement.

The other wrong turn was the supremacy of the council as conceived by Simon and his fellow radicals. Ironically, the failure of the council to rein them in during their spring sedition left the body discredited. It was barely functioning even before the October parliament convened, basically assigning all authority to Henry again, but he knew this was only temporary. Things were quiet now because Simon was then in Paris, where he had gone to help his wife sue her Lusignan relatives for a share of their mother's estate. The king could be sure that he would attempt to revive the council as part of the unholy trinity he had formed with Clare and Edward.

The only way out of this dilemma was to have the pope quash his oath to observe the Provisions of Oxford. Local reform legislation would stay in place, but it was clear that government by committee was no longer feasible. Since overthrowing the Provisions would cause an outcry, even among moderates, the two kings, Henry and Richard, and their advisers devised a strategy to catch the barons and clergy off guard. By the end of the Christmas court, everything was in place.[12]

7

CONSOLIDATION AND UPHEAVAL
1261–1263

From Windsor, Richard travelled fifty kilometres west to Wallingford to conduct the affairs of his realm and earldom from afar. He was back in London on 13 February when all Londoners twelve and older took an oath of fealty to Henry and Edward at St Paul's Cross. At that time Richard procured a pension of £13 for Arnold of Wetzlar and a murage (tax) for the 'good men of Exeter' to maintain their city walls. Later in the spring he was visited by a member of the house of St Mary of the Teutons. The business they transacted was not noted, but may have been related to the recent uprising in neighbouring Prussia against the Teutonic order.

The king of Germany's hopes of obtaining the imperial crown now rested with the college of cardinals in Rome. Spearheading his campaign was John of Toledo, who had been at the papal court since 1220. He was an Englishman who got his name from the years he spent studying in Spain, where he picked up enough medical skills allegedly to cure the pope when he was struck down by blindness. John was among the cardinals imprisoned by Frederick twenty years earlier in 1241 and would have known of Richard's efforts back then to get them freed. His gratitude notwithstanding, he worked to secure Richard's exaltation because it represented the interests of his Guelf faction at court. When they learned that the Ghibellines planned to make Manfred a Roman senator, they decided to get there first with Richard.

Naturally Richard was expected to provide the money needed to win the votes of the various city wards. His candidacy was welcomed by Italian merchants with extensive moneylending operations in the Rhineland. He could facilitate not just more business for them, but also the collection of their debts, principally from deadbeats like Archbishop Konrad. In April 1261 in the Capitol, Richard was elected a Roman senator for life. He received various letters urging him to accept the dignity and come to Rome immediately. The pope continued to have his doubts, however. In an undated letter at this time, he cited Richard to appear, calling him 'king of the Romans', but he added that Alfonso had had the majority of votes and was seeking to have his election confirmed.

Two events in quick succession put an end to whatever Richard may have been planning. Alexander IV died on 25 May and two months later Constantinople was lost to the Latin Empire. The new pope, Urban IV, gave the Christian empire in the east priority over the Christian empire in the west. Richard was informed he should not take his election as senator seriously nor to give any thought to being crowned emperor until Urban and all the new cardinals around him could thoroughly study the dispute over who the rightful king ought to be.[1]

The change in popes also left Henry in a quandary. As planned back in December, his proctors in Rome secured a papal bull from Alexander nullifying all oaths to preserve and protect the

Provisions of Oxford. To avoid any doubt, the proctors asked the new pope to confirm the nullification of his predecessor, only they found Urban in a confused state of mind. He claimed to have just issued letters that confirmed the Provisions, whatever they were. An investigation was launched and revealed that Simon de Montfort had planted an agent in Rome to take advantage of Urban's newness in the job to get him to reverse Alexander's nullification. It took the proctors several months to expose the deception.

Simon's action went back to a series of confrontations between the king and barons that Henry deliberately staged earlier in the year. He lambasted them for using the council to usurp his authority and for making a mess of the realm through negligence and selfishness. They had even forsaken the promise of quick and free justice because too many complaints had been raised about themselves. In short, their attempt to rule alongside their sovereign lord had been woeful. In June, Henry published Alexander's bull nullifying the Provisions and retreated to the Tower of London. If the barons wanted a fight, they could attack him there.

Clare and the moderates were outraged and united with Simon and the radicals to organise resistance. They countered Henry's appointment of sheriffs with their own baronial anti-sheriffs, but few were willing to risk a war. They had already lost their most militant ally when a heavily indebted Edward returned to parental obedience in the spring. When Simon proposed hiring mercenaries abroad and holding an anti-parliament, Clare had enough and entered talks with the queen and his stepfather Richard about ending the standoff. Henry sought outside help just to be on the safe side and looked to his brother for assistance. Writing from Berkhamsted on 23 October, Richard told him to leave the task of finding mercenaries to him.[2]

The peace talks that ensued at Kingston, southwest of London, resulted in a treaty on 8 December 1261. A panel of six, three for the king and three for the barons, convened to consider the whole framework of government to everyone's liking. It was only a face-saving gesture for the barons. Henry's shrewd use of diplomacy and propaganda allowed him to win back all the power he enjoyed before 1258 without resorting to bloodshed. He kept the wiser aspects of reform in place but would no longer suffer the indignity of his vassals ordering him around. That, of course, was the only arrangement acceptable to Simon. When even his closest associates crumbled, he grew disgusted and left for France, vowing never to return until truth prevailed.

The barons agreed to let Richard break any deadlock, even on the contentious issue of sheriffs. He was chosen for his elevated status. Kings, so went the belief, were the highest form of earthly judge. It was not in their nature to take sides. As for Richard's relationship to the king at the centre of the controversy, it would not have been viewed as a conflict of interest because his history of opposition to Henry was well known.

While the talks were underway at Kingston, Richard worked out a temporary compromise that invited every county to offer four nominees for sheriff. Henry would then choose one of the four for the post. Richard informed his brother of it in a letter from Wallingford on 28 November. He also used the same letter to reply to Henry's request for his opinion on a marriage proposed for the king's son Edmund. He had none, he curtly told him, because Henry had not bothered to give him any details about it.[3]

Apart from the political situation at home, Richard also had to worry about Sanchia, who was bedridden at Berkhamsted. As tensions mounted in October, she grew weaker. At the beginning of November, the executors of her will were given permission to dispose of her wardships 'for the good of her soul'. Richard was not at her bedside when she died on 9 November, aged thirty-three. The queen of the Romans was buried at Hailes Abbey six days later with her uncle Archbishop Boniface officiating. Her other uncle, Peter of Savoy, who had arranged her marriage to Richard, was there, but no mention was made of her husband's presence.

The little surviving evidence suggests Sanchia was a vigorous lord who did not shy away from litigation or royal officials. In England, she belonged to a circle of noble ladies who shared the same books and she enjoyed the company of her older sister Eleanor. She remembered her stepson Henry of Almain in her will, and she herself was well remembered by the king and queen in the masses said for her soul.

Here again, Richard appears indifferent. Unlike for his first wife Isabel, he organised no commemoration for Sanchia and made sure the first thing he did after her death was gain complete custody of their eleven-year-old son's wardship and marriage. Whatever problems he and Sanchia had in their marriage of eighteen years, his womanising and illegitimate children had surely been an unpleasant spectre. Indeed, the *Flores Historiarum* notes that only three months before Sanchia's death a certain Richard died in Winchelsea who was also said to be one of his.[4]

It was another death that took Richard away from Berkhamsted during Sanchia's final days. Konrad von Hochstaden, the archbishop-elector of Cologne and driving force behind Richard's coronation, had died at the end of September. Richard was summoned to Westminster to receive the news from the bishop of Lübeck, who extended by proxy the homage of the new archbishop, Engelbert of Valkenburg. As the Valkenburgs were loyal supporters, there was no need to plan an immediate trip to his kingdom.

The situation changed abruptly in the spring. In April 1262, while Richard was in Dorset building his new castle of Mere, Urban declared himself unable to choose between him and Alfonso. His inaction coincided with archbishop-elector Werner of Mainz falling out with Richard's chamberlain, Philip of Falkenstein, a stepbrother of the Valkenburgs. Werner plotted with other electors to have Conradin, now ten years old and in full possession of Swabia, elected king of the Romans. Learning of it from Ottokar, the pope responded with thanks to the king of Bohemia and warnings to Werner and other ecclesiastics not to persist in their designs for Conradin.[5]

Informed of the plot by Engelbert, Richard began making plans for a third trip to Germany. It was bad timing for Henry, who was going abroad himself in the summer. He wanted to visit France to implement outstanding articles of the peace treaty and either to make peace with Simon de Montfort, who was still a threat, or destroy him. He asked to meet Richard at his manor of Cippenham, near Windsor, but his brother wrote back to say it was impossible. He had too much to do with all the reports and embassies arriving from Germany.

Richard suspected that Henry was anxious about the arbitral award he was about to issue. As expected, the royal-baronial panel had failed to agree on the appointment of sheriffs and so left it up to Richard to determine if they should be men local to their counties, as the barons insisted, or they could be whomever the king wanted. He was given until the end of May to announce his award, although it should have been clear from the start he would come down on his brother's side. His own history suggested as much.

During King John's reign, the people of Cornwall had always paid for the right to name their own sheriff. When Richard became earl in 1227, he refused to renew the grant. He was happy to appoint somebody from Cornwall to the post, but only if that person turned a blind eye to the hard-driving bailiffs he employed to wring the maximum profit from his estates. In 1261, for example, his bailiffs were summoned twice for their transgressions against the rights of peasants and freemen under reform legislation, and Richard again used the loopholes enacted by parliament the previous year to forestall any settlement.[6]

With his sheriffs award out of the way, Richard left London on 21 June in the company of his son Henry of Almain, who went on to France while he embarked for Flanders. He first went to Ghent, where on 2 July he reconciled the two sides of Countess Margaret's children after their two-decade long dispute. Reaching Aachen on 13 July, he presented the cathedral with new coronation regalia consisting of a jewel-encrusted gold crown, orb, sceptre, and vestment robes bearing his coat of arms. In fact, they may not have been so new. Richard probably had them made in 1257 when he could not be sure the old imperial regalia would be made available to him. Although Aachen was the traditional coronation city, the regalia had always been kept elsewhere. His gift of the new regalia was meant to remove another kink in the flawed electoral system.

Still in Aachen, his next move had an even greater impact on the future of the empire. In the more than five years since Ottokar supposedly gave his consent to Richard's election, the king of Bohemia had kept his distance. Things now changed because he needed Richard. Back in 1252, Ottokar had married the much older Margaret of Babenberg, who was of such an age that Henry had unsuccessfully vied for her hand when he was still the teenage king of England. Ottokar knew the marriage would produce no issue, but he wanted possession of her lands of Austria and Styria.

The lack of an heir began to gnaw at him, so in 1261 he had his marriage to Margaret annulled and took the granddaughter of his rival, the king of Hungary, for his second wife. The only authority who could legitimise his retention of his former wife's lands was the king of Germany. Ottokar had thwarted the recent attempt to elect Conradin king of Germany because neither he nor any German prince would ever concede the loss of so much imperial territory. Richard, on the other hand, was happy to do so because it was tantamount to the king-elector of Bohemia finally acknowledging him as the rightful king of Germany. On 6 August 1262, Richard confirmed Ottokar's possession of Austria and Styria, thus setting the stage for the major conflict of the years following his reign.[7]

Two weeks later he set off on his familiar tour up the Rhine. At Boppard, Duke Ludwig of Bavaria came to meet him for the first time. The duke was an enemy of Ottokar and concerned that his name had been insinuated into the plot to elect Conradin. All opposition from Archbishop Werner of Mainz had ceased, allowing Richard to enter Frankfurt freely on 17 September. Further south, he crossed the river into Alsace to end the violent dispute between the bishop of Strasbourg and his diocese. There he received the homage of various German nobles, including Rudolf of Habsburg, who came from an area just north of Savoy.

With Rudolf at his side, Richard continued south on the Alsatian side of the Rhine because Swabia lay on the opposite bank. At Basel, he turned east to Zürich and took that city, which Conradin had tried to wrest away, under his protection. Citing imperial encroachments, Richard declared the youthful pretender's possession of Swabia forfeited despite an earlier promise to Ludwig (Conradin's uncle) not to take such action. Unable to enforce his ruling in any case, Richard only wanted to put his rival, who was more than forty years younger than him, in his place.

It was November, late in the year for crossing the Alps into Italy, but Richard may have planned to do so when his journey began three months earlier. Prior to leaving England, he had extracted a promise of support from his brother. In October, while Richard was in Alsace, he received a letter from Henry to say that it would not be forthcoming. The king had been stricken by a mysterious illness while in Paris and was only now recovering. He assured Richard he would tend to the business once he was back in England.

The support was never specified, but was clearly expected, as Richard had asked Peter of Savoy to remind Henry of it. Whether men or money or intense diplomatic pressure of some sort, Richard was disappointed if not angry it never materialised. All the times he had come through for his brother, which Henry admitted in his letter, and here he was leaving him in Zürich with nothing to do except admire the view of the snow-covered mountains.

Richard retraced his route through Alsace and on 3 December came to Mainz. He spent Christmas with Archbishop Werner in order to patch up relations between him and Philip of Falkenstein. It also meant saddling the seditious prelate with an uninvited guest for the holidays, as well as all the entertainment and expense that went with hosting the royal court. The king left in January, making his way leisurely to the coast and landing in Dover on 10 February 1263.[8]

Where Richard's third visit to Germany had been regal and successful, Henry's third visit to France was beset by misfortune practically from the start. Two days after his party left Dover on 12 July 1262, Richard de Clare was dead. He may have intended to cross over with them, for he died nearby in Kent. The Dunstable annalist accused Peter of Savoy of inviting Clare to dinner and poisoning him there, if for no other reason than Peter left England with the court and did not return with it.

Clare's heir was his redheaded son Gilbert, who at eighteen expected to come into his inheritance immediately. His uncle Henry of Almain and William de Valence took him to see the king, but he was told to be patient. There were issues to work out, such as the rights and privileges his father had usurped from the crown under the cover of reform, as well as the proper assignment of his mother's dower from the estate. Seeing it all as an affront to his dignity, Gilbert went back to England seething and swearing retribution.[9]

Prior to departure, it had been agreed that Henry and Simon would put their grievances before Queen Margaret in Paris and she would decide who was in the right. Henry charged Simon with being an insubordinate ingrate who almost cost him Gascony through his tyrannical rule there. Simon replied that he had received only his due, and if others had been treated harshly by him, that was their due too. Before Margaret could render judgement, a deadly malady struck the court, killing the earl of Devon and scores of others, and almost killing the king.

Simon was unaffected and left for England, where he rallied the faithful with the papal bull his agent had obtained in Rome. He then stole away before the justiciar and regent, Philip Basset, could slap him in irons. Upon recovery, Henry undertook a pilgrimage to Reims, the coronation city of France, and did not arrive in Dover until 20 December. He took ill again. The winter was bitterly cold, and some wayward hot coals set his bedroom and adjacent buildings ablaze. In February, royal proctors in Paris reported that Louis and Margaret had failed in their last-ditch effort to reconcile Simon. By then, Richard had been home a week.

His two previous arrivals from Germany had generated much speculation and this one was no different. The king's prolonged illness had drawn him homeward, it was said, or perhaps it was something untoward like replacing him as king of England altogether. Edward had proved a huge disappointment. He was still lingering on the continent, showing no signs of returning despite his lordships in Wales coming under attack again. Such was the agitated state of the kingdom that the sheriffs were ordered to take oaths of fealty to the king and his son. Gilbert de Clare not only refused to do so, but the mouthpiece for his family, the annals of Tewkesbury, ran an obituary for Henry on 23 March 1263. It was a very moving tribute, but an obituary just the same.[10]

A month later Simon reappeared in England. Henry had tried to undercut his base before then by reissuing the Provisions of Westminster, the reforms that protected ordinary people from oppressive lords, but it fell on deaf ears. Simon and his supporters had long since co-opted the word 'Provisions' as their rallying cry. Theirs was a grassroots movement, the first political party in English history, and it was all the work of the church. Preachers and friars were everywhere in the countryside espousing him and his cause. They were led by bishops like Walter Cantilupe, who saw Magna Carta and the Provisions of Oxford as their bulwark of protection against king and pope. Since Simon was the only high-ranking baron not to abandon the movement, he was their final hope.

Barons certainly formed the core of Montfortians who gathered in early May at Oxford to plot their strategy. Hugh Despenser, who had served for a spell as justiciar, had grown close to Simon during the recent turmoil, and Henry of Almain remained committed to him even after Edward repudiated Montfortianism. Almain had arrived in England on 6 March together with his cousin Henry de Montfort and John de Warenne in order to prepare the way for Simon's return. Other members of the younger baronial crowd had idealist notions about their leader, which led Thomas Wykes to call them wax in his hands. Most, however, could take him or leave him. They were a vindictive lot, resentful and spoiling for a fight. They included Gilbert and his neighbours in the Marches, who had been great friends of Edward until the previous year when the king and queen banished them on account of their corrupt and violent behaviour. Their aim was not the submission of the king, but the restoration of their friendship with the man who would be king after him.

According to the Dunstable annalist, Richard was also at this inaugural meeting of Montfortians. Like Simon, he was a man forever vigilant for his own advantage, yet the two of them were nothing alike in temperament. Simon was pushy and uncompromising, Richard ponderous and slippery. Their shared history went back a quarter of a century to 1238, when Simon had to get down on his knees before Richard and beg him for forgiveness for eloping with his sister. A year after that, Richard saved Simon from the king's wrath, but as Henry knew better than anyone, gratitude would never be Simon's strong suit.

Richard may have been alerted to the meeting by his son and decided to come because he too had an axe to grind with his brother, or he just wanted to make sure his properties were spared in the coming upheaval. If their discussion included the possible deposition of Henry and Edward, then the installation of Richard on the throne, with Henry of Almain to follow him, would have also been on the agenda. That was, of course, provided they accepted the semi-figurehead status of kingship under the Provisions of Oxford. For Richard, that was no comedown from his current position in Germany.[11]

The first indication of their rebellion occurred when Edward returned from the continent with a body of foreign knights to repel the Welsh, but the Marcher lords refused to aid him. His campaign then stalled and ended ignominiously. Simon moved in to conclude an alliance with Llywelyn while his men launched their initial assaults. The fighting that broke out along the River Severn was eerily reminiscent of Richard Marshal's rebellion exactly three decades earlier: a disaffected noble with the support of the bishops teaming up with a Welsh chieftain named Llywelyn to wage war against the king and his courtiers.

Henry took immediate measures, but he lacked time and money to counter their offensive. On 19 June, the royal family, including Richard, retreated to the Tower. Ten days later Edward, Walerand and the foreign knights pulled off a full-scale robbery of the vaults at the New Temple, stuffing their saddlebags and making their way to Windsor. London erupted in riots at the news of the heist, with the houses of loyalists, foreigners, and Jews looted and destroyed. Boniface of Savoy fled the realm together with John Mansel, who was charged with escorting a group of 'ladies from overseas' to the safety of France.

Richard's mansion at Isleworth was untouched. He was there on 29 June when he wrote to his brother to say he was on his way to Wallingford, where he hoped to catch up with Simon, now at the head of an army approaching London, to work out a truce. He wrote again the next day to say that their brother-in-law had no time to meet. He had swung his troops south and was making for the coast. His intention was to secure it against Henry bringing in mercenaries. By 12 July, Simon was in Canterbury and his sweep was complete.

As his army next targeted London, the riots in the city grew worse. It had become open season on foreigners and Eleanor of Provence carried the highest profile among them. The Tower was no longer deemed safe enough a fortress for her, so on 13 July she boarded a barge at the wharf to make her way upriver to Windsor. The mob outside, however, dogged her moves and rushed to intercept her at London Bridge. As the boat came within distance, they hurled objects and filth at her and the crew, calling her, their queen, a witch and a whore. They might have succeeded in sinking her craft altogether had not the mayor, who declared for the Montfortians, intervened with his militia. On Henry's orders he conveyed her to St Paul's, where the bishop of London, another Montfortian, took her under his protection.

On 15 July, Simon entered London, and the next day Henry agreed to reinstate the Provisions of Oxford. A second, more ominous condition imposed by the victors was the expulsion of all foreigners 'never to return'. Since that category included Simon and the queen, an exemption was made for all those deemed acceptable by the council. Ten days later, Edward was prised out of Windsor and his foreign knights were escorted to the coast and put on ships for France. It took Simon less than two months to overturn Henry's victory in 1261, but it would forever be remembered for the violence and xenophobia that made it possible.[12]

At no time did Richard participate in the talks to end the conflict. As the situation in London worsened, he left Isleworth for Berkhamsted and stayed there for the duration. Given his rank and prestige, the peace settlement also carried his seal, but it was only a matter of formality. Henry simply had it procured and attached to the instrument, as if it made no difference to him what Richard thought about it. It had become clear to him that his brother, if not actually part of the uprising, had certainly aided and abetted it.

The first sign of it was in Richard's letter of 29 June and his request that Henry keep Edward from attacking the Montfortians. Simon's whole strategy depended on the mindset that the king himself was not the problem. It was the evil advisers around him causing all the trouble. Simon was making war on them. He was trying to save the king, not rebel against him. Engaging Henry or Edward in combat would have exposed that fiction for what it was and subjected Simon and his followers to charges of rebellion, which entailed the penalty of disinheritance.

One of these advisers was John Mansel, a courtier from a humble background whose rise to power coincided with Simon's disgrace in 1239. Hearing of his flight abroad, Henry of Almain bolted to the continent to bring him back in chains, but the queen learned of it and had Almain himself detained when he landed. Richard warned his brother to have young Henry freed at once or else face 'inestimable peril' and 'loss of honour', which amounted to a threat to openly side with the Montfortians. The king ordered his nephew released on 10 July and Richard thanked him for it.

Then there was Simon's army. After entering London, his troops bivouacked in Richard's park at Isleworth, almost as if by invitation, and their ranks included German mercenaries provided by the archbishop of Cologne and others. How they got there remains a mystery, but it was damning evidence that Richard had conspired with Simon all along. In his fury, Henry had his proctors in Rome denounce his brother to the pope. Urban wrote to Richard immediately, exhorting him to 'consider the boisterous fluctuation of the storm, which shakes the solid foundation of the kingdom of England.' Either he had permitted the rebellion or else stirred it up himself. He was advised to return to his brother's side at once.

Richard was unmoved. Urban had already written to him earlier, on 7 August 1263, to announce that both he and Alfonso were to call themselves 'king-elect' and appear before him on 2 May 1265 to receive final judgement. It was another blow to his imperial ambitions and the most outrageous one yet. Richard had been to Germany three times and demonstrated on each occasion that he was the king in name and authority. Alfonso was still nowhere in sight. But Urban had a new plan. He wanted to let uncertainty rule in the north so that he could finish up the business in the south. To that end, and to Henry's great disappointment, the pope took the kingdom of Sicily away from his son Edmund and gave it to Charles of Anjou. The great prize was to go to France, not England.[13]

Through the course of Simon's new regime, Richard remained at Berkhamsted attending continental affairs. Peter of Savoy, whose estates in Sussex had been raided by the Montfortians, came to see him. Peter had succeeded his nephew as the count of Savoy that summer and he wanted possession of imperial lands northeast of Lake Geneva, which Rudolf of Habsburg claimed. Richard granted the lands to Peter on 17 October, but in doing so initiated a war of attrition between the Savoyards and Habsburgs that pushed Rudolf into Conradin's camp.

The day after making the controversial grant, Richard received one of his own. It was the very profitable Mowbray wardship in the north of England and it came directly from Henry. The king and his son had just seized Windsor, where they began chipping away at Simon's power with offers of patronage and favours to his supporters. Richard topped the list of those to win back in this fashion. Henry was somebody who could never be angry for long, and he would always need his brother, despite his occasional treachery.

Within a week, the desertions began en masse and Simon grew desperate enough to send his bishops to Henry to negotiate. Richard went to London and got both sides to agree to a truce while arrangements were made for Louis to arbitrate. Henry continued to reclaim his kingdom in the meantime, and in late November, with Richard and most of the magnates by his side, he broke the truce by marching on Dover. The garrison there refused to surrender, but Simon was clearly on the ropes. He and his dwindling core of Montfortians just missed being trapped by Henry when their position south of London was betrayed by loyalists.

On 13 December, Simon made his formal submission for arbitration, Henry followed three days later. The king's thirty-one witnesses, all of whom swore to abide by whatever Louis ruled, had a far greater representation of the baronage but no clergymen. They included Philip Basset, Hugh Bigod, the earls of Norfolk, Hereford, and Surrey (Warenne's fourth change of sides since 1258) and the Marchers. Simon's twenty-four sworn witnesses included two bishops (Worcester and London) but no earl other than himself. Despenser was the highest-ranking baron among his backers.

Missing from his list, but appearing in Henry's, was Henry of Almain. While it was reported that he had been bribed with a manor to cross over, young Henry told Simon that he was simply no longer able to oppose the king and subsequently his father and so he felt compelled to leave the movement. He nevertheless assured his uncle that he would never take up arms against him. Simon received the news with scorn. 'Lord Henry, I welcomed you for your loyalty, not your arms. Raise them against me all you want. They are of no concern to me.'

A conspicuous absentee from both camps was Gilbert de Clare. He had come into possession of his earldom under Simon's regime but chose to hold aloof pending the outcome of the arbitration and aftermath. Richard also neglected to commit himself but remained firmly by his brother throughout December and spent Christmas court with him at Windsor. What level of Henry's trust he managed to regain can only be speculated, but it is significant that while Richard acted as regent once the king and Edward left for France, he was never officially appointed to the post.[14]

Family trees of the 13th century

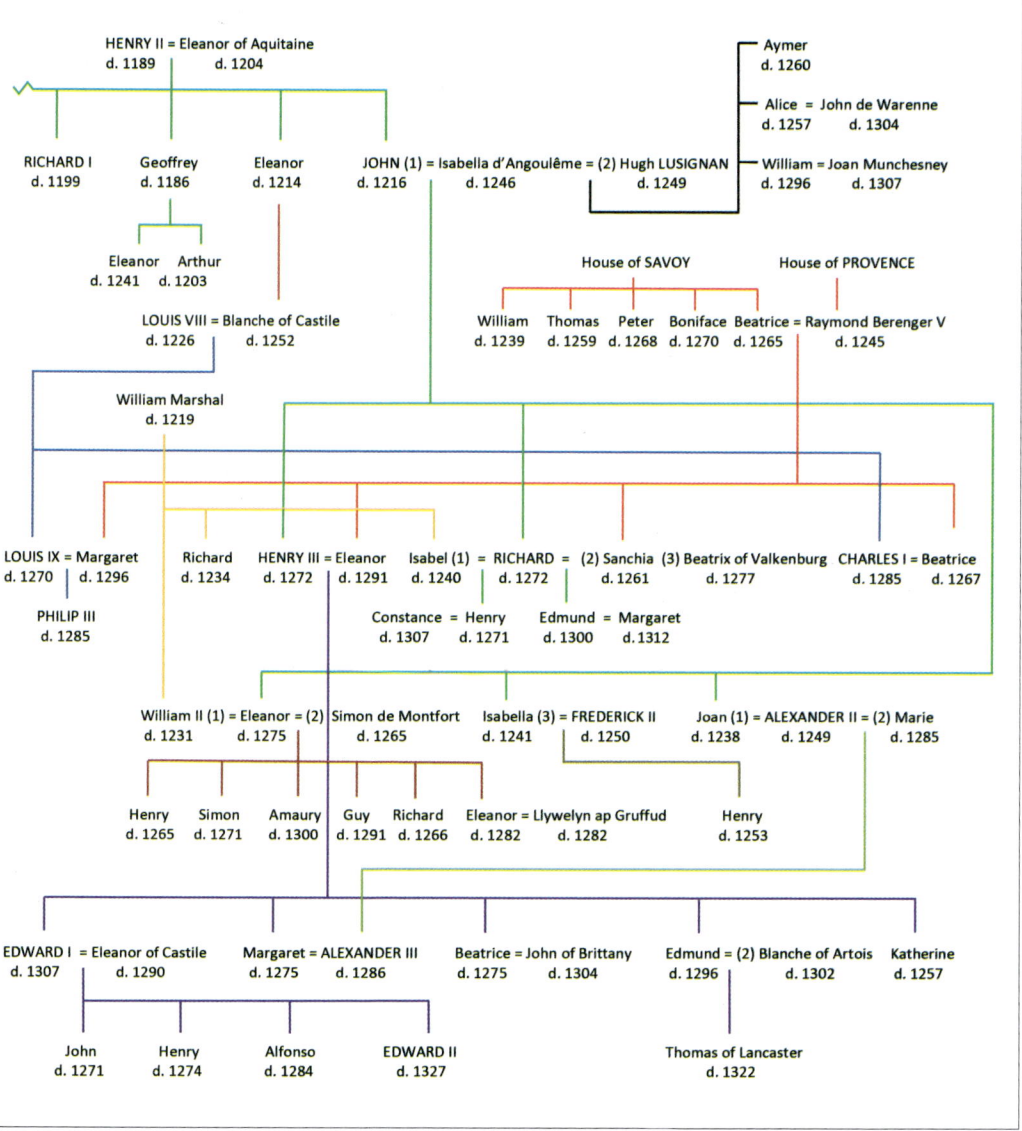

This genealogical line shows the five legitimate children of King John. 1) The oldest was born in 1207 and succeeded him as Henry III in 1216. His reign of 56 years was longest of any medieval English monarch. 2) Richard was born in 1209 and made earl of Cornwall by Henry in 1227. Thirty years later he was elected the king of the Romans and served in that dignity until his death in 1272. 3) Isabella, born in 1214, was actually the middle girl. She became the second and last English empress at age 21 and died in childbirth six years later. None of the children born to her and Holy Roman Emperor Frederick II are shown here. 4) The youngest daughter, Eleanor, was born in 1216. She was married first to William Marshal II, then after his death in 1231 to Simon de Montfort. Her death in 1275 made her the last-surviving of the siblings. 5) Joan was the oldest daughter, born in 1210. Her marriage to King Alexander II of Scotland produced no issue at her death in 1238.

Richard's two sons Henry of Almain and Edmund of Cornwall are shown at left on the bottom row together with their de Montfort cousins Henry, Simon, Amaury, Guy, Richard and Eleanor. The families would be wrenched apart by the war launched against the crown by Simon in 1263. After wavering between both sides, Richard and his son Henry deserted Simon, whose death and dismemberment at the battle of Evesham in 1265 created a blood feud between them and the de Montforts. Simon's sons avenged their father in 1271 when they caught up with Henry of Almain in a little chapel in Italy.

pres Richard regna son fim frere en ky tenf Engleere
fuit entrodyt. vi. aunz e. iii. quaters e. i. moys par

Richard's father King John died in the midst of a baronial war to replace him on the throne with the crown prince of France. The barons had significant help from the church, who despised the king for his quarrel with the pope that put England under interdict, then by his capitulation to that same pope that made their church subservient to Rome. Although dysentery killed the king in 1216, the image above shows a monk and his brethren doing the work with a poisoned chalice.

The effigy of Richard's mother Isabella of Angoulême at Fontevrault Abbey in France next to that of his namesake uncle Richard the Lionheart. Denied any role in the minority rule of her son Henry III, Isabella went back to her homeland in 1218 and never returned. Richard was five when she took him on his first overseas trip and they probably met for the last time during the Poitevin campaign of 1242, when he was thirty-three. He inherited all of her dower lands in England.

Richard's older brother Henry III was crowned as a 9-year old boy at the death of their father. Pious, generous and untiringly ambitious, Henry struggled all his long reign to assert the authority of kingship in the age of Magna Carta and to recapture the glory of the kingdom that had been lost to France.

Henry's wife Eleanor of Provence, shown in the back of the boat, was Richard's rival for his brother's favour and patronage. She eventually won him over by marrying him to her sister Sanchia. Richard served as the queen's chief adviser during her groundbreaking regency while Henry was abroad in 1253–54. The parliaments they held in the king's absence were among the most notable and innovative in constitutional history.

The promontory in Cornwall where Richard resurrected Tintagel, the fabled castle of King Arthur. In Richard's day, the island and mainland courtyards were linked by a saddle of rock that has since disappeared. The bridge on the right spans the divide today.

The ruins of Wallingford Castle in Oxfordshire. Located on the Thames between Windsor and Oxford, Richard used it as one of his primary residences and Henry often stopped there on his jaunts upcountry. After the battle of Lewes, Richard was imprisoned there with other royal captives until a failed rescue attempt resulted in their removal to the more secure environs of Kenilworth.

Richard's first wife Isabel on her deathbed in 1240, with her head shaven and the tresses next to her. The daughter of William Marshal, she was the widow dowager countess of Gloucester when she and Richard married in 1231. Despite having tried to divorce her a few years later, he was heartbroken when she died in childbirth aged forty.

Richard's sister Isabella, the Holy Roman Empress, who was 27 when she too died in childbirth. She had seen her brother a few months earlier when he stopped in Sicily on the way home from the Holy Land in 1241.

Isabella's husband Frederick II was happy to receive his brother-in-law at his court in Palermo and enlisted his aid in his ongoing quarrel with the papacy. On Richard's journey homeward, the city of Cremona in northern Italy welcomed him enthusiastically with a band playing atop an elephant.

The row above shows the heraldic shields of England as drawn by Matthew Paris, with a modern rendition below. The three lions of the Plantagenet kings is first, followed by Richard's crowned and rampant lion in black border, then the shields of the earls of Gloucester (Richard and Gilbert de Clare), Arundel, Leicester (Simon de Montfort) and Surrey (John de Warenne).

The vast chronicle that Matthew Paris kept from 1235 until his death in 1259 includes this self-portrait. The Benedictine monk drew several portraits of Henry, but oddly none of Richard. He knew both brothers well and they visited him several times at St Alban's with gifts and information to impart, but little did they realise that the chronicler was a sneaky, mean-spirited xenophobe who ranted against Henry for his foreign relations and oppressions of the church, and against Richard for always selling out the opposition. His real gripe, however, was money, and how he saw Henry greedily collecting and wasting it and Richard just collecting it.

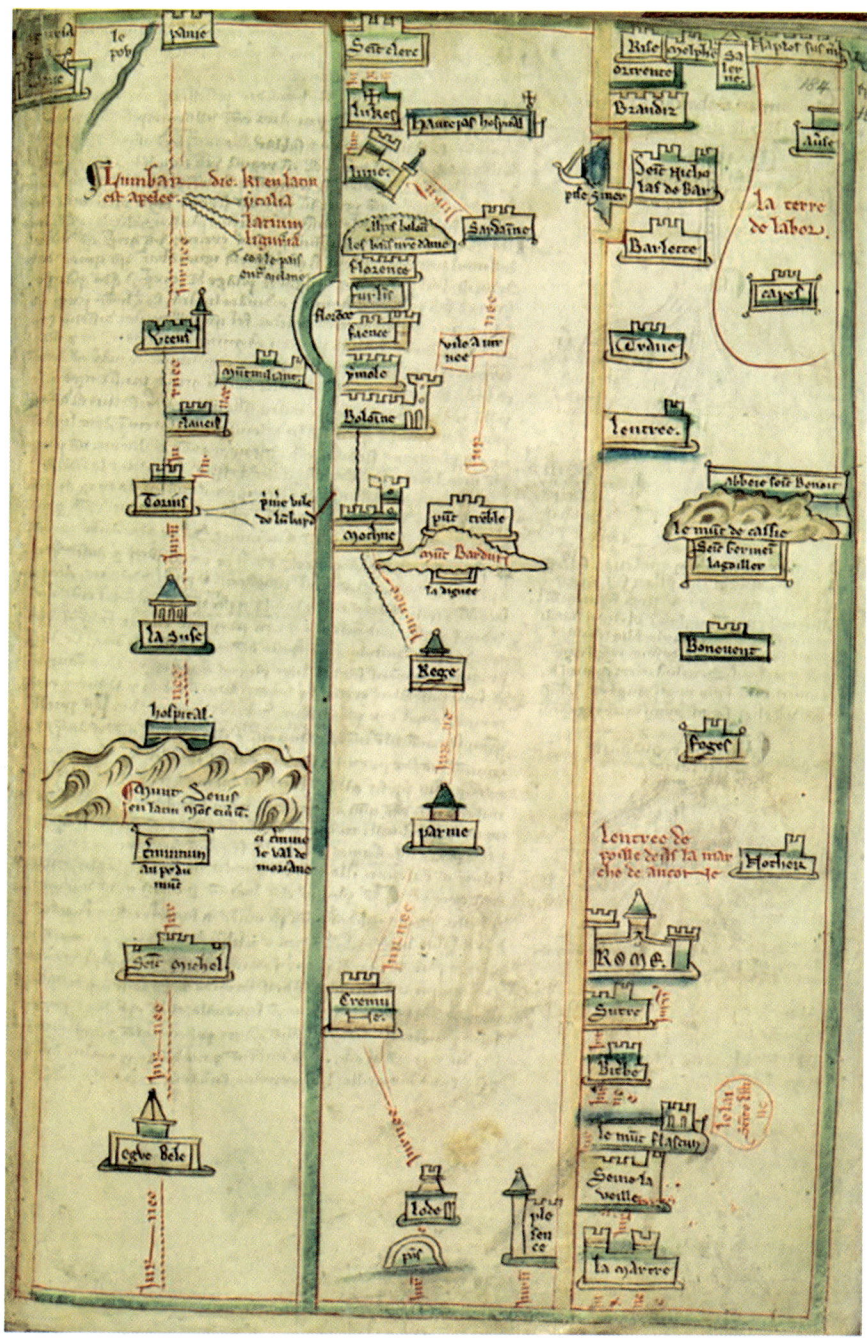

An itinerary, or the stopping points along a particular journey, in this case from London to Apulia in southern Italy. Paris drew it after Richard informed him that the pope had offered him the crown of Sicily but he had turned it down when his conditions were rejected.

Innocent IV was one of the ablest if most controversial of popes in the Middle Ages. He succeeded in deposing Frederick II but failed to drive out his heirs from the empire.

Richard eventually vied for the crown of Germany and might have attained the empire itself were it not for the strenuous opposition of another candidate, Alfonso X of Castile. Culturally brilliant but politically inept, Alfonso was later deposed himself by his own son.

Rudolf of Habsburg, the German nobleman who succeeded Richard as king but strove to erase all memory of his 15-year rule.

Richard and his second
wife Sanchia of Provence
as the crowned king
and queen of Germany.
These statues, at Meissen
Cathedral, were erected
around 1260, a year
before Sanchia's death.
Completely beholden to
his image, Richard made
sure he looked much
younger than his 51 years
at this point.

The rebuilt castle of
Trifels, where Richard the
Lionheart spent most of
his captivity at the hands
of Frederick's father,
Emperor Henry VI. As the
repository of the imperial
regalia, it was here that
Richard's son Edmund
acquired a brooch that
contained drops of the
holy blood.

In 1262, Richard donated a brand new set of regalia to Aachen Cathedral to ensure it remained the coronation city of the empire. He also had a special chest made out of cedar wood and emblazoned with coats of arms in the form of forty copper-gilded medallions. Known as *Wappentruhe*, the function of the chest was to transport relics. Today it forms part of the collection of the cathedral treasury.

The knight on horseback bears the coat of arms of Simon de Montfort, named after his crusader father. The younger Simon first arrived in England in 1230 to reclaim the earldom of Leicester for his family. He became the rising star at court and married Richard's youngest sister, Eleanor. Ousted by Henry in 1239 over financial chicanery, he fell under the influence of churchmen opposed to the king's interference in their affairs. Driven out again by Henry in 1252 over his harsh rule of Gascony, Simon used the reform period begun in 1258 to exact revenge against the king.

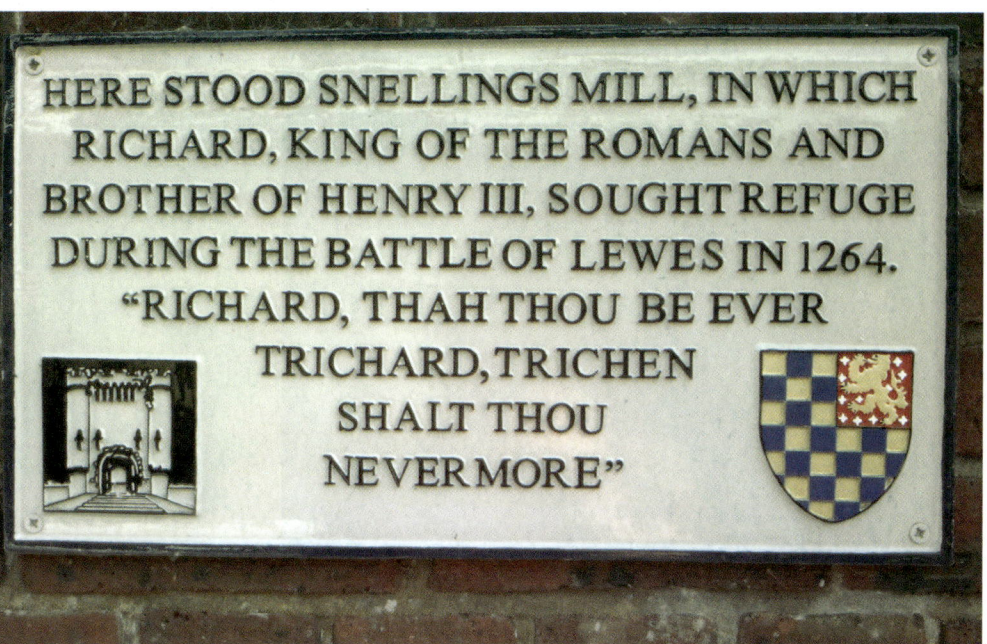

HERE STOOD SNELLINGS MILL, IN WHICH RICHARD, KING OF THE ROMANS AND BROTHER OF HENRY III, SOUGHT REFUGE DURING THE BATTLE OF LEWES IN 1264. "RICHARD, THAH THOU BE EVER TRICHARD, TRICHEN SHALT THOU NEVERMORE"

In 1263, Simon led an armed revolt that had Richard's support until Henry won his brother back to his side. Richard aimed to win glory by spearheading the royalist attack at the battle of Lewes, but his division was roundly defeated and he fled for the safety of a windmill. That bit of ignominy wound up in a popular song of the day, remembered in this plaque that was erected where the windmill once stood.

Simon heaped the humiliation on Richard by threatening to chop off his head if Henry did not surrender. Eventually seizing the king and government, Simon kept Richard locked up and out of sight in Kenilworth, above left, for more than a year. For the first few months Richard would have been able to see a great comet, described as fiery red, which appeared in the low horizon of the sky, and depicted above right in this artistic rendition.

Left: Following his coronation as king of Germany in 1257, Richard made three more trips there in 1260, 1262 and 1268. On his last visit he wed Beatrix of Valkenburg, a teenager forty years his junior, shown in this stained glass window. She died in 1277, still in her early twenties.

Below: The murder of Richard's son Henry of Almain in 1271 by his cousin Guy de Montfort. It was revenge for Evesham, even though young Henry had not been at the battle.

The ruins of Berkhamsted Castle give an idea of its impressive size. It was the administrative centre of Richard's vast estates and it was here that he died on 2 April 1272.

Richard built Hailes Abbey in the Gloucestershire countryside in thanks for surviving a rough sea passage. His son Edmund made it a popular place of pilgrimage for centuries by donating the holy blood he had brought from Germany. The serenity and beauty of the abbey did not prevent the Tudors from plundering and destroying it in the mid-1540s.

This excavated mound is where the shrine of the holy blood was located. The bigger mound in the middle contained the high altar, and the smaller mound in front of it the grave of Henry of Almain. Richard, Sanchia and Edmund were buried to the left of the altar, where the tall grass stands today. The Tudors made their destruction of England's cultural and religious heritage complete by failing to preserve the graves of monarchs like Henry I at Reading, Eleanor of Provence at Amesbury, and here, at Hailes, Richard of Cornwall, the only English king of Germany.

8

WAR AND IMPRISONMENT
1264–1266

When Richard was asked to arbitrate between the king and
barons in December 1261, he was given until the holiday
of Whitsuntide in June the following year to issue his award. He
took it all the way down to the wire. Now, two years later, Louis
was given the same condition, but with war threatening across the
Channel none of them wasted any time about it. Neither Henry
nor Simon argued before him. Henry had a rough passage over
and Simon failed to arrive at all. His horse tumbled on the way to
Dover and he was taken back to Kenilworth with a broken leg.

In his verdict at Amiens on 23 January 1264, Louis held nothing
back. He quashed the Provisions of Oxford in their entirety and
forever extinguished the experiment in government at the heart of
all the dispute. It was another case of a king coming down on the
side of a king, but where Richard's award about the sheriffs was
received with resignation by the barons, the Montfortians were
outraged by Louis's obvious favouritism and refused to accept his
ruling. They went home and prepared for war.[1]

Simon launched it by renewing his alliance with Llywelyn and sending an army under his two oldest sons to attack Roger Mortimer, a ruthless Marcher baron who, like Simon, had stewed over a personal grievance for the entire reform period. His grandmother had given him her plush manor of Lechlade on the Thames even though it was not hers to give. At her death in 1252, Henry gave it instead to Richard as part of the dowry he still owed him for Sanchia. Mortimer considered it an act of injustice, but Richard was unyielding and fought off all his attempts to get it back. That drove Mortimer into Simon's camp for the 1263 summer offensive.

Henry had used patronage to lure the Marchers away from Simon. In Mortimer's case, he offered him three manors close to his lordship to compensate him for Lechlade. These manors had been royal property until Henry was forced to give them to his sister and Simon to drop their obstruction of the peace treaty with France. Still seething over their extortion, Henry told Mortimer the manors were his if he could take them. Mortimer set out to do it in December, but Simon restrained himself from retaliating. He could see that Henry was trying to goad him into a war before the arbitration. Now that the war was on, at least as far as he was concerned, he told his sons to go to Mortimer's castle at Wigmore and avenge their father. Mortimer fled at their approach, leaving his wife and men to deal with their pillaging and destruction.

To keep the Montfortians and Welsh from joining forces, Richard ordered the sheriff to destroy all the bridges over the Severn except for the one in Gloucester. He then went to the Marches himself, reaching as far as Hereford on 18 February, before news that his brother had returned from France drew him back to Windsor. There he met the king, who summoned parliament and the feudal host to assemble at Oxford.[2]

Edward and Henry of Almain went immediately to Mortimer's aid, but after some initial success, they found themselves trapped in Gloucester by Henry de Montfort and his allies. Playing on their cousin's gullibility, Edward and Almain arranged a truce through Walter Cantilupe and escaped to join their fathers at Oxford. Cantilupe and the other bishops then arrived at Oxford to restart peace talks, but they were overtaken by events in London. The properties of prominent loyalists were sacked by armed mobs. In mid-March, at the toll of the great bell of St Paul's, the various mobs gathered in militia formation. They were met by Hugh Despenser, the keeper of the Tower, who told them to follow him.

Without knowing where they were going, they marched due west for eighteen kilometres until they came to Richard's sumptuous mansion at Isleworth. Despenser told them it was all theirs. The mob went on a rampage, setting fire to the house and mills, emptying the pond of fish, and destroying the dam that created the pond. Another mob went to Westminster and razed Richard's mansion there to the ground. According to Wykes, they ripped out all the trees and bushes in his orchards and in general turned the place into a wasteland.

It was revenge for Richard deserting Simon, much as he had deserted Richard Marshal three decades earlier. Richard had been furious then about the damage inflicted on his properties and hounded the perpetrator Richard Siward for years afterwards. Now he was completely beside himself, especially as the initiative came from Despenser, a former friend and tenant who had witnessed his coronation at Aachen. It was an attack on an anointed king that demanded the stiffest of reprisals, which is what the Montfortian leadership hoped to gain from it. They wanted Henry and Richard to bring the feudal host against the strong walls of London while they secured the countryside. Simon himself had just arrived in the capital in a carriage specially designed to haul him around in with his broken leg. Henry, however, refused to take the bait, and Richard had to settle for having his men scouring Oxford for Londoners to round up and rough up.[3]

On 3 April, Henry unfurled his famous dragon standard and led his army northwards to Northampton. Two days later they stormed the town and castle and captured the entire garrison, including the younger Simon de Montfort. This spectacular victory for the king threw London in a panic. A mob fell on the Jewish quarter and massacred as many as five hundred men, women and children. Several leading Montfortians were involved in it, although apparently not Simon himself. He nevertheless demanded they surrender their loot so he could launch an assault on Rochester, which was held by Warenne and Henry of Almain. He sacked the town with help from Gilbert de Clare, who decided to throw in his lot with the losing side of the moment, but their attempts to take the castle were repulsed by their former allies. When the king learned of their siege, he raced south and chased them back to London.

Henry and Richard spent the next week harrying the ports and abbeys of Sussex that were friendly to the Montfortians. When the king's favourite cook and other men in his train were killed by Welsh archers concealed in the surrounding woods, he had a large group of insurgents captured near Flimwell brought before him. After taking counsel with Richard, he sent them all to the chopping block. They then proceeded to Battle Abbey, the lordship of the executed men, and extracted both money and wine from the monks and harassed the abbot. It was there that they learned Simon had left London with his army and was heading in their direction.[4]

Simon stopped his men just north of Lewes, where Henry and Richard set up headquarters in the priory while Edward lodged in the castle. Knowing he was vastly outnumbered, Simon sent two sets of churchmen to negotiate. The first group, led by the bishop of Chichester, told the king that the Montfortians were compelled to observe their oath to the Provisions but were willing to submit them to a special commission for review. Henry had conducted a masterful campaign against Simon, but he longed to bring the country back to peace. He was thinking of accepting their offer when the second group led by the bishops of Worcester and London arrived.

The two prelates repeated the first offer, only now sweetened it to include £30,000 in compensation. The implication here was obvious. They thought Richard was of such shallow character that he would persuade his brother to accept their offer just to get his hands on the money. Simon and the bishops were astute men, but they completely misread him on this one. Burning with revenge, Richard disabused Henry of any notion of compromise. He argued that, however much the Provisions of Oxford might be amended, the Montfortians would always seek to 'disinherit the king of England and his heirs and depress their power'.

The next day, 13 May 1264, Simon and Gilbert sent the king a letter assuring him that their fight was not with him, but with his evil advisers. He was their lord and they emphasised that fact by their grovelling tone. Henry replied with contempt. 'We care nothing for your assurances or for your love, but defy you as our enemies.' Having understood that they were the evil advisers spoken of, Richard and Edward wrote their own letter, jointly and on behalf of the barons, the majority of whom stood firmly by the king:

Your verbal defiance has already been sufficiently proved to us by your hostility, the destruction of our property by fire, and your laying waste to our possessions. We therefore wish you to know that you are defied by all of us as public enemies, and that from this time forward we will, with all our mind and strength, wherever we shall have the means of so doing, do our utmost to inflict injury alike upon your persons and your possessions.[5]

In the early hours of 14 May, Simon led his men up to the crest of the high ground overlooking Lewes. Royal sentries were either asleep or derelict in their duty and his army was not spotted until dawn by foragers. Henry, Richard, and Edward all had to be roused from their sleep. The night before Henry dictated a letter to Louis asking him to provide £500 in relief for the Holy Land. He was worried about dying with his crusader's vow still unfulfilled. With the battle about to be joined most unexpectedly, he decided to acquit Louis of all the money he owed under their treaty despite lacking the true figures. Knowing the chancery would raise all kinds of questions about it, he dictated the letter to Richard's right-hand man, Arnold of Wetzlar, in front of Richard, Edward, and his war council.

Henry had wished to avoid battle. His greatest pride was the peace his long reign had given his people, but he was also unwarlike to begin with and could never inspire men in the field the way Simon could. Richard was the same, but he was eager to fight and not just out of his desire to punish his troublesome brother-in-law. He was a man who understood the odds, and the odds were stacked wholly in his favour. Vanquishing the Montfortian rebels would do wonders for his career which, for all its success, still lacked military distinction. He would finally evoke the fear and admiration his uncle Richard the Lionheart had enjoyed. He also still had his German mercenaries with him. Returning with them to their homeland as victors in the war would gain him the respect he needed to demand the imperial crown once and for all.

It was with this profile in mind that Richard took the centre position of the royalist line that emerged from the town. So confident was he of victory that he had his fourteen-year-old son Edmund with him. He faced his step-grandson Gilbert de Clare, while the king, on the left, had with him one nephew, Henry of Almain, to do battle against two other nephews, Henry and Guy de Montfort. Theirs was going to be a tough fight uphill, with enemy slingers pummelling them from above.

Edward had most of the cavalry and used it to smash the Montfortian left wing, which contained the lightly armed London militia. All he had to do was drive the survivors into Simon's centre line and the battle would be over. But hot-headed youth that he was, he could not wait to exact his revenge against the Londoners for their vile treatment of his mother at London Bridge. He chased the fleeing urban warriors headlong towards the river and in the process completely left the field of action.

At his vantage point up the slope, Simon kept a small but adequate division in reserve. Seeing Edward's flight, he threw these reserves into the fight. They went bowling down the hill and provided the impact needed to snap Richard's line and send his men running for their lives. As Edward should have done, Simon next wheeled his men around into Henry's flank and scattered his attack. The king, who was in the thick of the fighting, managed to retreat to the priory while the Montfortians descended on the town. They were still trying to take the castle when Edward reappeared. They dispersed his charge, forcing Valence, Warenne, and Hugh Bigod to flee to the nearby coast. Edward and Mortimer fought their way into the priory.[6]

Richard was not in the priory. During the rout, he and Edmund came across a windmill that was in the line of retreat. They took refuge inside and barred the door behind them. The soldiers who tracked them there could not believe their good fortune. They had Richard of Cornwall trapped, the man who had fleeced them on the currency exchange, hounded them for crusade legacies, and used all that money to buy his pretentious title of 'forever Augustus'. They had great sport with his predicament. 'Come out, come out, king of the Romans,' they hollered. 'Come out, you poor excuse for a miller!'

As dusk fell, Richard emerged to the jeers of his captors, one of whom, John de Befs, claimed him for Gilbert. They delighted in putting him in chains and marching him through the town. He was their highest-ranking prisoner, Edmund their youngest. They were locked up together with his friend Philip Basset, who endured more than twenty wounds before he was taken. Simon threatened to execute them and 'stick their heads on lances to serve as standards' unless Henry surrendered. When the king called his bluff, Simon was forced to offer terms. He agreed to submit the Provisions to arbitration and allow the prisoners to go free. Henry's brother, son, and nephews, however, were to remain hostages for his acquiescent behaviour under the new Montfortian regime.[7]

The victors put the princes in Dover and brought the two kings to London. Richard went to the Tower of London, still in the keeping of his mortal enemy Despenser, and Henry to St Paul's. In June, all the royal captives save the king were confined at Wallingford, doubtless an act of consolation to Richard arranged by his sister Eleanor de Montfort, who was put in charge of their custody. That quickly came to an end when a troop of loyalist knights under Walerand rode in the night from Bristol to try and spring them in a dawn raid. They were working in coordination with Eleanor of Provence, who was putting together an invasion force on the continent. The knights breached the outer walls of the castle but were eventually beaten back. Simon responded in late June by having his wife move the captives to the more secure environs of their castle at Kenilworth.

It was at this time that a great comet appeared in the early morning sky and remained there until the end of September. According to Robert of Gloucester, its long red tail was a portent of much bloodshed to come. Indeed, Eleanor of Provence was ready to launch her fleet from Flanders, and Simon mobilised the peasantry on the south coast to defend the realm against their queen. Her hand was stayed, however, by a papal legate dispatched by Urban to deal with the crisis. Although Simon refused to admit the legate to England, he sent representatives to discuss a peaceful outcome with him at Boulogne.

He was only stalling for time. Even a soldier of lesser skill could see that his peasants stood no chance against the knightly force preparing to invade. To show that he was acting in good faith, Simon released Henry of Almain on bail to carry proposals back and forth. On Almain's second mission to Boulogne, he was nearly killed when his party was attacked and robbed by locals. The talks went in circles and the death of Urban in October deprived the legate of his commission. He excommunicated the Montfortians and went back to Rome. By then the queen had run out of funds and her army disappeared along with the comet. The Montfortian regime was a pariah state, but a secure one.

Through all of it, Gilbert was technically Simon's co-ruler, but being thirty-five years younger and lacking experience, he was forced to maintain a low profile. With the invasion no longer a threat, he demanded the release of the royal hostages. His motives were plain. Since his men had captured his step-grandfather Richard, he could claim a king's ransom for him.

He dared not go as high as the £100,000 paid for Richard the Lionheart seventy years earlier, but the £17,000 in silver and £5,000 in gold he demanded was 'a sum worth having', notes the Melrose chronicler. Simon, however, refused to release Richard.

He was right to worry about letting Edward on the loose, especially with the northern barons and Marcher lords still actively hostile to his regime, but Richard posed absolutely no problem and no one pretended that he did. He did not even figure in the peace talks. Simon's reason for keeping him locked up were the same as Gilbert's for wanting to free him. Richard's estates in Devon and Cornwall and their extremely profitable tin mines were given to Simon's son Guy to hold. Another son, clergyman Amaury, was given Richard's Cornish church of St Wendron, one of the richest in the land, and Eleanor de Montfort was in possession of his favourite residences, Wallingford and Berkhamsted. As a hostage, Richard was too valuable to the Montforts to let go.[8]

The feast ordered for the Christmas court of 1264 was magnificent, but it was not for Henry, who was left alone at Woodstock. Simon and his family took the boar, oxen, and venison to Kenilworth, where they spent the holidays in their family castle (given to them by Henry twenty years earlier) with 140 household knights and the hundreds of squires and orderlies attending them. The endless eating, drinking, and singing must have been unbearable for the royal captives there, Richard in particular. Far from covering himself in glory, Lewes and the windmill had made him a laughingstock. One of the songs belted out with gusto at this time, believed to be the first of its kind in Middle English, heaped on the shame and humiliation. The rhyming of 'Richard' with 'trichard' added to their merriment at his expense.

Sitteth alle stille ant herkneth
to me!
The Kyn of Alemaigne, bi mi
leauté,
Thritti thousent pound
askede he
For te make the pees in the
countré,
ant so he dude more.
Richard, thah thou be ever
trichard
trichen shalt thou never more.

Richard of Alemaigne, whil
that he wes kyng,
He spende al is tresour opon
swyvyng.
Haveth he nout of Walingford
o ferlyng,
Let him habbe, ase he brew,
bale to dryng,
maugre Wyndesore.

The Kyng of Alemaigne wende
do luI wel,
He saisede the mulne for a
castel,
With hare sharpe swerdes he
grounde
the stel,

Sit still everyone and listen
to me!
The King of Almain, by my
loyalty,
Thirty thousand pounds he
asked
To make peace in the country,
And so he did more.
Richard, though always
treacherous,
Treacherous you shall be never
more.

Richard of Almain, while he
was king,
He spent all his treasure on
luxury.
Not a yard of Wallingford he
has.
Let him have his brew, an evil
potion,
In spite of Windsor [i.e. the
king]

The king of Almain thought to
do well,
He seized the mill for his castle.
With their sharp swords he
ground
the steel,

He wende that the sayles were mangonel	He thought the sales were a mangonel
to helpe Wyndesore.	To help Windsor
Richard, thah thou be ever trichard	Richard, though always treacherous,
trichen shalt thou never more.	Treacherous you shall be never more.

Just as bad was the much more serious *Song of Lewes*, a long poem extolling Simon and composed in Latin in order to reach a wider audience. In the nearly one thousand lines, Richard appears just once, and not by name but only as a king 'subdued' for being a 'transgressor of the laws'. Except for a song and laugh, the first ever English king of the Romans had become a non-entity. There was no more visible sign of it than the parliament that convened in January 1265, the one that made Simon forever famous.

All those invited to it were Montfortians and their supporters, hardly a democratic ideal but good enough for later historians to pinpoint it as the first House of Commons. The assembly concluded on 11 March with a grand ceremony in the great hall of Westminster. There in front of nine bishops and a host of dignitaries, Henry and Edward were made to swear that they accepted the constitutional monarchy that England had become under Montfortianism. Edward was released to the custody of his father's household, still under the ever-watchful eye of Simon's knights, and Henry of Almain promised to stand surety for his cousin's good behaviour. Richard of Cornwall was given no role to play in the ceremony at all. He was left at Kenilworth, his fate on no one's agenda.

Only thanks to his sister Eleanor was he not completely forgotten. Knowing his taste and fondness for luxury, she regularly sent him spices and treats like raisins and dates. Her accounts for 29 March show that she purchased for Richard and Edmund twenty pounds of almonds, five pounds of rice, two pounds each of pepper, sugar and cinnamon, a pound of ginger, and twenty slices of whale meat. She also had robes of scarlet red and miniver made for him and his son for Pentecost, which fell on 24 May.⁹

On that day, the court was in Hereford. Simon had taken it there to try to appease Gilbert, who had left parliament in a high temper over the way Simon and his sons were hogging all the glory and riches. He went back to Gloucester to conspire with the queen and Marcher lords to bring his partner down. On 28 May, Gilbert's people on the inside, working together with Roger Mortimer and his wife Maud, helped Edward escape from custody. It coincided with Henry of Almain's failure to return from France, where Simon had sent him for negotiations with Louis. Simon's first response was to order the garrison at Kenilworth to put Richard and Edmund in irons. He was worried about a wide-ranging conspiracy to free all the royal captives, but it also reflected the anger and confusion he felt at the moment.

It took Edward and the Marchers less than two months to trap Simon behind the River Severn. Things were looking bleak for him when his namesake son arrived at Kenilworth on 31 July with reinforcements. Edward sought to neutralise the threat with a pre-dawn raid on the troops camped outside the walls. He and his horsemen pounced on the Montfortians in their sleep. Caught completely unawares, Simon the younger, whose life Edward had saved during the assault on Northampton, scampered to safety completely naked.

The raid was of questionable benefit. It did not knock out the relief force but did allow Simon to get across the Severn.

Edward had to strike again fast if he hoped to keep father and son from linking up. On 4 August, he cornered his uncle's meagre, exhausted forces at Evesham and annihilated them. Simon was cut down by Mortimer and his men, his body chopped up into trophy parts. When Simon the younger arrived and caught sight of his father's head pitched up on a lance, he mournfully led his men back to Kenilworth. They were in a vengeful mood and wanted to mete out the same fate to Richard, but his nephew intervened to save him.

   In the days after Evesham, Eleanor de Montfort arranged the surrender of Richard's castles of Berkhamsted and Wallingford. She was then at Dover, which she occupied following Edward's escape, and was preparing to go into mourning for her husband and son Henry, who was also killed at Evesham. When she emerged in late August, she got into contact with Kenilworth, where negotiations were underway for Richard's release. On 6 September 1265, he and his son Edmund walked free after almost sixteen months of imprisonment. Remembering her kindness, he issued letters that same day promising to protect 'my lady Eleanor, our sister, countess of Leicester, and all her children'. Three days later Richard returned to Wallingford to much joy and acclamation by his household.[10]

From Wallingford Richard continued south to Winchester to attend the special parliament that Henry, who had been wounded at Evesham, summoned to reassert his power and authority. There on 12 September he ordered the people of Cornwall not to stand in the way of his brother retaking possession of the county. In what had to be a calculated jibe, the king reminded them that the earl of Cornwall had always been faithful. Exeter received a similar order, along with protection for the merchants there who were again purchasing tin from Richard.

The main issue before parliament was whether Henry should disinherit the Montfortians on account of their rebellion. The majority of loyalists were for it. The butchery on the battlefield, which was unprecedented in that age, helped make the land grab easier to execute. The only magnates to oppose it were Richard, Philip Basset and Roger Bigod, none of whom played any part in Simon's downfall. Richard and Philip had remained in custody the whole time, whereas the earl of Norfolk, who missed both Lewes and Evesham, had actually supported the Montfortian regime.

Henry and Edward wanted an end to the conflict and pursued a policy of mercy in exchange for submission. The Tower of London and Windsor surrendered and London was about to follow, but Kenilworth and Dover remained defiant. Since both fortresses were directly controlled by the Montforts, Simon the younger was given a safe-conduct to come to parliament and make his peace with the king. He may have left Kenilworth together with Richard and remained in his suite until they arrived in Winchester. The terms he was offered were generous. His family had to forfeit Leicester, which would go to the king's son Edmund, but they would receive an annual payment close to its value and Eleanor would continue to receive her dower payment.

Unwilling or unable to bring his mother and compatriots on board, Simon the younger went back to Kenilworth to resist with the garrison. That settled it for Henry. On 17 September, the Montfortians were disinherited by official proclamation. Edward went to Dover to deal with his aunt. Mindful of the slaughter of her husband and son and imprisonment of Guy de Montfort, who was wounded at Evesham, he promised to protect her household if she sailed away without a fight. Having already sent her sons Amaury and Richard to the continent with the family treasure, Eleanor left with her daughter on 28 October.

The queen and her son Edmund arrived the next day. They were accompanied by Cardinal Ottobon Fieschi, appointed as legate for England by the former legate, who was now Pope Clement IV. Ottobon's mission was to help restore peace to the land and preach a new crusade, but his first priority was to crack down on the English clergy for their support of Montfortianism. Of the bishops and abbots he cited for abetting the rebellion, Walter Cantilupe died soon enough, but four others were suspended from office and dispatched to Rome to explain their conduct. Unlike the nobility, churchmen were safe from disinheritance, but not from taxes, and Ottobon, with Clement's blessing, imposed a stiff one to help the king and queen recover their financial footing. Ironically, it yielded the same amount of money Henry had wrung out of the church for his Sicilian business.

Richard knew the legate well. Second only to John of Toledo, Ottobon had been his biggest supporter at the papal court, and in 1261 he had written to urge him to accept his election as a Roman senator. Together with Henry, Richard went to meet him and the queen at Canterbury. On 29 October, the day of their arrival, Henry issued the following extraordinary appeal.

Whereas Richard, king of Almain, the king's brother, was taken at the conflict at Lewes and imprisoned for a year and more whereby his lands and chattels were occupied, aliened and scattered during that time; and whereas he is now, for reasons of which the king is silent at present, charged with debt, for which the king pities him, the king requests the tenants of the said Richard their lord to give him such an aid for the relief of his said goods, chattels and debts that he shall be bound to show himself favourable to them in the future and so that they shall deserve the king's special thanks.[11]

Normally Henry granted Richard permission to tax his tenants without any comment, but here he used his 'silence' and 'pity' to remind him in front of everybody that it was still not too late to come out in favour of disinheritance. Richard certainly needed the help. The damage to his properties was everywhere, from burnt buildings and stolen cattle to the stock and valuables missing from his castle at Eye. Some of the plundering had occurred after the proclamation of peace, as in the case of his woods in Norfolk and Suffolk, where the trees were mysteriously razed and the timber carted off. On 3 November, Henry ordered the sheriff there to apprehend the malefactors so that he 'may have their bodies to answer to Richard'.

On the same day that Henry made his appeal on his brother's behalf, he granted Henry of Almain the manor of Gringley in Nottinghamshire. It had belonged to William de Furnival, a Montfortian who had been captured at Northampton and probably died at Evesham. Almain was likewise given the London houses of a former king's clerk who had openly served in Simon's regime, but his biggest prize were the extensive estates of Gilbert de Gaunt in York and Lincoln.

Richard travelled with the royal family and legate to spend Christmas court at Northampton. Edward and Henry of Almain preceded them to the north in order to suppress their cousin Simon the younger, who left Kenilworth on 23 November to ravage the Lincoln countryside from a base of banditry he had established on the Isle of Axholme. It was a brief contest. The Montfortians were routed and scattered and Simon himself was captured and brought to Northampton, where his fate was left to Richard, Philip Basset and Ottobon to decide.

In gratitude to his nephew for saving his life, Richard overcame objection from Gilbert de Clare and decreed that Simon the younger could still have the pension he was originally offered, but only provided he procured the surrender of Kenilworth and that he left the country to live in peaceful exile along with his mother and siblings. Negotiations for the surrender floundered and, suspecting that life imprisonment awaited him, Simon eluded Edward and his guards and escaped to France in February 1266. Later that spring his brother Guy bribed his jailer at Dover and also fled abroad. They joined their mother at the nunnery of Montargis south of Paris, where Eleanor de Montfort spent the last decade of her life.[12]

The royal family remained at Northampton until mid-January. On the 10th, Henry pardoned London for their transgressions against him, the queen, Richard and Edward, in return for a fine of £13,333. How much of that money went to Richard is unknown. On 25 January, Richard was granted lands that belonged to Adam Newmarket, a leading Montfortian landowner from York who had served on Simon's council. It was done very secretively, probably because of Richard's opposition to disinheritance, and so neither the extent nor value of the grant were officially enrolled.

To be sure, not all Montfortians were disinherited. Those who submitted before the end of the Winchester parliament were pardoned. Simon and Eleanor de Montfort's steward Richard de Havering and their former ward Gilbert de Umfraville were among those to do so. Henry also allowed the widows and widowed mothers of fallen rebels to receive their dowers from the confiscated estates, if not always the full one-third. On 14 April, while the court was at Windsor, thirty per cent of the Furnival lands granted to Henry of Almain were returned to William's widow Ada 'by way of humanity and grace'.

Four days later the king crossed the Thames to visit Richard at his manor of Cippenham, which was eight kilometres northwest of Windsor. He was there, along with Edward, Henry and Edmund of Almain, and a host of dignitaries, to witness his brother's foundation of a new religious house for an abbess and nine nuns of the Augustinian order down the road at Burnham. The grandiose opening of the charter shows that the old Richard was back. 'Richard, by the grace of God, King of the Romans, ever Augustus, to all the faithful of Christ, present or future, to whom the present writing shall come, eternal health in the Lord.' Later on the same day a group of Cornish burghers witnessed him issue a charter for the foundation of the borough of Liskeard.[13]

The court left Cippenham for Reading and Oxford before settling in at Northampton. It was going to be Henry's base for forcing the surrender of Kenilworth, where the rebel garrison was terrorising and plundering the local population. On 5 May, he ordered Henry of Almain, whom he appointed commander of royalist operations in the north, to bring all his troops to Northampton in early June. Almain was just then stalking a new insurgency emerging in Derbyshire under Robert de Ferrers, the earl of Derby.

Ferrers had joined the Montfortians in early 1264, not out of political ideals but because he nursed a long-standing grudge against Edward. He took advantage of Edward's imprisonment to wreak havoc on his territories. Since Simon was about to come into possession of those same lands, he wanted Ferrers neutralised. He lured him to parliament in 1265 and had him locked up in the Tower. The young earl was released after Evesham and given a pardon for his transgressions in exchange for a golden cup, but he deluded himself into believing that, with the exile of Simon the younger, he was now head of the Montfortians.

With Edward in the south subduing rebel pockets, Ferrers put together a formidable band of the Disinherited at Chesterfield. Almain had with him a strong force led by seasoned warriors John Baliol and John de Warenne. On 15 May 1266, they struck. Using covered wagons as concealed troop carriers, they caught the insurgents by surprise and scattered or slaughtered those not cut down in the initial assault. Ferrers, whose gout had left him unable to flee, was captured and hauled away in chains to Windsor.

In the two years of unrest following Evesham, Chesterfield was the only full-scale engagement of the War of the Disinherited. It paled in comparison to the far more spectacular storming of Northampton in 1264, but Henry and Richard's victory there was quickly overshadowed by their defeat at Lewes. They had no time to rest on their laurels in the way that Henry of Almain could for Chesterfield, even though his triumph was in no way decisive. Twenty-two insurgents of knightly status had gone out hunting the night before and got away. Some went to Kenilworth, others followed the redoubtable John Deyville to the Isle of Ely to carry on the struggle there.[14]

The siege of Kenilworth commenced in the last week of June. After Henry gave him the castle in 1243, Simon de Montfort put his knowledge of siege warfare acquired from his father, the Albigensian crusader, to good use on the defences. The occupants, who were said to number a thousand men, women and children, repelled everything thrown at them, including a monstrous siege engine known as the Bear. Not even a fairer settlement for the Disinherited could induce them to surrender. It took starvation, disease and squalor to make that happen on 14 December.

Having been locked up inside Kenilworth for more than a year and threatened with dismemberment by the garrison, Richard might have been expected to emulate his brother's zeal and determination to retake the fortress, but apart from a brief attempt at mediation, he took no active part in the siege. He also had no role on the committee that met at Coventry to draw up terms for the new settlement. It was a measure of the esteem his son Henry of Almain now enjoyed that the king chose him to work with Ottobon on approving the final form of what became known as the Dictum of Kenilworth. Richard was over a hundred kilometres to the south at Wallingford when the dictum was published on 31 October 1266.

Under the terms, the Disinherited were allowed to redeem their lands in proportion to their involvement in the rebellion. The value of property at that time was reckoned to be ten times the income it produced on an annual basis. The scale of the redemption fines started with those who had been coerced into supporting Simon. They had to pay one year's worth of revenue. At the top end were those who had borne arms against the king. They had to pay five times their annual income, or half the value of their property. Taking Gilbert de Gaunt as an example, his vigorous adherence to Simon earned him a redemption fine of five times his annual income of £400. To recover his estates, he had to pay Henry of Almain £2,000.

It was up to the principals to work out the final amount and payment of the redemption. Wardships, marriages, and all feudal rights save those belonging to the crown figured into the bargaining between the new owners and old. Nothing is known about the arrangements made between Richard and Adam

Newmarket. The debts Adam had incurred in order to get his lands back, however, haunted his grandson well into the reign of Henry's great-grandson Edward III. It suggests that Richard had somehow exploited the redemption process to the hilt before returning the lands.[15]

9

BRINGING PEACE TO TWO KINGDOMS
1267–1269

Richard's absence from the political scene in England during the previous year can be attributed to his diminished status in the political order after Evesham. His power was nothing like it had been a decade earlier when, if Wykes can be believed, he 'managed the king and the affairs of state, and on his nod hung all the business of the realm'. His only true rival then had been the queen. Now he had to compete with Ottobon, Edward, Mortimer, even his own son Henry of Almain.

The shame of his capture and imprisonment also suggested he keep a low profile. With nothing else to lose, the Disinherited stepped up their campaign to include mockery of the sacred institutions of church and state. When Ottobon put on an elaborate show of excommunicating the garrison at Kenilworth, they responded by dressing up a priest to look like a legate and have him stroll up and down the walls of the castle cursing Ottobon and Henry with the same sentence. Had the insolent anti-legate seen the king of Germany standing beside them, he might have started singing the windmill song loud enough for the whole countryside to hear.[1]

The political situation in Germany also diverted Richard's attention from English affairs. In February 1266, Charles of Anjou defeated and killed Manfred at the battle of Benevento. Charles won the kingdom of Sicily that Henry III had endeavoured so long to bring under Plantagenet hegemony. The Ghibellines turned to Conradin as their new leader and sought to elect him king of the Romans as a prelude to challenging Charles in the south. In his 'congratulations' to Richard on his release, Ottokar assured him he would keep Conradin and his supporters in check but expected the king to cede more imperial territory to him.

The impasse over the rightful king of the Romans was supposed to have been settled in May 1265, but Urban died before then and Richard was in captivity. The new pope hoped that Alfonso, who had yet to set foot in Germany, might withdraw his candidacy. With Richard away indefinitely, Clement IV wanted to insinuate a third candidate onto the throne. Alfonso not only refused his request but sent an emissary to the pope demanding that he put off the decision no longer.

Richard's freedom shortly after that gave Clement some breathing room. He urged Richard to pick up where he left off and gave Ottobon legatine powers in Germany to help him reassert his authority there. He did not favour Richard over Alfonso, rather he was anxious to thwart Conradin. To keep up appearances, he ordered both parties to make their cases before him in February 1267. Richard sent Henry of Almain to plead for him, but Alfonso, according to the pope, lacked adequate representation. Given the gravity of the matter, it was only fair to give him another chance. On 9 May, Clement cited both parties to try again on 26 March 1268.[2]

Henry of Almain returned to a land again in turmoil. Pockets of the Disinherited had rejected the Dictum of Kenilworth because it made no provision for the return of their estates before they paid their redemption fines. They found an unlikely supporter in Gilbert de Clare, who felt his betrayal and destruction of Simon had been insufficiently appreciated. In April, while Henry and Richard dealt with insurgents on the Isle of Ely near Cambridge and Edward was doing the same in the north at Alnwick, Gilbert marched on London and duped Ottobon into opening the gates. He and his men swarmed into the capital with ease, forcing the legate to retreat to the Tower for safety. The Jews wisely followed him there. One of Gilbert's henchman had led the massacre of their community three years earlier, as Gilbert himself had butchered the Jews of Canterbury around the same time.

Henry was of a mind to bring in mercenaries from abroad and storm the city, but he allowed Richard and Philip Basset to work for a peaceful end to the occupation. In the end, the Disinherited won two major concessions. The king agreed to 'diligently' ask those in possession of the confiscated lands to return them to their former owners so that they might work off their redemption fines, and Ottobon promised to secure a tax from the church to help them pay off their fines. The arbitral award, which carried Richard and Henry's seals on it, was published on 16 June 1267, one day after Gilbert vacated the city. According to the Osney chronicler, Richard's work on the arbitration was 'pleasing to Jesus Christ'.

Although Gilbert had to provide money, castles and children as surety for his good behaviour in the future, Henry pardoned the Londoners for their part in the occupation. He did, however, suggest they might show their own goodwill by compensating Richard for the destruction of his property at Isleworth. The city agreed to pay him £666, but Richard also wanted accountability. It took a year, but in June 1268 Henry appointed an official to find the perpetrators who had set fire to his buildings and carried off all his fish and timber. Nothing more is known about the case, but by this time the estate had already been largely rebuilt. He and Edmund were at Isleworth on 26 July when Richard made a grant for the new college founded by his friend Walter Merton.[3]

For all the messiness of the disinheritance policy, it proved to be another of Henry's lasting if unacknowledged success stories. Not only did the vast majority of the Disinherited recover their estates within a few years, but Montfortianism as a political and social force completely vanished. Simon's leading adherents were assimilated, some going on to glittering careers under Edward. His miracle cult at Evesham, which had been outlawed under the Dictum of Kenilworth, withered and disappeared until he was remembered only in songs and tales as a folk anti-hero type anticipating the Robin Hood legends of later centuries.

Disturbances and lawsuits continued to linger. Ruffians drove away all the beasts Richard kept at his park in Beckley, then stole the livestock of his tenants at Woodstock. The effects of the war and settlement would go on for decades, but the weather that had helped bring on the onset of troubles in 1258 was especially gorgeous that year. The land blossomed and produced a harvest like no other in living memory. Fruit, bread and wine became plentiful as 'swords were turned into ploughshares and spears into pruning hooks'. Henry even allowed his son and nephew to organise a multitude a tournaments to celebrate.

Having brought the War of the Disinherited to a peaceful end, Richard intended to do the same for the conflict with Wales, but he was quickly rebuffed by Llywelyn. When the court left for Montgomery to conduct treaty negotiations, he chose not to accompany it. He was not with Henry and Edward when they passed through Evesham, almost two years to the date after the battle, and so missed out on what would have been an exclusive tour of the battlefield. The treaty concluded on 29 September 1267 was mostly Ottobon's work, with Richard's name mentioned nowhere in the instruments.[4]

His decision to shun the proceedings also had to do with his brother, who had not fulfilled a promise to provide him with £2,000 in wardships and land from the Disinherited. He had, moreover, broken a promise not to make peace with the Londoners without consulting him first, a sign that Richard had expected more compensation for his devastated properties. In November, he rejoined the court at Marlborough for a special parliament tasked with codifying the good that had come out of the reform programme into statutes of the realm.

While there, Richard took up his issues with Henry, who was apologetic and promised him redress. He offered to put in a good word for him with Clement and expressed his wish that Richard spend Christmas with him at Winchester. Henry was not exaggerating his pull with the pope. Clement not only approved the tax he requested from the clergy but assigned the collection of it to royal agents. The monks who wrote the history of this period bitterly resented it, but the bishops had learned their lesson and raised no opposition.

Clement was just then vexed by the latest developments in the former empire. In May 1267, Charles of Anjou moved into central Italy to crush Ghibelline resistance. Conradin responded in September by marching into northern Italy at the head of an army whose ranks included Duke Ludwig and Rudolf of Habsburg. As the two sides jockeyed for position, Rome was lost to the Ghibellines and Clement had to remain confined at Viterbo, the papal enclave north of the city. The hearing between Richard and

Alfonso's advocates scheduled for March 1268 was called off and rescheduled for the following year.

Even with Conradin's departure, the situation in Germany was hardly less quiet. In the nearly six years since Richard left, the Germans had succumbed to what Wykes called a 'raging madness'. Merchants and travellers using the River Rhine were forced to stop at each approaching castle and pay a toll for their passage. Various turf wars broke out as a result, one involving Archbishop Engelbert of Cologne when he tried to corner his own piece of the action. He was defeated and imprisoned at Nideggen Castle, where he was sometimes suspended outdoors in a cage for the amusement of onlookers.[5]

Despite the imperial crown again being out of reach, Richard began amassing another fortune to return to his kingdom. In February 1268, Henry asked Ottobon to pay his brother £1,333 he still owed him out of the church tax. The legate was preparing to leave England himself and brought his mission to a close by preaching the crusade at the church of the Holy Sepulchre in Northampton. There, on 24 June 1268, Edward and other young nobles took the cross. It had been at that same church three decades earlier that Richard renewed his crusader vow and went on to lead the last successful crusade in the Holy Land.

Henry of Almain also took the cross, but he first went west. On 12 July, the king ordered him to go to Ireland to recover the estates that Edward had unwisely alienated there. Neither Henry III nor Richard ever went to Ireland in their lifetimes, nor would Edward. Since Almain would be gone when his father left, Richard appointed Basset, Walerand and Merton to watch over his affairs while he was away. On 2 August 1268, he and his son Edmund, now nineteen years old, departed from Dover with a small retinue.[6]

Even as they arrived at Cambrai two weeks later, Conradin was leading his army out of Rome to have the decisive showdown with Charles of Anjou. They met at Tagliacozzo on 23 August 1268. Conradin won the initial clash, but Charles fell on his forces in ambush and won the day. The German prince fled but was captured and taken to Naples. Charles was convinced he would never be secure on the Sicilian throne as long as the sixteen-year-old boy lived and so had his head chopped off on 29 October.

The Hohenstaufens were finally extinguished. The papacy had won its thirty-year-long war with Frederick's dynasty, but it took all the energy and effort and ultimately lives of five popes to accomplish it. They included Clement, who died on 29 November, one month after Conradin's execution. Richard must have received the news of the pope's death with weariness and disbelief. His quest for the imperial throne was back to square one and there was no telling when the election of a new pontiff, to be the fourth during his reign, would take place.

Two days after leaving Cambrai on 20 September, Richard and Edmund arrived in Aachen. Conradin's demise did not upset the balance of power in Germany because most of the German princes did not march with him to Rome. Their interest was the north of Italy, not the south. Rudolf of Habsburg was back, but Richard did not have to contend with his anger over his earlier grant of contested land to Peter of Savoy. The two Swiss rivals had concluded a peace treaty before Peter's death in May 1268. But Richard's arrival coincided with an even deadlier dispute and one right on his doorstep.

Just northwest of Aachen was the ancestral home of Dieter of Valkenburg, who had supported his brother Engelbert in his struggle against the patrician overlords of Cologne. To help procure the archbishop's freedom, Dieter embarked on a mission to tunnel his way into the city and force the patricians to negotiate at sword point. His opponents were tipped off, however, and Dieter was killed when he and his men struck on the night of 14 October. His wife and children were forced to seek protection from their uncle Philip of Falkenstein, who was Richard's chamberlain.

Richard went to Cologne to smooth over relations. He spent the Christmas holidays in the city and probably celebrated his sixtieth birthday there on 5 January 1269. During this time he became enamoured of Beatrix, the second of Dieter's four daughters, who was around fifteen years old. His first two wives Isabel and Sanchia had both been beautiful and Beatrix was no exception. The Osney chronicler described her as a 'jewel among women' and Richard put plans into motion to marry her.

He began his now very familiar trek down the Rhine. When he reached Worms in March, he summoned the princes and prelates to a diet to deal with the general state of extortion inflicted on river traffic. With Archbishop Werner of Mainz leading the way, they all agreed to abolish their private tolls. Trade naturally began to flourish again as a result and Richard gave it an added boost by proclaiming a general peace throughout the land, the first such proclamation since 1235. The lawlessness of the Germans had been reined in by the earl of Cornwall.

During the diet, Falkenstein surrendered the castle of Trifels, about ninety kilometres southwest of Heidelberg, to Richard's control. It housed the original imperial regalia and for a while had served as the home of Richard the Lionheart during his captivity. Edmund came to Trifels at this time, whether to oversee the transfer of the castle or because he had spent part of his boyhood there and so was a favourite of Falkenstein's relatives. He came across a brooch in the collection of regalia that was said to contain the blood of Christ and somehow or other he retrieved a portion of it to bring back to England, along with other relics.

In May, Richard moved downriver to Frankfurt and from there 120 kilometres southwest to Kaiserslautern for his wedding to Beatrix of Valkenburg on 16 June 1269. By marrying into the ancestral nobility, Richard may have hoped to establish a future Plantagenet dynasty in Germany, perhaps even endear himself closer to his subjects, but Wykes thought it was just Richard being Richard. The older man was enraptured by the incomparable beauty of the teenager. 'The innate grace of the new bride so transfixed the heart of the king that he could not bear to be separated from her for one single night, whatever the reason.'

In July, the couple were guests of the archbishop of Mainz. After delegating powers to him and various imperial officials to enforce the decrees of Worms, Richard started homeward. It had been his most successful visit to Germany so far, but no new pope had yet been elected and Richard was as ever dependent on his resources in England. He may in fact had been eager to show off just how rich he was to his young bride. They set sail and arrived in Dover on 3 August.[7]

Three days later they reached Gravesend at the mouth of the Thames. Edward and Henry of Almain were just then leading a group of noblemen to France to discuss the upcoming crusade with Louis. They put off their journey by a day to have a long conference with Richard. It was the first opportunity for Almain to meet his new stepmother, whose dower entitled her to one-third of the vast estate that he stood to inherit. At thirty-three, he was at least twice her age.

He was also recently married himself. His bride was Constance de Bearn, who was probably then in her late twenties. They celebrated their wedding at Windsor on 21 May and were on their way to the continent, first with the other crusaders to Paris and then alone to her ancestral home of Bearn in the foothills of the Pyrenees. As the daughters of noble families, Constance and Beatrix would have used the French and Latin they learned growing up to bridge the communication gap between their Occitan and German.

The marriage of his son had been in the works for four years, but at no time did Richard take part in the negotiations. Constance's father Gaston was a southern strongman who had been consistently at odds with English rule over Gascony. He and Simon de Montfort clashed frequently when Simon was the governor in the early 1250s. Both of their families had a claim to the county of Bigorre, which bordered Bearn, and Simon never forgave the king for, as he saw it, siding with Gaston (who was a cousin of Queen Eleanor). Richard's promise to help his sister Eleanor de Montfort would have rung hollow if he actively supported a union between his son and the daughter of her dead husband's mortal enemy.

From her base in France, Eleanor had appealed to Louis to intervene on behalf of her and her children. Louis got Henry to agree to return Leicester to Simon the younger, but on condition that he sell it to him whenever asked to, and that if there was a dispute about the price, Richard would decide what was fair. Nothing came of this arbitration, and in 1267 Simon and his brother Guy went to Italy to serve under Charles of Anjou, who was their second cousin and a long-time friend of their father. Guy distinguished himself at the battle of Tagliacozzo, fighting like a 'wild boar among dogs', and rose to become one of Charles's trusted aides.

The driving force behind Henry of Almain's marriage was his aunt, Queen Eleanor, who conceived it while she ruled Gascony during the Montfortian regime. She was also behind the lucrative marriage of her son Edmund in Westminster Abbey on 9 April. He had been granted Simon's earldom of Leicester and in 1267 Henry created the earldom of Lancaster for him. From that time on he was known as Edmund of Lancaster. His marriage to the heiress of Albemarle and Devon would put two more earldoms in his future. With the help of his brother Edward and cousin Henry of Almain, he soon made it five.

Since being captured by Almain at Chesterfield in 1266, Robert de Ferrers had languished in the dungeons of Windsor while Edmund held custody of his earldom of Derby. Under the Dictum of Kenilworth, Ferrers was required to pay a redemption of seven years, which should have made his fine a hefty £9,000, but on 1 May 1269 he told the council that he had in fact agreed to pay £50,000 for both his estates and freedom. He informed them that a group of peers, led by Henry of Almain, were ready to stand surety for the money. The king was satisfied and ordered his release.

Ferrers was handed over to his mortal enemy Edward, who took him from Windsor to Richard's nearby manor of Cippenham. There Ferrers agreed, under duress he later claimed, that Henry of Almain and the other sureties might keep his lands and give them to Edmund until Ferrers paid the money. Edward then took him to Wallingford before setting him free three weeks later. Unable to raise the enormous sum, his earldom of Derby was lost to Edmund and the Lancasters. All future attempts to get it back were thrown out of court on the technicality that he had been a 'free man' when he agreed to the arrangements.[8]

Richard's history of crusade legacies and currency exchanges shows he was no stranger to the art of swindle and would have thought nothing of his son using two of his homes, Cippenham and Wallingford, for this unsavoury transaction. After seeing him off, he and Beatrix continued their journey upriver to London, which the court had left after Edward's departure. The royal couples first met in Winchester on 24 August. No description survives of the impression Beatrix made on Henry and Eleanor, although Henry was said to have been very affable and gracious to the teenage Sanchia when she first arrived in England in 1243.

By leaving Germany when he did, Richard was home in time to celebrate what would be the crowning achievement of his brother's reign. Henry's reconstruction of Westminster Abbey had taken him six times longer than it took Richard to build Hailes Abbey and it cost him six times as much, or £40,000, and while still incomplete, enough of the cathedral was ready to translate the remains of Edward the Confessor on his feast day to the new jewel-encrusted shrine. The ceremony of 13 October 1269 was a solemn occasion. Henry, Richard, Edward, Philip Basset and other nobles bore the saint's coffin in front of a multitude of dazed onlookers. Two of them, said to be Irishmen possessed by the devil, walked away with a new lease on life.

The new cathedral itself stole the show. The artistry and masonry truly made it one of a kind. The stones of the wondrous pavement in front of the high altar were set in a pattern that evoked the creation of the universe. The Confessor himself was mostly lost to history after that. In rebuilding the abbey around him, Henry wanted to give the English people a patron saint to call their own, but they eventually expressed their preference for a foreigner instead and gave the honour to St George.

Henry had hoped the translation would mark the final reconciliation of the realm. He even allowed the coat of arms of Simon de Montfort, who had been posthumously absolved by Ottobon, to hang in the abbey with his and other heraldic shields.

The day itself, however, was marred by rivalries among clergymen and between the men of London and Winchester. The endless disputes meant that the full splendour of the ceremony had to be scaled back.

While doubtless a disappointment, no one could have been surprised. For the king, dealing with endless gripes and grievances was just another day at the office, and he had now spent nearly twenty thousand days on the throne. In the words of one historian, 'Henry had never been free of his exacting people.' Observing it all for the same lifetime, Richard had to wonder if he was in fact the luckier of the two.[9]

10

THE END OF TWO REIGNS
1270–1272

The talk before and after Richard's last visit to Germany had been all about the crusade. The situation in the crusader states had become desperate as the Egyptians reduced the original Frankish conquests to just a coastal strip of land. Henry was eager to fulfil the vow he took back in 1250, but that put him in conflict with Edward's intention to come to their relief. They both could not leave when the country was still recovering from a decade of strife. Pope Clement settled it in April 1268 by deciding that Edmund of Lancaster could go as proxy for his father.

Brothers Edward and Edmund, Henry of Almain and the rest of the English contingent were to serve under Louis, who had taken the cross again to atone for the failure of his earlier crusade. Their meeting with him in Paris just after Richard's return from Germany was as much about procuring financing from him as it was about coordinating strategy. Under severe terms that included handing over one of his sons as a hostage, Edward borrowed £17,500 from his uncle the king of France, but it was nowhere near enough for the anticipated costs. It took taxing the church again, the third time in four years, and getting parliament to approve a subsidy in return for laws that restricted Jewish debt collection, before the English crusaders could set out.

One who had thus far withheld men and money from the planning was Gilbert de Clare. He had also taken the cross at Northampton in 1268, only to become discouraged as Edward grabbed all the attention and glory. He suspected him of sleeping with his wife Alice and refused to attend the consecration of the new Westminster Abbey for fear that Edward was plotting against him, perhaps even trying to poison him. To soothe his ego, he was invited to France to discuss the crusade with Louis, but he returned obstinate and dissatisfied as ever.

Richard was called in to arbitrate their dispute, just as he had done between Edward and Gilbert's father a decade earlier. Wykes praises Richard's efforts here, calling him 'the most fervent enthusiast for the tranquillity of the realm'. The award he issued on 27 May imposed a list of conditions on his step-grandson. Gilbert had to sail for the Holy Land within six months after Edward's departure, he would receive a certain amount of money if he agreed to serve under Edward, less if not. He had to maintain the peace in the meantime at the risk of excommunication and hand over two castles to be held by the king until he left. The earl of Gloucester grumbled about the unfairness of the award, but he went back to Wales and caused no more problems.[1]

It was at parliament in Winchester that the crusaders said goodbye. They all knew the risks they were facing with a long expedition of this sort. Henry at sixty-two and Richard at sixty-one might never see their sons again. On 2 August, just before sailing from Portsmouth, Edward committed his castles, lordships, everything he owned to a committee headed by Richard. Since his wife Eleanor of Castile was going with him, Edward also entrusted the care of their three children to him.

Why to Richard and not to their grandmother Eleanor of Provence was based on political considerations. Eleanor's strong, dynamic queenship had not been to everyone's liking, and the church historians of the period tended to blame her for the upheavals of the last decade, in part because she was a foreigner. Despite being a foreigner himself, Simon de Montfort had risen to power on a wave of xenophobia, and Edward wanted to keep the biggest xenophobe of them all, Gilbert de Clare, from exploiting it while he was away.

Henry of Almain and his wife Constance left separately for Gascony on 15 August. From there he joined Edward and the main body on the Mediterranean coast of France. Having arrived two months behind schedule, the English contingent found Louis long gone. Not only that, but he took the crusade to Tunisia in North Africa. It seemed like a terrible betrayal of the crusader states in the Holy Land, and Charles of Anjou was accused of somehow talking his brother into going in that direction as part of his dream of creating a Mediterranean empire. Whatever advantage Charles derived from striking at the emir of Tunisia, the king of France knew perfectly well what he was doing.

Louis's aim for this crusade was victory, something less likely now against the Mamluks than when they crushed him twenty years earlier. The emir of Tunisia was not only a soft target but was reportedly ready to convert to Christianity with a little applied pressure. Neither turned out to be the case and the Christian army that landed outside the ancient ruins of Carthage was quickly decimated by heat and disease. Almost a quarter of the eighteen hundred knights perished. Louis himself wasted away from dysentery until it carried him off on 25 August, five days after the English crusaders left for France.

Word of the disaster reached London just after the feast of St Edward on 13 October. Edward learned about it two weeks before then, during a layover on Sardinia, but sailed for Tunisia anyway, where he and his men arrived on 10 November. They were dismayed to learn that Charles, who had arrived in Africa a day after Louis's death, and Louis's son Philip III, the new king of France, had concluded a peace treaty with the emir and were ready to leave. Unwilling to concede that the crusade was over for him before it got started, Edward decided to winter in Sicily as Charles's guest before taking his couple of hundred knights and attendants to the Holy Land.[2]

Henry conveyed his displeasure with his son's decision in a letter of 6 February 1271. His poor health had put the burden of running the realm on Richard, and a month later, on 7 March, he named 'the king of Almain' regent for the duration of his illness. Even so, Richard declared his intention of leaving straightaway for Rome once a new pope was finally elected. Losing him would be grave for Henry at this point, because save for Philip Basset, who was also getting on in years, no other member of the committee or council had the same prestige or authority.

They were also dealing with two particularly troublesome affairs. First, the death of Archbishop Boniface in his native Savoy during the previous summer led to an unseemly squabble between Canterbury and the priory of Dover. Richard summoned the chief instigators to Wallingford to defuse the situation, but the controversy outlived him and Henry. Then in September 1270, the countess of Flanders precipitated a trade war with England. When Edward learned of it, he beseeched his parents and Richard to harass the countess. Otherwise, he was staying the course to the crusader states. If there was one thing he had learned from his uncles Richard and Simon, it was the importance of public image. He had no chance to accomplish anything militarily in the

Holy Land with his meagre resources, but returning home with a crusade under his belt would add to the legend he had been cultivating since escaping from Simon's grasp.

To help both his father and uncle, Edward detached his cousin Henry of Almain from the crusade. Now thirty-five years old, Almain had been indispensable to the English king and his son since their restoration. The terms of Edward's agreement with the committee back home allowed young Henry to assume control of his affairs from his father Richard if need be. As the new king of France was returning home for his coronation, Almain joined his entourage. His plan was to go to Gascony to attend to those affairs and pick up his wife Constance before heading to England.

King Philip was going overland through Italy with his uncle Charles of Anjou. They wanted to stop at the papal enclave of Viterbo to see if they might not induce the college of cardinals to break their deadlock, now in its thirtieth month, and finally elect a successor to Clement IV. It was a good opportunity for Henry of Almain to scope out the chances of his father finally receiving the imperial summons, as well as his own chances of becoming emperor after him. Their party arrived in Viterbo on 9 March 1271.[3]

When Charles of Anjou left on crusade, he took many of his senior aides with him. One who did not go was Guy de Montfort, his vicar-general for Tuscany. It was not the ongoing conflict between Guelfs and Ghibellines that kept Guy in Italy, rather the expected arrival of Edward in North Africa. The mutilation of Simon de Montfort's body at Evesham had created a blood feud between his surviving sons and the ranking royalists. Letting Guy or his brothers Simon and Amaury, who were also in Italy at the time, anywhere near the English contingent was simply out of the question.

Edward realised the gravity of the situation. He had openly wept at the funeral of Henry de Montfort at Evesham and had been extra kind to his aunt Eleanor when he forced her out of Dover. It was no secret that Guy was coming to Viterbo for talks with Charles, but the risk that posed to Henry of Almain was judged negligible. While it was true that Almain had both deserted Simon and married into the Bearn family, he had not been at Evesham, and he was, moreover, travelling under the protection of the kings of France and Sicily.

Guy arrived on 12 March 1271 with Simon, his father-in-law, and fifty knights in his retinue. The next day, while Charles and Philip attended services elsewhere, Henry did his devotions in a little parish church across from his lodgings. Suddenly Guy appeared in the doorway and shouted, 'Henry of Almain, you traitor, you shall not escape me.' How the Montforts found him there is unknown. Edward later claimed that he had asked Henry to undertake a mission of reconciliation between their families. Almain may have sent word to the brothers that he wanted to meet them and provided them his location. It is also possible that they simply chanced upon his presence in the city. In either case, they went berserk. All the wealth and power they had accumulated in Italy far outweighed what their father had achieved in England, but they were ready to throw it all away now to avenge him.

Seeing Guy with his sword drawn, Henry dashed for the altar. Mayhem broke out in the congregation as Guy and his men chased after him. Henry begged for mercy, but Guy replied that he had shown none to his father or brother. Given they were in a church, they attempted to drag him outside, but Henry gripped the altar so tight that Guy ended up chopping off the fingers of his left hand. In the hail of blows that followed, he and his men cut down two priests who tried to intervene, killing one and severely wounding the other. Guy left the church confident he had had his revenge, but when one of his knights reminded him that what had happened to his father had been far worse, he went back inside, grabbed Henry by the hair and dragged him onto the square. There, for public viewing, he and the other killers hacked away at the corpse in retribution for the desecration at Evesham.

While the Montfort brothers and their gang fled north for refuge, the kings of France and Sicily set about the painful task of informing Henry's relatives of his murder. Charles wrote to Edward, still on Sicily, swearing to pursue these 'children of perdition to their ruin and extermination'. Edward took him at his word and left for the Holy Land in May, but Edmund of Almain did not go with him. He had reached the crusade sometime after 14 September 1270, when he led a procession from Winchcombe to Hailes to present the abbey with a portion of the holy blood relic he brought back with him from Germany. He now set off for England to convey his brother's body home.

Richard was at Isleworth on 23 April when the letter from the king of France arrived. Philip was his first cousin twice removed and thirty-five years younger. Addressing Richard as his 'most dear cousin and friend', he opens by wishing he could bring him news of a 'more pleasing nature' but that divine mercy has refused to indulge him:

> We are compelled to announce unto you certain tidings full of sorrow and of sadness, which we, being at Viterbo on the morrow of the Blessed Gregory, and hearing the divine service of the Mass in the Church of the Friars Minors at Viterbo, from the relation of certain trustworthy persons have heard; to the effect that Guido and Simon de Montfort, knights, on the same day and

at the same hour, with an armed force attacked our most dearly beloved cousin Sir Henry, your eldest son, while in a certain other chapel at Viterbo, in front of his hostel there, for the purpose either of hearing Mass or of offering up his prayers; and there, at the instigation of the devil, slew him; a matter which we impart to you not without intense grief and anguish of heart.

As far as justice was concerned, Philip assured him that he would get 'real results', but his present worry was that Richard might hold him and the French responsible for the tragedy. One of Philip's household knights had a son who, being a friend of Edward's children, was just then under Richard's care in England. Philip wanted Richard to know that the knight had 'always been against Guido and Simon'. Just the same, the king of France prayed that no 'inconvenience' might arise to the child on account of the murder and asked Richard to send the boy back safely as soon as possible.

The only surviving testament of Richard's grief over the murder of his son comes from the letter he wrote to the Friars Minors of London on the following day.

We are compelled to announce unto your devotedness, news most dreadful and full of anguish, to the effect that Simon and Guido, the sons of that most wicked traitor, the late Simon de Montfort, satellites of Satan, on the morrow of Saint Gregory, at Viterbo, with an armed force attacked our dearly-beloved and eldest son Henry, while hearing the solemn service of the mass in a certain chapel there, intent upon his prayers and imagining no evil, and cruelly slew him. And this, not without great bitterness of heart do we, sorrowing, announce unto you, making request that, devoutly celebrating his obsequies, you will for him suppliantly intercede with God, that so we may be enabled forth with to return you worthy thanks for the same.

If his sister Eleanor, writing from her home among the nuns, sent any condolences for the monstrous deed of her sons, none have survived. In mid-May Edmund arrived with his brother's bones and heart (the flesh having been boiled away and buried in Viterbo). Henry of Almain's heart was encased in a gilded silver vase and placed near the shrine of Edward the Confessor at Westminster Abbey. The monks did it in gratitude for a gift of land that Henry made to the abbey in July 1270 to fund the lighting of candles at the shrine. His bones were interred at Hailes Abbey on 21 May, on what would have been the second anniversary of his marriage to Constance.[4]

However much he was consumed by the tragedy, Richard still had two realms to run. On the day before his son's burial, he met messengers from Cologne at Wallingford. After three and a half years, Archbishop Engelbert had been released from his cage. Fearful of reprisals, the city sought and received Richard's promise of support should the prelate again try to disturb the peace there. In September, he ordered the count who had held Engelbert prisoner to pay him 2,000 marks out of the money that the count owed to him, the king, or else he was to acquit the archbishop of the money that he owed for his ransom.

After an illness lasting several months, Henry III was finally well, but that created a new set of problems. Despairing that this was truly it, the king had made another vow to go on crusade and was miraculously cured after that. On 16 April, he handed over control of royal income to Richard and the council to raise money for his departure, but just keeping the current crusade afloat required constant injections of cash. Richard himself provided £2,000 in loans, but the upside of controlling the purse strings meant that he was finally able to get the grants of wardship that Henry had promised him more than three years earlier.

Richard also had Edward's affairs to worry about, including his children. There was the eldest John, who was born to great fanfare in the summer of 1266, thirty-five years after the birth of Richard's own son John. A second son Henry was born two years after that, followed by Eleanor, who was one when her parents left on crusade. Like Edward and Henry of Almain, they were being raised at Windsor. On 1 August, new tragedy struck when five-year-old John died. Richard had the boy's body brought to Westminster Abbey for interment in front of his grieving grandparents.

The next month Richard proceeded north to Yorkshire, perhaps with Edmund at his side, to take custody of properties that had belonged to Henry of Almain. On the way home he would have heard of the death of Philip Basset, which occurred on 29 October. The Osney chronicler eulogised Basset as 'exceedingly faithful, a strenuous warrior who greatly loved England and the community of the realm'. Wykes adds that he was a 'discreet noble and generous provider of food'. From enemies in Marshal's rebellion, now four decades past, to fellow crusaders a few years after that, Philip had been Richard's oldest and most trusted friend.

By December, father and son were back at Berkhamsted. On the 12th of that month, Richard granted letters of protection for an abbey in Hainault. He seems to have been ill that day, for a barber was brought in to bleed him. Sometime during the following night he suffered a stroke. The right side of his body was paralysed and he was unable to speak or make himself understood.

He lingered in this condition for several months. It would be pleasing to report that his brother paid him a visit in his stricken state, but it seems Henry was himself overcome by a life-threatening malady. He was on his way back from Christmas court at Winchester when, having crossed London Bridge, he was taken to the Tower of London. He never used the Tower as a place of residence unless he had to, the last time being in 1261 when he overthrew the baronial council. This time he remained there for three weeks, not leaving until 7 February.

When Henry returned to Westminster, he was probably informed that his brother had recovered somewhat, because eleven days later the king of Germany issued a charter from Berkhamsted for the new bishop of Verdun. It was to be his last known piece of business, however. He grew worse and, knowing the end was near, drew up his will and 'lamented his past deeds in most sincere repentance'. On 2 April 1272, Richard of Cornwall 'exchanged the fleeting glories of the world for the heavenly kingdom'. He was sixty-three.

No mention was made of Beatrix or Edmund being at his bedside when he died, although Wykes speaks of the 'inconsolable grief and anguish' that accompanied his decline. Richard's funeral was held on 13 April at Hailes Abbey, where he was buried next to his second wife Sanchia and his son Henry. His heart went to the Franciscan church at Oxford. His brother, still ailing, did not attend his funeral, nor did he leave Westminster Palace for the next two months.[5]

The first official notice of Richard's death came on 5 April. The bishop of Coventry was commissioned to take Wallingford, Berkhamsted and other properties 'of R. sometime king of Almain, lately deceased' into the king's hands until Edmund did homage for them. It provides another hint that the bishop, Roger de Meuland, was Richard's illegitimate son and therefore Edmund's half-brother. On 1 May, Roger was told that Edmund's homage had been taken and that he was to hand over the lands and castles to him.

In his will, now lost, Richard left £5,333 to the Holy Land, £333 to the Dominicans of Germany, and money to establish a college of canons at Oxford. A dispute quickly arose involving one of the executors, Michael of Northampton. Richard had presented him and another clerk to two churches that fell vacant in one of the wardships he held. He did so in violation of Henry's right to install his own clerks in these offices. At a personal meeting with the king, Edmund and the other executors agreed to give way to the king's clerks, and Henry, 'to show grace to his nephew for his assent', granted Edmund the right to fill the churches the next time they fell vacant.

Edmund also had immediate trouble with his stepmother. On her wedding day in 1269, Beatrix issued a charter protecting the rights of her husband's children, but with his death she launched a series of suits in eleven counties to enrich her dower at her stepson's expense. She and Edmund remained in litigation until a few months before her early death in October 1277. She was buried in the Franciscan church in Oxford, where Richard's heart was interred.

Strong in piety, Edmund solicited prayers for the souls of his parents, his uncle Henry and brother Henry, but none for Beatrix. He also remembered his father's natural children while they were alive. He became close to Richard, who received two manors from him and was made steward of Knaresborough in 1284. Twelve years later, this Richard of Cornwall was struck by a spear during the siege of Berwick and died shortly afterwards of his wound. Another half-brother Walter served as the coroner of Cornwall for a spell. He died in 1313.

During his first summer as the newly ennobled earl of Cornwall, Edmund began a lifelong service of lending money to the royal family, as his father had done before him. Through the agency of his aunt, Eleanor of Provence, he dispatched £2,333 for the use of his cousin Edmund of Lancaster in the Holy Land in return for the custody of his earldom of Leicester. The queen may have also been the matchmaker behind Edmund's marriage to Gilbert's sister Margaret, although the king himself must have desired it. In 1252, Henry forged links between the Clares and his family by marrying Gilbert to his niece Alice Lusignan, but that union had famously ended in divorce and recrimination. Marriage between Margaret and Edmund may have been meant to mend that miscalculation.

Their wedding was held on 6 October at Ruislip. One week later Henry knighted Edmund at the feast of St Edward, but the king was sinking fast. More riots and disturbances in Norwich and London had sapped his remaining energy. Henry died at Westminster Palace on 16 November 1272, after a reign of fifty-six years. Gilbert finally stepped up as the statesman he always imagined he was and helped keep the country at peace until the return of Edward from crusade. He never went himself.

It was more than eighteen months before the new king returned. Having barely escaped an assassin while in Syria, Edward landed in Sicily in December 1272 to learn of the deaths of his father, his son and heir John, and his uncle Richard. He delayed his homecoming in order to conduct various business while on the continent, including hunting down the killers of Henry of Almain. Despite their promises, neither King Charles nor King Philip made any effort to apprehend the Montforts.

Simon the younger died in the same year as the murder, but Guy enjoyed the protection of his Italian in-laws. Edward appealed to the new pope, Gregory X, whom he had met in England when the cleric served as an aide to Ottobon. Gregory took action right away, but Guy eventually returned to service under Charles until captured in a fight off Naples. Edward reportedly blocked all attempts to have him ransomed and Guy died in prison in 1292.

Dante, who as a boy in Florence may have seen Guy in person, immersed him in a river of boiling blood for killing Henry of Almain, whose 'heart is yet honoured on the bank of Thames'.

Edward never blamed his aunt Eleanor for his crime. Passing through Paris on his way home, he undertook to settle her dower issues and even lent her money. She died in 1275, almost three years after Richard's death, without any reconciliation with her brothers. The most vengeance Edward got was when his men captured brother and sister Amaury and Eleanor de Montfort trying to sneak into Wales for her marriage to Llywelyn. Not until 1282, after an imprisonment of more than six years, did Edward release Amaury. Both Llywelyn and Eleanor died in that same year.

Charles had been accused of having a hand in the murder and his failure to bring Guy to justice seemed to suggest it. The idea was that he wanted to prevent Henry of Almain from succeeding Richard as the king of Germany in order to make the imperial throne available to his nephew King Philip III. As emperor, Philip would give Charles a free hand to consolidate the old empire under his control. Such a scheme never had a chance, not just because of the sheer lunacy of it, but there was still the problem of Alfonso. Even after fifteen years he had not given up his claim. But the pope ignored both him and Charles, just as Ottokar was ignored by his fellow electors when he put himself in the running to succeed Richard. They wanted a petty German nobleman they could boss around and assumed they had one in Rudolf of Habsburg, who was crowned king of the Romans in Aachen on 24 October 1273.

Despite his background in Germany, Edmund's name never figured in the election. He was content to be the earl of Cornwall and, unlike his father, his loyalty was never in doubt. He served as Edward's regent for the more than three years that the king and queen spent on the continent between May 1286 and August 1289. It was not an easy time for him. Wales erupted in revolt, which he put down vigorously, and his fellow magnates, angered by what they saw as Edward's ingratitude and interference, were restless.

Like his father, Edmund was not a natural warrior and so struggled to inspire fear and respect. His regency also coincided with the breakdown of his marriage. Edmund and Margaret had no children and the only recorded pregnancy, which did not come to full term, occurred twelve years into the marriage. It was over by 1290, and Edmund's hostility towards his wife may have been owed to attempts by her obnoxious brother Bogo to force him to take her back. She received £800 of land in their divorce settlement, an impressive figure but hardly a dent in his massive fortune.

He died in 1300, aged fifty, without any heirs. His lands and wealth reverted to the crown and the earldom of Cornwall went into abeyance until the end of Edward's reign seven years later. Edmund of Cornwall would have been forgotten to history had it not been for the relic of holy blood, which he divided between Hailes Abbey and the College of Bonhommes he founded in 1283 at Ashridge, close to Berkhamsted. It turned both institutions into major pilgrimage sites. In terms of popularity, they far outstripped the holy blood that his uncle Henry had famously deposited in Westminster Abbey in 1247. This was due not only to their pastoral settings, but to the legend of the Holy Grail associated with this particular relic, coming as it did from Charlemagne's empire and donated by the man whose father had restored King Arthur's castle.

By the fifteenth century, the relic had made Hailes so renowned that it was mentioned in Chaucer's *Canterbury Tales* and in the writings of the mystic Margery Kempe. During the Reformation, the holy blood was declared to be an 'unctuous gum' and the shrine dismantled. Minions of Henry VIII then moved in to destroy the rest of the abbey. No care was taken to preserve the graves of Richard, Sanchia, or his sons. Over the centuries their tombs were plundered and lost, and the only fragments of bone discovered came to light during excavations in 1900. They were found at the spot in front of the high altar where Henry of Almain was interred. Henry's gilded silver heart vase at Westminster also disappeared, likely melted down by the same minions.[6]

While England grappled with the destruction of the Tudor era, Rudolf of Habsburg's descendants brought the Holy Roman Empire to the zenith of its power. He had made it possible by exerting strong kingship from the outset, but he did it at Richard's expense. His court presented Germany as a kingdom mired for years in despair and anarchy thanks to all the outsiders coming in with their money, thinking they could rule the Germans by buying the throne. His aim was to ward off challenges from Ottokar and Alfonso, but in doing so he painted Richard's reign as a corrupt, phony monarchy. He showed he meant business by revoking his predecessor's grant of imperial land to Ottokar, which led to war and the defeat and death of the Czech king in 1278.

Otherwise Rudolf maintained the realm as bequeathed to him by Richard, including cracking down on private tolls and proclaiming the peace. Like Richard, however, he had to deal with a high mortality rate among popes and so never did achieve imperial coronation by the time of his death in 1291. His dynasty almost did not survive him, but because it did and prospered over the centuries, historians looked back on his reign as the glorious beginning of it all, when King Rudolf I lifted the darkness that had beset the land under a presumptuous and pretentious Englishman named Richard of Cornwall.[7]

This mindset was not abandoned until the eighteenth century, when the first attempt to collect documents associated with Richard's reign was undertaken. Interest in him grew, but only in Germany, where four scholarly works about him had been produced by the early twentieth century. In that same period not a single biography of Richard came out in England. By the time the first one appeared, there were already five of Simon de Montfort.

Why this should be is best explained by the advent of democracy under the French and American revolutions. Seemingly overnight, England's long constitutional history had been unjustly swept aside. To recapture their rightful place, English historians promoted the Barons' War against King John as an earlier struggle against tyranny. They emphasised the evolutionary nature of their own democracy by drawing a straight line from it to the conflict of Henry's reign and dubbed it the Second Barons' War, even though it was nothing of the kind. Since Simon's martyrdom added an edge to their argument, they threw in the bogus claim that he founded parliament.

It was desperate and outlandish, but it was supported in spirit by the highly critical chroniclers of the thirteenth century. They had admonished Richard for cheating his tenants and peasant crusaders, for turning the currency exchange into an extortion racket, for selling out his peers during crucial confrontations with the king. One of them remembered him as 'a most greedy hoarder of treasure and violent oppressor of the poor'. But then everyone knew that, as the jeers that greeted his surrender at Lewes made abundantly clear.[8]

Richard might have argued they were all like that. Simon de Montfort admitted the oppressive nature of his own lordship and his obstruction of the peace treaty with France was just one more instance of money influencing his actions. It was also no secret that he owed his rise to power to people whose complaints against the crown were personal and not political. His allies in the church were of a similar calibre. They regularly engaged in the kind of worldly practices they denounced the king and pope for.

None of this mattered to those who saw Richard's virtual disappearance under the Montfortian regime as proof of the shallowness of the man and his ambition. Not even his triumphant return to Germany, where his role as lawgiver was welcome and appreciated, made any difference back home. They took no pride in the only Englishman to be elected king of the Romans and later historians viewed the whole episode as quirky and disastrous. He should have exercised good sense and stayed home to mind a kingdom that was faltering under his feeble brother.

It was this slap at Henry that allowed some room to resurrect Richard's reputation. His success with money and arbitration came to be seen as qualities that made him a fitter ruler than his brother. The only problem was the peace and prosperity that England enjoyed for most of the half century that Henry sat on the throne. The uncertainty of proving that Richard or anyone else could have done it better is likely one of the reasons why no singular biography of Henry appeared until the present century.

Failing that argument, an attempt was made to blame Henry for his brother never becoming emperor. It is true that trouble in 1258 brought Richard's first trip to Germany to an end, but that had to do with the peace treaty, which was vital for his recognition as king of the Romans. His next visit, in 1260, was abruptly terminated by events in Italy. He returned to find Henry had emasculated the baronial council and was surprised as anyone to see him standing there. Richard's third return in 1263 was the sinister one. Learning of an uprising planned against his ailing brother, he threw in his lot with Simon, perhaps in the expectation of being crowned king of England. Six years later he capped off his fourth visit to Germany by marrying a beautiful young woman. If he sped home for any reason at all, it was to show her off.

The quibbling about whose fault it was that England never had an emperor is important in the sense that Richard, judging by what he managed to accomplish as king of Germany, would probably have made a success of it. Matthew Paris thought his preference for negotiation to warfare was a hindrance, but the belligerent tone of Richard's letters, his surefootedness in the limited military experience that he had, and his willingness to execute prisoners demonstrate a readiness to impose his authority on those who stood in his way. Using the battle of Lewes as the barometer of his and Henry's soldierly skills is unfair in any event. The storming of Northampton by the brothers was a brilliant stroke and they almost certainly would have rolled over Simon and his army at Lewes had it not been for Edward's catastrophic blunder in the field.

We should also not make too much of Paris's offhand remark that Richard was 'not well or strong in bodily health'. The first English study of his life took this to mean he was a sickly character incapable of great exertion, whether in war or politics, but here Paris was clearly speaking from hearsay. Neither he nor any other contemporary provided a physical description of Richard, but he must have enjoyed a fair amount of robustness to come as far as he did in his career. From the Alps and Levant to the Rhone and Rhine, his journeys and missions were typically long and arduous. Nothing for the sickly.[9]

While that sense of adventure boosts Richard's appeal as an historic figure, there is also the rakishness that stands in sharp contrast to his brother. Henry was the virtuous one of the two, all-forgiving and generous and deeply devoted to his wife and children, but these are not the kind of values to stir the imagination. Rather in Richard we get a life full of quest and desire. We see him rebuilding King Arthur's castle and treasure hunting on the Isle of Wight, searching for a princess bride and marrying ever younger ones, freely trading on his loyalty and lustfully producing little Richards, acting bold and threatening and happily stealing the thunder of others, and finally the greatest outrage of them all, going out and buying himself a kingdom with money fleeced from the working stiff.

And yet it was from that same kingdom that he came to the rescue when famine plagued his homeland. It was just one of many charitable acts and good works that also informed his life. But apart from a few artefacts in Germany and scattered ruins in England, nothing remains of them today, nothing to recall the legacy of a younger son who quite literally made the world his stage. He may not be remembered as one of the great kings of the Middle Ages, may not be remembered as a king at all, but in the end just being Richard of Cornwall has proved distinction enough.

Appendix I

LETTERS OF RICHARD OF CORNWALL AND A DESCRIPTION OF HIS CORONATION

Richard was famous for his boastful letters, as in the account he gave of his crusade to the Holy Land in 1240–41. His success there was built largely on the efforts of the French crusaders who preceded him, but since they failed to stick around and claim the credit, he did it for himself and took a swipe at them in the bargain.

Of the great desolation and grief of which the Holy Land has long been the seat, and how difficult the matter has been its reparation and relief since the catastrophe at Gaza, wise men are sensible, and experience of the truth has reached those dwelling near, and report has carried to those at a distance; and, but that the present letter might disclose our secret, and being opened on the way to you, give occasion to a sinister interpretation, many things would be explained in it which now sleep and like concealed in the bottom of our heart. From the time when kings and kingdoms turned aside from Jerusalem, owing to its being divided and held by iniquitous and unjust possessors, we have been consumed with no small grief, and cannot altogether be silent, but must loosen our tongue in bitter complaint, as there is no pleasant matter to occupy it; for the sword of compassion has pierced to our soul, so as not to be able to contain itself.

For some time past, indeed, in the Holy Land, this court has reigned instead of peace, schism instead of union, hatred instead of affection, and justice has been totally excluded. A such seed there have been many planters in that land, and many have become collectors of the fruit springing from it; but I hope they are now eradicated. And there is no one amongst all its beloved ones to console it. For twin brothers disagreeing in the bosom of their mother, whose business it was to defend her, becoming proud in their affluence, have nourished and fomented these humours at the roots, and because the branches of it to spread far and wide. For an abundance of good things produces such an itching after mutual contention that the reprimands of the father who presides over the see of Peter, are encountered with the utmost indifference, provided that the stronger party dazzled the world with their renown. To the pacification of these discordant parties we have applied no small portion of care; but, as yet, the footsteps of peace leave no impression, inasmuch as the followers of discord do not acquiesce in the words of peace. Those who have money easily allure others to them as long as it lasts; but when the time for vindicating the modesty of their mother arrives, they leave the peace-makers, and feigning secret impediments, show no regard to bring consolation to their mother.

From this cause, and the great number of the Gallic cavalry, almost twice as numerous as the Saracens, utterly prostrated by evil habits, the enemies of the cross were so unexpectedly encouraged, that a small body of them thought little or nothing of numbers of us. Owing to this, on our first arrival here, the nobles who were thought likely to help us were taking their departure, and it appeared to be a serious and difficult matter to relieve the country; yet, the Divine clemency, when it wills it, suffers injuries to be without their remedies, and sorrow to be without means of consolation. For when we were expecting, on our arrival here, in conjunction with the rest of the Christians, to the utmost of our power, as was incumbent on us, according to our vow, to revenge the insults offered to the cross on the enemies of that cross, by attacking their territory and afterwards occupying and restoring them to good condition, behold the king of Navarre, the then head chief of the army, and the count of Brittany, although aware of our approach for fifteen days before we arrived at Acre, took their departure with an immense host.

Before they left, however, in order that they might appear to have done something, they made a kind of truce with Nazir, the lord of Crach, by which it was agreed that he should give up all the prisoners taken at Gaza, whom he had in his custody or power, together with some lands contained in the conditions of the truce, as a security for which he gave his son and brothers as hostages, fixing on a term of forty days for fulfilling the terms of the truce. Before that period, however, had elapsed, the said king and count departed, paying no heed to the time agreed on, or to the terms of the truce. Within this said period, namely, on St. Dionysius's eve, we, as we have before informed you, arrived at Acre ; and by the general advice of all, we at once sent to the aforesaid Nazir, to ask him if he could observe towards us the truce he had made with the said king, and we received word in reply, that he would willingly do so if possible, owing to his respect for the said king of Navarre, although he should gain but little by it; we therefore, by the advice of the nobles, awaited the completion of the term fixed on, to see the result.

At the expiration of the term, however, we received another message from him, stating that he could on no account abide by the aforesaid agreement; on hearing which, by the common consent of all, we betook ourselves to Joppa to improve with all possible caution the condition of the Holy Land, which had deteriorated from the aforesaid causes. At this place a man of rank and power came to us on the part of the sultan of Babylon, and told us that his lord was willing to enter into a truce with us if we pleased. After hearing and perfectly understanding what was to be set forth to us by him, and having with all sincerity invoked the grace of God, we, by the advice of the duke of Burgundy, Count Walter de Brienne, the master of the Hospitallers, and other nobles, in fact, the chief part of the army, agreed to the under-mentioned terms of truce, which, although at our first arrival appeared to be a difficult matter to accomplish, is yet a praiseworthy one, and productive of advantage to the Holy Land, since it is a source of delight and security to the poor people and to travellers, advantageous and agreeable to the middle classes of the inhabitants, and useful and honourable to the rich and to religious men.

Nor did it appear to us, on looking at the melancholy condition of surrounding events, that we could then employ ourselves more advantageously than in releasing the wretched prisoners from captivity, as there was a deficiency of men and things (although we alone still had money about us), and profiting by the time of the truce to strengthen and fortify against the Saracens the cities and castles that had become ruinous. We have thought proper to insert the names of the places and territories which were given up in accordance with the terms of the truce, although it may be tedious to you, lest perchance some evil interpreter may ascribe our deeds by way of glory to others or perversely and maliciously pervert their character. For some, although but few, refused to consent to the terms of the truce, which are as follows...

All this territory, with the castles therein before named, the Christians are allowed to fortify during the truce if they wish; the noble captives taken at Gaza are also to be restored, and all the prisoners taken in the war with the French are to be released on both sides. As soon as the aforesaid truce was arranged, we took our way to Ascalon, and that the time might not hang idly on our hands, by the advice of all the Christian chiefs we began to fortify a large castle. From that place we sent messengers to the sultan of Babylon, to induce him to swear to observe the said truce, if he would do so, and at the same time to send the aforesaid prisoners; he, however, for what reason we know not, detained our messengers, without giving us any reply, from St. Andrews day till the Thursday after Candlemas; but during this time, as we afterwards found by his letters, he, by the advice of his nobles, swore to keep the said truce.

We, during all this time, remained at Ascalon, assiduously intent on building the aforesaid castle, which, by God's favour has, in a short time, progressed so far that at the time of despatching these presents, it is already adorned and entirely surrounded by a double wall with lofty towers and ramparts, with four square stones and carved marble columns, and everything which pertains to a castle, except a fosse round it, which will, God willing, be completed without fail, within a month from Easter. And this was not done without good reason; for as we could not be certain that the truce would be confirmed, we thought it best to employ our time in building and fortifying this castle; so that if the truce should be broken by any casualty, we might have, in the march and in the very entrance of their territory, this place, which was formerly under their dominion, as a safe and strong place of refuge, if it were necessary for us to retreat there. And those who remained therein would have no occasion to fear the result of a siege; for although the besiegers could cut off all assistance and provisions from them by land, yet all necessities could reach them by sea. In times of peace, too, we believed that this castle would not be without its advantages, since it is the key and safeguard, both by land and sea, of the kingdom of Jerusalem, but will be a source of destruction and ruin to Babylon and the southern parts of the country.

On St George's day, then, after peace had been sworn to be observed on both sides, and after the truce had been confirmed, we received, according to the terms of the truce, all the Christian captives whom we had been so long expecting. After duly completing all these matters, we took leave of the Holy Land in peace, and on the festival of the Finding of the Holy Cross we embarked at Acre to return home; but owing to the fair wind failing us on the voyage, and being much fatigued, we landed at Trapani in Sicily, in the octaves of St John the Baptist. At that place we heard of the capture and detention of some of our bishops, and of other lamentable sufferings of the Church; wherefore, in order to restore peace as far as we were able, amongst those at variance, and to urge with all our power the release of the captives, and to give comfort to our mother, we turned aside from our course, and went to the court of Rome; and as soon as, by God's favour, the Lord disposes all events, we purpose returning to England with all possible speed.[1]

In the summer of 1253, Henry led an expeditionary force to Gascony, leaving behind his wife Eleanor of Provence as the regent and Richard as her adviser. The king asked them to summon parliament to ask for money to subsidise further operations. Below is the draft of the letter written by Richard that was subsequently incorporated into the official letter sent by the queen.

We received your letter on Christmas day last past, desiring us to convoke on the day following St Hilary, the archbishops, bishops, abbots, priors, earls, and barons of the kingdom of England, to show them your position, and announce to them the arrival of the king of Castile in Gascony against you. And because the said nobles, through the shortness of the notice, were unable to meet on the said day, we summoned them to appear at Westminster, on the fifteenth day after the said feast of St Hilary. When they were assembled, and the arrival of the said king and your position had been explained to them, we received answer:

That the earls and barons would be in London three weeks after the approaching Easter, prepared without delay to go to Portsmouth and embark with a strong force for your assistance in repelling the said king of Castile, if the said king of Castile is about to oppose you in Gascony. And this is what the earl of Gloucester and all the other nobles promised. Moreover, the archbishop of Canterbury, the bishop elect of Winchester, the bishops of London and Worcester, promised to assist you with a strong force. And the other bishops and abbots of England who were then present, promised to assist you with money, as much as lay in their power, against the said king of Castile, yet they were unwilling then to name the sum. However, each one of them, as they all formally declared, will have the sum which he intends to give, in London, at the time aforementioned, that is, three weeks after Easter, if it should so happen that the said king of Castile should oppose you in Gascony.

But they were unwilling to make any concession to you with respect to their clergy, on account of the tithe to be collected on your behalf for the succour of the Holy Land. But we with your queen will come to you according to your command, besides Edward your son, and Beatrice your daughter; and I Richard, your brother, the earl of Cornwall, will not be wanting to you, but will come to you with a force for your advantage and my own honour, if, as you announce to me, the king of Castile should oppose you in Gascony, provided that you and your heirs are well disposed with the help of God to me forever. And by the advice of our lady the queen, and of others well disposed towards you, I will entrust your kingdom of England to the hands of faithful subjects, by the help of God for your advantage and honour.

And if it should please and seem good to you that our lady the queen should come with your nobles and barons of England, let her know this in due time, if it is pleasing to you, that with Edward your son, and Beatrice your daughter, she may be able to come to you the more safely and befitting. But the aforesaid prelates and nobles wish, before they undertake the journey and give succour, that your letters patent may be sent to them from Gascony, to the effect that, on account of the present succour both in money and effective services, there may not accrue at any future time any disadvantage to their successors or heirs, be it in your own time or in the time of your heirs.[2]

Richard's coronation in Aachen on 17 May 1257 was a splendid and historic affair and he wanted everyone in England to know it. In this letter to the mayor and citizens of London, he proudly adds the formula semper Augustus *('ever exalted') to his title, thus styling himself 'Richard, by the grace of God, King of the Romans, ever August'.*

We do the more joyfully and in especial retain in our heart the more propitious and marked events that attend our elevation, inasmuch as we do believe that the pleasures thereof are doubled by congratulation: and the more especially do we find a threefold degree of exhilaration in our joyousness, when we feel assured that the same has reached your ears, confident as we are that the same are always ready, in the purity of your good faith and the zeal of your warm affection, attentively to listen to news of our well-being; while at the same time, in our own affection towards you, we do feel a longing regret which tells us how much more rejoiced we should have been rather to converse with you personally hereon, and upon certain other festive matters, than give you information thereof through the agency of writing, acting as our interpreter.

To the end, however, that a full and certain knowledge may be imparted to you of all the joyous events that have befallen us since we took our departure from among you, we have deemed it proper that the present page, indicative of the events aforesaid, should unto you be directed; intimating thereby, as matter for your congratulation, that on the Sunday next after the Feast of Saint Mark the Evangelist (25 April), attended by our suite, we took ship at Jernemue (Yarmouth). On the Tuesday following, the day, namely, of the blessed Apostles Philip and James (1 May), all, as well ourselves and our family as our suite, being well alike in person and in effects, we reached the town of Dordrecht, situate in the midst of the dominions of the Count of Holland; and, after staying there two days to take some repose after our fatigues, on the third day we took our departure therefrom, and then continuing our progress, through the countries of Holland and Gelderland, on the Friday before the Feast of Our Lord's Ascension arrived at Aachen; the more illustrious and more worthy of the men thereof, clergy, that is to say, as well as laity, nobles, knights, and all other the citizens, meeting us at our entrance into the said city, and receiving us magnificently and honourably amid the greatest joyousness and jubilation, glad and rejoicing, without any obstacle or difficulty whatsoever intervening.

And it is our belief, so far as in these lands the testimony bears witness of general and widespread report, that for the last two hundred years, no one of the Roman Emperors or Kings, upon newly commencing his rule, has ever without grave offence, or opposition and gainsaying thereon, entered the city of Aachen. And while after so entering the said city, it was necessary for us to make a somewhat long sojourn therein, behold ! certain rumours, cherished by our warmest desires, reached us, joyously making known unto us that the Archbishop of Trier, the enemy of our advancement, who, to the detriment of our name and honour, with a vast multitude of armed men had laid siege to our Castle and Palace of Boppard, and had prepared many engines for the capture thereof had been attacked by our beloved prince, the venerable Archbishop of Mainz; who, with the aid of a great body of warriors from among our faithful subjects, out of respect for our name had hastened to the relief of the said Castle, and to the assistance of the people there besieged, and on the Wednesday next after the Feast of Saint John Port Latin (6 May) had manfully engaged the said Archbishop of Trier; not without slaughter of his partisans, while many of his knights and other accomplices were made prisoners, the Archbishop himself, at the close of the battle, by the aid of a disgraceful flight avoiding the punishment of death, or at least the peril of being taken captive.

And thus, our said Castle being, by the aid of the aforesaid Archbishop of Mainz and other our faithful people, happily relieved from the blockade of the besiegers and the assaults of the foe, and excellently well supplied with provisions and such other valiant defenders as were needed, the same Archbishop of

Mainz at Aachen presented himself before us. Where, on the Feast of Our Lord's Ascension, himself and the Archbishop of Cologne being present, as also many other Bishops, Dukes, Counts, and Barons, peers and nobles of our realm, and faithful subjects of ours, we did, upon the throne of Charlemagne, with all befitting solemnity, in the name of Him 'Who resisteth the proud, but giveth grace to the humble' receive the sceptre of the Holy Roman Empire, and the crown thereof; our most dear consort being in like manner on the same day solemnly crowned together with us, as was befitting.

At length, the feast of our coronation having been celebrated with great solemnity and rejoicing, and the counsels of our well-beloved princes and other our faithful subjects as to our own affairs having been communicated to us, it seemed unto ourselves and to them, that it would be most in accordance with the elevation that had by vote been conferred upon us, that we should immediately, without loss of time, proceed to the humbling of those who were rebelling against us, and more especially, and first thing of all, turn all our endeavours towards breaking the horns of him of Trier who had raised them against us; that so, as he was the first of all, in our matters, to show himself not so much a just and a reasonable opponent as a willing embroiler, he may be the first to experience and to learn what and how much to his detriment our hand both can and may effect.

As to this however we would especially have you informed, that we do now trust that so great is our power in Almain, through the aid of our faithful subjects and supporters, that, while they continue to cherish their fealty towards us, and remain zealous in their devotion in our behalf, the power of no man living will be an object of fear to us. Given at Aachen, this 18th day of May, in the first year of our reign.[3]

The thousand words of the letter above oddly contain no description of Richard's coronation ceremony itself. Doubtless it followed the familiar pattern outlined below.

Richard would have camped outside Aachen for a period of at least three days, and then presented himself at the Cologne Gate, one of the entrances through the city walls of the later twelfth century. There, he was met by the dean and canons of the church with a processional cross, leading him to the church of St Mary, the cathedral, with its polygonal nave and westwork with two spiral staircases. These were the parts of the building which Charlemagne had actually had constructed, joined from the late fourteenth century almost incongruously to the enormous Gothic choir.

The king-elect approached the church from the north and then passed through the atrium at its west side, with before him the great niche of the westwork, and above it the later medieval gallery, the purpose of which was to display the imperial regalia and relics of saints to those assembled in the atrium. He then passed through the great eighth-century bronze doors and so under the gallery, where the symbolic significance of the eighth-century bronze she-wolf (the emperor should guard his people as fiercely as this animal would do her young) and the somewhat later pine-cone fountain (his people would have as many tongues as this pine-cone), and so into the polygonal nave.

In the centre of this was the shrine of Charlemagne, adorned with figures of the line of rulers who were his successors. Above it was the great candelabra given by Emperor Frederick Barbarossa in the twelfth century, inscribed with words invoking Aachen as the Heavenly Jerusalem. Before the shrine, the king elect prostrated himself with his arms outstretched like a cross while a Te Deum was sung. After this, he went to his lodging, to return the next day for the actual coronation and enthronement itself.

On the day of his coronation, he was taken to the high altar of St Mary, the dedicatee of the church to which Charlemagne was supposed to have given relics of the Passion of Christ. There he swore an oath on the Coronation Gospels, received oaths of obedience from the lay and ecclesiastical lords, and was anointed with holy oil. He was then washed, dressed in the appropriate garments and was crowned by the Archbishop of Cologne. He was girded with the sword believed to be that of Charlemagne, in fact a tenth-century Hungarian weapon, and he used it to dub knights. Taken then up into the gallery of the Carolingian nave, the newly crowned king was enthroned by the archbishop of Mainz and the Bishop of Trier on the throne which was believed to have been the throne of Charlemagne.

From the church, a two-storyed corridor led directly northwards across what is now the open square of the Katzhof to the great hall of Charlemagne's palace, the building converted into the town-hall in the fourteenth century. The king proceeded along the upper storey of this corridor, which opened directly from the western gallery. At the great hall, he gave a great feast, at which the principal nobles acted as his servants, and an ox-roast was held outside for the citizens of Aachen.[4]

Richard's election as king of the Romans was disputed by his brother's ally Alfonso X of Castile. The Spanish king's persistence in claiming the title, despite never once setting foot in Germany, caused Pope Alexander IV to waffle over whether to extend the imperial crown to Richard. In response, Richard wrote this scathing letter about his rival to the holy father.

Richard, by the grace of God King of the Romans, ever August, seeks justice and beseeches the grace and favour of his most holy mother church of Rome. The canonical election which preceded the proper and solemn coronation, the oaths given and the homage received from the loyal subjects of the empire and from vassals, the rightful and full possession of the cities and castles pertaining to the imperial crown, are proof enough that entitlement to these certainly requires no other formal recommendation, as this well shows.

For our sovereign rule benefits all, is burdensome to none, and prefers rather to be loved than feared. And so, with few fawning flatterers about it, it will prevail against countless others. Furthermore, it ardently pursues the profit of each and everyone and the security and growth of the empire. For a ruler is called Augustus not because he always increases the empire's borders but because he always strives to do so. What I have written, I have written. This glorious title was inscribed by the finger of God into the canon of imperial nomenclature, from which it will never ever be removed, uttered as it now is throughout the diverse regions of the world. Because of this, he who has challenged it in any way or attempts to diminish its integrity, or falsely gives himself that name, let him be declared anathema, for he offends against the majesty of God and the dignity of our rule.

Surely I am hearing what I can scarce believe? Whilst the commonly accepted understanding of the title rejects it and common sense argues against it, it appears that the illustrious king of Castile is adding the glory of this title to his many styles, calling himself king of the Romans, of Castile, Leon and the other names of that country. On what grounds can this be justified? For before there was any mention of his nomination as emperor, he knew or could have known that the lord king Richard had been elected and solemnly crowned as king of the Romans. This prince, owing so great a debt of honour to his kinsman, ought to have spat it out (*respuere*) when first asked and stepped back from the offer when invited. God forbid, then, that he should now suddenly creep up (*obrepat*) and seek self-aggrandisement.

When his father was near death and the people demanded he become king, Herenes, son of Anatholeus, answered that had no desire to presume to the kingship for as long as his father was expected to live, or otherwise someone else might be found whose ability to govern the state was proven. When the emperor Decius proposed that his son Decius be invested with the imperial crown, Decius Minor refused and said, 'I fear that if I am made emperor, I will forget that I am a son. So let someone else take command, and let my power be to humbly obey him who commands'.

Valerius Maximus tells us that when a certain Sericus, a man of proven valour, was offered the imperial robe, he refused to accept it, saying, 'This piece of cloth brings fame rather than good fortune, and if someone understood how much grievous anxiety, danger and misery came with it, he would not pick it up even if it was lying on the ground'. When the multitude he had fed wanted to make him king, the King of kings and Lord of lords fled to the mountain. Gideon also, when offered mastery, rejected it. These men knew the burdens which press upon a ruler's honour and his task of ruling.

I ask myself whence came this presumption. I suppose that the oft-mentioned lord king of Castile is just, a magnificent and distinguished ruler. If just, what of the natural law by which he is obliged to the king of Germany? What of the oaths he gave to the lord king of England, that he or his men would in no wise cause him offence? Is it just when he does not strive for what belongs to him but usurps another's right?

If he is magnificent, where is the magnificence in his puffing himself up in name only? He tries to take another's title and calls himself king of the Romans, but really resembles a dead lion (*leo mortuus*) or even a painted picture of one. If he is wise, where is the wisdom in trying to claim a higher rank and contending for what he cannot have? It is the mark of a wise man that he understands the measure of his power and does not exceed it.

I hear though that some people are suggesting that it was revealed to him in a dream that he is to be the future emperor. Well, I will grant you that Gaius Caesar, when in his youth, used to dream of committing incest in his mother's bed. Overcome by its carnal shamefulness, he referred the dream to astrologers, who one and all told him that the entire world would come under his dominion; upon this was built the foundation of this great man's hope of seizing imperial power. And again, when Getro was setting out to war, an eagle perched upon his shield, presaging that he would be victorious and a future king.

But dreams and night-time fantasies fade away and we read that many dreams were illusions, for we know that Alexander was deceived by Apollo's oracle. But why am I wasting time on such things? We have no opportunity to overcome this infamous king of Castile by conquest, as he does not attack us with arms and fighting-men but with letters and the representations of his minions. Nor ought we fret over this, for as Antony said to Tiberius, 'Tiberius, my friend, do not be worried if someone speaks ill of you. It is enough that he cannot harm you'. Socrates, too, answered someone asking how he might gain good repute by saying, 'Do your best and say little'. Now this blustering bragging will assuredly be put to a stop, indeed it will, for king Richard seeks justice and beseeches the grace and favour of the most holy church of Rome.[5]

In early May 1264, the Montfortians had all but lost the war to the king. Simon de Montfort marched out of London to chance everything on one pitched battle. In a grovelling letter to Henry, he explained that he was not making war on him, his lord, but on his evil advisers. Richard and Edward believed he was referring to them and wrote their own letter in response.

Richard, by the grace of God, King of the Romans, ever August, and Edward, of the illustrious King of England the first-born, and all other the Barons and nobles, who in the works of sincere fealty and devotion do testify their constant adherence unto the aforesaid King of England, to Simon de Montfort, Gilbert de Clare, and all and singular other the accomplices of their perfidy. From your letters which you have sent unto the illustrious King of England, our most dear lord, we have heard that we by you are defied; although this your verbal defiance has already been sufficiently proved unto us by fact of your hostility, in the destruction by fire of our property and the laying waste of our possessions.

We therefore do wish you to know that you, as public enemies by enemies, are defied by all and singular of us; and that from this time forward we will, with all our mind and our strength, wheresoever we shall have the means of so doing, do our utmost to inflict injury alike upon your persons and your possessions. And further, whereas you do falsely impute unto us, that we do give neither faithful nor good counsel unto our said King, you do say that which is not the truth. And if you, Sir Simon de Montfort, or Gilbert de Clare, do wish to assert that same in the Court of the said King, we are ready to procure for you a safe-conduct to come unto the said Court, and by another, your peer in nobility and in birth, to make proof of our innocence herein, and, as being a perfidious traitor, the falsehood of yourself. We all are content with the seals of the Lords aforesaid, that is to say, of the King of the Romans, and Sir Edward. Given at Lewes, this twelfth day of May.[6]

Appendix 2

LIFELONG ITINERARY OF RICHARD OF CORNWALL

An indication of Richard's well-travelled life are the locations where his presence can be documented. The list below is by no means complete, as he must have stopped in Greece or Cyprus on his way to and from crusade, nor can excursions to Jerusalem and Spain be ruled out.

1209
Devizes (5 Jan)

1212
Marlborough

1213
Durham (Jan)

1214
La Rochelle (Jul)
Corfe (Oct)

1215
Corfe (Apr)
Dover (Sep)

1216
Dover
Corfe (May)

1220
Corfe
Westminster
(20 May)

1223
Lambeth (Apr)
Canterbury (Aug)

1225
Westminster (2
Feb)
Portsmouth (9 Apr)
Bordeaux (2 May)

1226
La Rochelle (Nov)

1227
Thouars (Feb)
Westminster (May)
Northampton (Aug)
Kinghorn, Scotland
(Nov)
Carlisle (Dec)
York (Dec)

1229
Cornwall
Portsmouth (Oct)

1230
Portsmouth (Apr)
St Malo (3 May)
Nantes (May)
Tonnay (July)
Pons
Mirambeau
Blaye (Aug)
Bordeaux
Luçon (Sep)
Nantes
Redon
Saint-Pol-de-Léon
Portsmouth (27 Oct)

1231
Fawley (30 Mar)
London (15 Apr)
Paincastle (10 Aug)

1232
Wallingford
(26 Oct)
Berkhamsted (20
Jun)
London (10 Nov)

1233
Radnor (Mar)
Worcester (Jun)
Oxford (Jun)
Westminster (1-3
Aug)
Westminster (28
Oct)

1234
Gloucester
(25 May)
Westminster
(2 Aug)

Marlborough
(12 Aug)
Marlborough
(26 Sep)

1235
Westminster
(25 Jan)
Rochester (31 Jan)
Westminster
(22 Feb)

1236
Westminster
(20 Jan)
Winchester (8 Feb)
Winchester (8 June)

1237
Westminster
(20 Jan)
Canterbury
(18 Feb)
York (Sep)
Woodstock
(26 Oct)

1238
Kingston (Feb)
Havering (4 Mar)
Tarrant (Mar)
Berkhamsted
(26 May)
Launceston (15
Jun)

1239
Northampton
(11 Nov)
Winchester (Dec)

1240
Launceston
(17 Jan)
Beaulieu (Jan)
Reading (8 Apr)
St Albans (May)
Wallingford (3 Jun)
London (5 June)
Dover (10 Jun)
Paris (24 June)
Acre (8 Oct)

1241
Trapani (1 Jul)

1242
Dover (7 Jan)
London (28 Jan)
Westminster (8 Mar)
Haughley (19 Mar)
Portsmouth (May)
Pons (24 May)
Saintes (15 Jun)
Tonnay (24 Jun)
Taillebourg
(30 Jun)
Saintes (1 Jul)
Pons (23 Jul)
Blaye (27 Jul)
Camp on the
Gironde (4 Aug)
Bordeaux (18 Aug-
16 Oct)
Scilly (18 Oct)

1243
Berkhamsted
Westminster
(23 Nov-1 Dec)
Wallingford (Dec)

1244
Reading (4 Feb)
Wallingford (9 Feb)
Newcastle (Aug)
Westminster (Nov)
Berkhamsted
(20 Dec)

1245
Wallingford
(9 May)
Woodstock (15 Jul)
Wallingford
(25 Nov)
London (Dec)

1246
Westminster (Mar)
Westminster
(20 Apr)
Beaulieu (17 June)
Winchester (7 Jul)
Wallingford
(15 Aug)

1247
London (19 Jan)
Windsor (24 Feb)
Oxford (15 Apr)
Reading (13 Jun)
Woodstock (27 Jul)
Paris (Sep)
Pontigny (Oct)
Westminster
(28 Oct)

1248
Westminster (Feb)
London (11 Mar)
Windsor (May)
Risborough (Jul)

Westminster
(13 Oct)
Wallingford
(Dec)

1249
London (5 Jan)
Risborough (10 Apr)
Launceston (Apr)

1250
Paris (Mar)
Lyon (6 Apr)
London (May)
Wallingford (1 Jun)
Westminster (1 Aug)

1251
Wallingford (26 Jan)
Wallingford (8 Feb)
Wallingford (30 Oct)
Hailes Abbey
(5 Nov)

1252
Bishopthorpe (4 Jan)
Wallingford (8 Feb)
Winchester (20 Jun)
Woodstock (4 Aug)
Winchester (25 Dec)

1253
Westminster
(13 May)
Winchester
(22 Jun)
Southwick (30 Jun)
Portsmouth
(5 Jul)
Wallingford
(1 Aug)

Portsmouth (6 Aug)
Westminster
(13 Oct)
Westminster
(29 Dec)

1254
Windsor
(28 Jan – 24 Apr)
Westminster
(29 Mar)
Winchester
(25 May)
Berkhamsted
Windsor (5 Jun)
Reading (13 Jun)
Oxford
(14–22 Jul)
Windsor (30 Jul)
Kingston
(3 Aug)
Westminster (4 Aug)
Kingston (12 Aug)
Kempton (13 Aug)
Westminster
(19 Aug)
Waltham (1 Sep)
Rotherfield (12 Sep)
Reading (15 Sep)
Westminster (7 Oct)
Windsor (9 Oct)
Westminster
(12 Oct)
Windsor
(26–29 Oct)
Westminster (5–19
Nov)
Canterbury (10 Dec)
Dover (20–27)
Canterbury (29 Dec)

1255
Westminster (5-24
Feb)
Wallingford
(26 Feb)
Westminster
(7 Mar)
Merton (5 Apr)
Woodstock (20
Jun)
Lincoln (Sep)

1256
Wallingford (28
Jan)
Woodstock (22
Aug)
Windsor (7 Nov)
Winchester (28
Nov)
Clarendon
(8 Dec)
London (26 Dec)

1257
St Albans (2 Jan)
Windsor (27 Jan)
Wallingford
(31 Jan)
London (18 Mar-8
Apr)
Great Yarmouth
(29 Apr)
Dordrecht (1 May)
Aachen
(11-22 May)
Cologne
(24 May-16 June)
Bonn (21 June)
Boppard
(13 July-Aug 16)

Bingen (Aug)
Mainz (26 Aug-16
Sep)
Oppenheim
(18 Sep)
Weissenberg
(20 Sep)
Alzey (25-26 Sep)
Neuss (22 Oct)
Luttich (29 Oct)
Neuss (28 Nov)

1258
Siegberg (27 Feb)
Mainz (Apr-May)
Oppenheim
(22-24 May)
Mainz (1 Jun)
Oppenheim
(16-20 Jun)
Worms (24-25 Jul)
Mainz (16-22 Aug)
Lausanne (26 Sep)
Speier (6 Oct)
Worms (19 Oct)

1259
Cambrai (Jan)
Arras (14 Jan)
St Omer (Jan)
Dover (28 Jan)
Canterbury
(29 Jan)
London (1 Feb)
Westminster
(10 Feb)
Hailes Abbey
(6 Apr)
London (7 Dec)
Mere (11 Dec)
Launceston (Dec)

1260
London (15 Feb)
Westminster (Apr)
London (Apr)
Westminster
(30 Apr-15 Jun)
London (19 May)
Westminster
(15-17 Jun)
Dover (20 June)
Cambrai (27 Jun-
8 Jul)
Worms (12 Aug-16
Sep)
Mainz (1 Oct)
London (29 Oct)
Windsor (25 Dec)

1261
Wallingford (7-8
Jan)
London (12 Feb)
London (9 Apr)
London (12 Jul)
London (Oct)
Berkhamsted (23
Oct)
London (8-9 Nov)
Beckley (9 Dec)
Wallingford
(28 Dec)

1262
Wallingford (Jan)
Mere (Apr)
Wallingford
(9 May)
London (20 Jun)
Ghent (2 Jul)
Brussels (4 Jul)
Lowen (5-8 Jul)

Andernach
(21 Aug)
Frankfurt (17 Sep)
Oppenheim
(27-28 Sep)
Hagenau
(16-25 Oct)
Strasbourg (3 Nov)
Basel (Nov)
Hagenau
(18-21 Nov)
Mainz (3-18 Dec)

1263
Trier (25 Jan)
Oxford (May)
London
(11-24 June)
Isleworth
(29-30 Jun)
Berkhamsted
(8 July-17 Oct)
Windsor (23 Oct)
Wallingford
(30 Oct)
Reading (21-23
Nov)
Canterbury (5 Dec)
Croydon (8 Dec)
Windsor (16 Dec)

1264
Risborough
(10 Jan)
Berkhamsted
(18 Jan)
Oxford (7 Feb)
Worcester (10 Feb)
Hereford (17 Feb)
Windsor (4 Mar)
Reading (7 Mar)

Oxford
(8 Mar-4 Apr)
Northampton
(5-10 Apr)
Nottingham
(13-20 Apr)
Grantham (20 Apr)
Aylesbury (26 Apr)
Croydon (27 Apr)
Tonbridge (30 Apr)
Battle (3 May)
Winchelsea
(8 May)
Lewes
(12-15 May)
London (28 May)
Berkhamsted (Jun)
Wallingford
(Jun-Jul)
Kenilworth
(Jul-Dec)

1265
Kenilworth
(Jan-6 Sep)
Wallingford (9 Sep)
Winchester
(12-22 Sep)
London (13 Oct)
Canterbury
(29-30 Oct)
London (2 Nov)
Northampton
(24 Dec)

1266
Abington (8 Jan)
Cippeham
(18 Apr)
Kenilworth (July)
Wallingford (8 Oct)

1267
Cambridge (1 Mar-
20 Apr)
Windsor (May)
Stratford
(May-16 Jun)
London
(18-21 Jun)

1268
Westminster
(3 Feb)
Westminster (26
May)
Windsor (5 Jun)
Woodstock
(8-10 Jul)
Geddington
(2 Aug)
Cambrai (16 Aug)
Cologne
(15 Dec)

1269
Worms
(7 Mar-20 Apr)
Mainz (8 May)
Frankfurt
(12-26 May)
Kaiserslautern
(16 Jun)
Mainz (9-11 Jul)
Dover (3 Aug)
Gravesend (6 Aug)
London (8 Aug)
Winchester
(24 Aug)
Westminster
(13 Oct)

1270
Berkhamsted
(20 Jan)
Westminster (Apr)
Winchester (2 Aug)
Risborough
(10 Sep)
Wallingford (13-24
Sep)

Westminster (25
Oct)
Windsor (30 Oct)

1271
Westminster (18
Jan-6 Feb)
Westminster (16-
24 Apr)
Isleworth (24 Apr)

London (15 May)
Hailes Abbey
(19 May)
Wallingford
(20 May)
Westminster
(20 Jun)
Westminster
(1 Aug)

Knaresborough
(7-13 Sep)
Westminster (14-
20 Oct)
Berkhamsted (11-
31 Dec)

1272
Berkhamsted
(1 Jan-2 April)

BIBLIOGRAPHY

Primary Sources

Annals of Burton, Annales Monastici, Vol. I, ed. H. R. Luard (London, 1864)

Annals of Dunstable, Annales Monastici, Vol. III, ed. H. R. Luard (London, 1866)

Annals of Nicholas Trivet, ed. T. Hog (London, 1845)

Annals of Tewkesbury, Annales Monastici, Vol. I, ed. H. R. Luard (London, 1864)

Annals of Waverley, Annales Monastici, Vol. II, ed. H. R. Luard (London, 1865)

Annals of Winchester, Annales Monastici,Vol. II, ed. H. R. Luard (London, 1865)

Calendar of Charter Rolls, 1903 (**CChR**)

Calendar of Inquisitions Post Mortem, Vol. I, 1904

Calendar of Liberate Rolls, 1930 (**CLR**)

Calendar of Papal Letters, 1893 (**CPL**)

Calendar of Patent Rolls, 1908 (**CPR**)

Close Rolls of the Reign of Henry III, 1932 (**CR**)

Chronicle of Battle Abbey, trans. M. A. Lower (London, 1851)

Chronicle of Florence of Worcester, Vol. II, ed. B. Thorpe (London, 1849)

Chronicle of John of Oxendes, ed. H. Ellis (London, 1859)

Chronicle of Lanercost, ed. J. Stevenson (Edinburgh, 1839)

Chronicle of Melrose, trans. J. Stevenson (London, 1856)

Chronicle of the Mayors and Sheriffs of London, 1188-1274, French Chronicle of London, ed. H. R. Riley (London, 1863)

Chronicle of Osney, Annales Monastici, Vol. IV, ed. H. R. Luard (London, 1869)

Chronicle of the Abbey of Saint Werburg at Chester, trans. R. C. Christie (London, 1887)

Chronicle of Thomas Wykes, Annales Monastici, Vol. IV, ed. H. R. Luard (London, 1869)

Chronicle of Walter of Guisborough, ed. H. Rothwell (London: Royal Historical Society, 1957)

Chronicle of William de Rishanger, ed. J. O. Halliwell (London, 1840)

Croniche Fiorentine of Giovanni Villani, trans. R. Selfe (Westminster, 1896)

Crusader Syria in the Thirteenth Century: The Rothelin Continuation of the History of William of Tyre with Part of the Eracles or Acre Text (Crusade Texts in Translation), trans. J. Shirley (London: Routledge, 1999)

Diplomatic Documents, 1101–1272, Vol. I, ed. P. Chaplais (London, 1964)

Documents of the Baronial Movement of Reform and Rebellion (**DBM**), ed. R. F. Treharne, I. J. Sanders, (Oxford: Clarendon Press, 1973)

Documents of the Christian Church, ed. H. Bettenson, C. Maunder, (Oxford, Oxford University Press, 1963)

English Coronation Records, ed. L.G.W. Legg (London, 1901)

Flores Historiarum, trans. C. D. Yonge, (London, 1853)

Foedera, Conventiones, Literae, ed. T. Rymer (London, 1816)

Geoffrey of Monmouth, *History of the Kings of Britain*, trans. A. Thompson (Cambridge: Cambridge University Press, 1999)

Historical Works of Gervase of Canterbury, Vol. II, ed. W. Stubbs (London, 1880)

History of the Dukes of Normandy and Kings of England, ed. F. Michel (Paris, 1840)

Layettes Du Trésor Des Chartes, ed. M. Alexandre Teulet (Paris, 1863)

Letters of Adam Marsh, Volume 1 and II, ed. and trans. C. H. Lawrence (Oxford: Clarendon Press, 2006)

Letters of Robert Grosseteste, Bishop of Lincoln, ed. F.A.C. Mantello, F. M. Goering, (Toronto: University of Toronto Press, 2010)

Manners and Household Expenses of England in the Thirteenth and Fifteenth Centuries, ed. T. H. Turner (London, 1841)

Matthaei Parisiensis, *Monachi Sancti Albani, Chronica Majora*, ed. H.R. Luard (RS, 7 volumes, 1872–83)

Matthew Paris' English History from 1235 to 1273, Vol. I, II, III, trans. J. A. Giles (London, 1854)

Memoirs of the Lord of Joinville, trans. Ethel Wedgwood (London, 1906)

Metrical Chronicle of Robert of Gloucester, ed. W. A. Wright (London, 1887)

Political Songs of England, ed. T. Wright (London, 1839)

Regesta Imperii, Vol. I, II, III, IV, V, VI, ed. J.F. Böhmer (Innsbruck, 1881)

Roger of Wendover's Flowers of History, Vol. I, II, trans. J. A. Giles (London, 1859)

Rotuli Litterarum Clausarum, Vol. I, ed. T.D. Hardy (London, 1833)

Rotuli Litterarum Patentium, Vol. I, ed. T.D. Hardy (London, 1835)

Royal Letters, ed. W. W. Shirley (London, 1866)

Scotichronicon IX, (112-13), Walter Bower (Aberdeen: Aberdeen University Press, 1987)

Shorter Latin Forms of Master Henry of Avarances Relating to England, ed. J.C. Russell and J.P. Hieronimus, (Cambridge: Medieval Academy of America, 1935)

Song of Lewes, ed. C. L Kingsford (Oxford, 1890)

Secondary Sources

Abulafia, D., *Frederick II: A Medieval Emperor* (London: Pimlico, 1992)

Allen, M., *Mints and Money in Medieval England*, (Cambridge: Cambridge University Press, 2012)

Arancón, M.R.G., 'Ricardo de Montfort al servicio de Teobaldo II de Navarra (1266)', *Principe de Viana*, 41, nos. 160-1 (1980)

Baddeley, W., *A Cotteswold Shrine* (Gloucester, John Bellows, 1908)

Baker, D., *Henry III* (Stroud: The History Press, 2017)

– *Simon de Montfort and the Rise of the English Nation* (Stroud: Amberley, 2018)

– *The Two Eleanors of Henry III* (Barnsley: Pen and Sword History, 2019)

Bappert, J., *Richard von Cornwall Seit Seiner Wahl Zum Deutschen König: 1257-1272* (Bonn: Hanstein, 1905)

Bayley, C.C., 'The Diplomatic Preliminaries of the Double Election of 1257 in Germany', *The English Historical Review*, Vol. 62, No. 245, pp. 457–83 (1947)

Bémont, C., *Simon de Montfort* (Oxford: Clarendon Press, 1930)

Blaauw, W. H., *The Barons' War* (London, 1871)

Brown, M.C., 'The "Three Kings of Cologne" and Plantagenet Political Theology', *Mediaevistik*, Vol. 30, pp. 61–85 (2017)

Burrell, M.A., 'The Classification of *Blandin de Cornouailles*: the Romance within and without', *Florilegium* 18.2, pp. 11–19 (2001)

Busson, A., *Die Doppelwahl des Jahres 1257* (Münster, 1866)

Carpenter, D., 'A Noble in Politics: Roger Mortimer' in A. Duggan (ed.) *Nobles and Nobility* (Woodbridge: The Boydell Press, 2000)

– *Henry III, The Rise to Power and Personal Rule* (New Haven: Yale University Press, 2020)

– *The Battles of Lewes and Evesham* (Keele, 1987)

– *The Minority of Henry III* (London: Methuen Publishing, 1990)

– *The Reign of Henry III* (London: The Hambledon Press, 1996)

Cassidy, R., 'Richard of Cornwall and the Royal Mints and Exchanges, 1247-59', *The Numismatic Journal*, Vol. 172 (2012)

– 'The Exchanges, Silver Purchases and Trade in the Reign of Henry III', *British Numismatic Journal*, Vol. 81 (2011)

Chaplais, P., 'The Making of the Treaty of Paris (1259) and the Royal Style', *The English Historical Review*, Vol. 67, pp. 235–53 (1952)

Church, S., *King John, And the Road to Magna Carta* (London: Basic Books, 2015)

Clanchy, M., *England and its Rulers, 1066–1307* (Chichester: Wiley-Blackwell, 2014)

– *From Memory to Written Record: England 1066–1307* (Oxford: Blackwell Publishers, 1979)

Cockayne, G., *Complete Peerage of England, Scotland, Ireland, Great Britain and the United Kingdom* (London: George Bell, 1895)

Cockerill, S., *Eleanor of Castile, The Shadow Queen* (Stroud: Amberley, 2014)

Cox, E., *The Eagles of Savoy* (Princeton: Princeton University Press, 1974)

Crouch, D., 'The Battle of the Countesses: the Division of the Honour of Leicester, March–December 1207', *Rulership and Rebellion in the Anglo-Norman World, c.1066–c.1216: Essays in Honour of Professor Edmund King*, (eds) P. Dalton and D. Luscombe (London: Routledge, 2015)

– 'The Last Adventure of Richard Siward', *Morgannwg, The Journal of Glamorgen History*, Volume XXXV, pp. 7–30 (1991)

D'Avray, D., *Medieval Christianity in Practice* (Princeton: Princeton University Press, 2009)

Denholm-Young, N., *Richard of Cornwall* (New York: William Salloch, 1947)

Ellis, C., *Hubert de Burgh, A Study in Constancy* (London, 1952)

Gebauer, G., *Leben und Denckwürdige Thaten Herrn Richards, Erwählten Römischen Kaisers* (Leipzig: Caspar, 1744)

Gransden, A., *Historical Writing in England: 550–1307* (Abingdon: Routledge, 1996)

Harding, A., *England in the Thirteenth Century* (Cambridge: Cambridge University Press, 1993)

Howell, M., *Eleanor of Provence* (Oxford: Blackwell Publishers, 2001)

Huffman, J.P., *The Social Politics of Medieval Diplomacy: Anglo-German Relations (1066–1307)* (Ann Arbor: University of Michigan Press, 2000)

Hutton, W. H., *Simon de Montfort and His Cause, 1251-1266* (London: David Nutt, 1907)

Jobson, A., 'A Queen in the Shadows: Sanchia of Provence, Richard of Cornwall and a Royal Life Unveiled', *Women's History Review* (2020)

– 'Richard of Cornwall and the Baronial Opposition in 1263', in *Thirteenth Century England XIII: Proceedings of the Gregynog Conference 2007*, (eds) J. Burton et al. (Woodbridge: The Boydell Press, 2009)

Jordan, W.C., 'Isabelle d'Angoulême, By the Grace of God, Queen', *Revue belge de philologie et d'histoire* vol. 69 (1991)

Kinkade, R., *Dawn of a Dynasty: The Life and Times of Infante Manuel of Castile* (Toronto, University of Toronto Press, 2019)

Knowles, C. H., 'The Disinherited, 1265–1280: A Political and Social Study of the Supporters of Simon De Montfort and the Resettlement after the Barons' War' (Doctoral thesis, University of Wales, 1959)

Koch, H., *Richard Von Cornwall: Erster Teil* (Strasbourg: Heitz, 1887)

Labarge, M. W., *Simon de Montfort* (London: Eyre & Spottiswoode, 1962)

Laborderie, O. D., Carpenter, D. A., Maddicott, J. R., 'The Last Hours of Simon de Montfort: A New Account', *English Historical Review 15* (2000)

Le Goff, J., *Saint Louis* (South Bend: University of Notre Dame Press, 2009)

Lemcke, G., *Beiträge zur Geschichte König Richards von Cornwall* (Berlin: Matthiesen, 1909)

Lewis, F.R., 'Beatrice of Falkenburg, the Third Wife of Richard of Cornwall', *The English Historical Review*, Vol. 52, No. 206, pp. 279–82 (1937),

– 'Ottokar II of Bohemia and the Double Election of 1257', *Speculum*, Vol. 12, No. 4, pp. 512–5 (1937)

– 'The Election of Richard of Cornwall as Senator of Rome in 1261', *The English Historical Review*, Vol. 52, No. 208, pp. 657–62 (1937)

Lloyd, S., *English Society and the Crusade, 1216–1307* (Oxford: Clarendon Press, 1988)

Lower, M., *The Barons' Crusade: A Call to Arms and Its Consequences* (Philadelphia, University of Pennsylvania Press, 2005)

Lucas, S.H., 'John of Avesnes and Richard of Cornwall', *Speculum*, Vol. 23, No. 1, pp. 81–101 (1948)

Lunt, W.E., *Financial Relations of the Papacy with England, to 1327* (Cambridge: Medieval Academy of America, 1939)

Maddicott, J. R., *Simon de Montfort* (Cambridge: Cambridge University Press, 1994)

– 'The Mise of Lewes, 1264', *English Historical Review*, Vol. 98 (1983)

– *The Origins of the English Parliament, 924–1327* (Oxford: Oxford University Press, 2010)

Marsh, F. B., *English Rule in Gascony, 1199–1259* (Ann Arbor: University of Michigan, 1912)

Martínez, H.S., *Alfonso X, the Learned* (Leiden: Brill, 2010)

Mayhew, N. J., 'From Regional to Central Minting, 1158-1464', *A New History of the Royal Mint*, ed. C. E. Challis (Cambridge: Cambridge University Press, 1992)

Mitchell, S. K., *Studies in Taxation under John and Henry III* (New Haven: Yale University Press, 1914)

Norgate, K., *The Minority of Henry III* (London, 1912)

Page, M., 'Cornwall, Earl Richard, and the Barons' War', *The English Historical Review* , Vol. 115, No. 460 pp. 21–38 (2000)

Page, W., *The Victoria History of the County of Bedford, Vol. 3* (London: Archibald Constable, 1912)

Pernoud, R., *Blanche of Castile*, (London: Collins, 1975)

Pollock, M.A., *Scotland, England and France after the Loss of Normandy, 1204–1296* (Woodbridge, The Boydell Press, 2015).

Powicke, M., *King Henry III and the Lord Edward Vol. I, II* (Oxford: Clarendon Press, 1947)

– *Ways of Medieval Lives and Thought: Essays and Addresses* (New York: Biblio and Tannen, 1949)

Prestwich, M., *Edward I* (Berkeley: University of California Press, 1988)

Ray, M., *Edward I's Regent, Edmund of Cornwall: The Man Behind England's Greatest King* (Barnsley: Pen and Sword History, 2022)

– 'Three Alien Royal Stewards' in M. Prestwich, R. H. Britnell, R. Fram (eds) *Thirteenth Century England X: Proceedings of the Durham Conference 2003* (Woodbridge: The Boydell Press, 2005)

Richardson, D., *Plantagenet Ancestry: A Study in Colonial & Medieval Families*, Vol. 1 (2011)

Ridgeway, H., 'Henry III (1207–1272)', *Oxford Dictionary of National Biography* (2004)

– 'Henry III and the "Aliens", 1236–1272', *Thirteenth Century England II*, (eds) P.R. Coss and S. Lloyd (Woodbridge: The Boydell Press, 1988)

– 'King Henry III's Grievances against the Council in 1261', *Historical Research*, Vol. 61 (1988)

– 'The Lord Edward and the Provisions of Oxford (1258)', *Thirteenth Century England I*, (eds) P.R. Coss and S.D. Lloyd (Woodbridge: The Boydell Press, 1986)

– 'What Happened in 1261?', *Baronial Reform and Revolution in England, 1258–1267*, ed. A. Jobson (Woodbridge: The Boydell Press, 2016)

Roche, T.W.E., *The King of Almayne, A 13th Century Englishman in Europe* (London: John Murray, 1966)

Rollason, D., 'From Tintagel to Aachen: Richard of Cornwall and the Power of Place', *Reading Medieval Studies*, 38, pp. 1–23 (2012)

Runciman, S., *The Sicilian Vespers* (Cambridge: Cambridge University Press, 1992)

Sanders, I.J., 'The Texts of the Peace of Paris, 1259', *The English Historical Review*, Vol. 66, No. 258, pp. 81–97 (1951)

Smith, J.B., *Llywelyn Ap Gruffudd: Prince of Wales* (Cardiff: University of Wales Press, 1998)

Soden, I., *Ranulf de Blondeville: The First English Hero* (Stroud: Amberley, 2009)

Stacey, R., 'Crusades, Crusaders and the Baronial *Gravamina* of 1263–1264', *Thirteenth Century England III: Proceedings of the Newcastle upon Tyne Conference, 1989* (3), (eds) P.R. Coss, S.D. Lloyd (Woodbridge: The Boydell Press, 1991)

– *Politics, Policy, and Finance under Henry III, 1216–1245* (Oxford, Oxford University Press, 1987)

Stewart, S., 'Simon de Montfort and His Followers, June 1263', *The English Historical Review*, Vol. 119, No. 483, pp. 965–69 (2004)

Stubbs, W., *The Constitutional History of England*, Vol. II, (Oxford: Clarendon Press, 1877)

Studd, R., 'The Marriage of Henry of Almain and Constance of Béarn', *Thirteenth Century England III*, ed. P.R. Coss and S. Lloyd (Woodbridge: The Boydell Press, 1991)

Treharne, R., *The Baronial Plan of Reform* (Manchester: Manchester University Press, 1932)

Turner, R.V.,'William De Forz, Count of Aumale: An Early Thirteenth-Century English Baron', *Proceedings of the American Philosophical Society*, Vol. 115, No. 3, pp. 221-249 (1971)

Vaughan, R., *Matthew Paris* (Cambridge: Cambridge University Press, 1958)

Vincent, N., 'Isabella of Angoulême: John's Jezebel', *King John: New Interpretations*, ed. S.D. Church (Woodbridge: The Boydell Press, 1999)

– *Peter des Roches: An Alien in English Politics, 1205–1238* (Cambridge: Cambridge University Press, 1996)

– 'Richard of Cornwall (1209–1272)', *Oxford Dictionary of National Biography* (2004)

– *The Holy Blood: King Henry III and the Westminster Blood Relic*, CUP (Cambridge, 2001)

Waugh, S., *The Lordship of England: Royal Wardships and Marriages in English Society and Politics, 1217-1327* (Princeton, Princeton University Press, 1988)

Weiler, B.K.U., *Henry III of England and the Staufen Empire, 1216-1272* (Woodbridge: The Boydell Press, 2006)

– 'Image and Reality in Richard of Cornwall's German Career', *The English Historical Review*, Vol. 113, No. 454, pp. 1111–42 (1998)

Werner, C., *Richard von Cornwall: Ein Engländer auf dem deutschen Thron - Historische Erzählung* (Hamburg: Tredition, 2022)

Westerhof, D., *Death and the Noble Body in Medieval England* (Woodbridge: The Boydell Press, 2008)

Wilkinson, L. J., *Eleanor de Montfort, A Rebel Countess in Medieval England* (London: Continuum Books, 2012)

– *The Household Roll of Eleanor de Montfort, Countess of Pembroke and Leicester, 1265* (Woodbridge: The Boydell Press, 2020)

NOTES

1 Second Son

1. *Waverley* (p. 264) and *Margam* (p. 29) say that Richard was born at Winchester, but *Gervase II* (p. 107) makes the stronger case for Devizes by writing that Isabella was confined (*includitur*) there, suggesting she was pregnant, and *Coggeshall* (p. 163) also has the queen confined at Devizes sometime in mid-February, just before she would have re-emerged in public after the birth of Richard. John himself had been at Winchester but moved to Aldingbourn near Chichester on 4 January and was there the next day as well (*Rot. Lit. Pat*, p. 19).

2. *Gervase II*, p. 103, *Dunstable*, p. 34; Denholm-Young, *Richard of Cornwall*, p. 3; Vincent, 'Isabella of Angoulême: John's Jezebel', p. 196.

3. *Rot. Lit. Pat.*, p. 117; *Rot. Lit. Cl. I*, pp. 173, 229; CR, 1242–47, p. 108; *Coggeshall*, p. 168 (who reports that Eleanor of Brittany was also taken to Poitou); Russell and Heironimus, *Shorter Latin Poems of Master Henry of Avranches*, pp. 56–7. *History of the Dukes of Normandy* (pp. 180–1) says that Isabella of

Angoulême was pregnant with Eleanor at John's death. My thanks to Rich Price for his translation of John's letters.

4. *Rot. Lit. Cl. I*, pp. 266, 540; *Foedera I*, pp. 145, 167; *Royal Letters I*, pp. 179–80; *Melrose*, pp. 173–4; Norgate, *Minority of Henry III*, p. 93.

5. *Foedera I*, pp. 177, 178; *Wendover*, pp. 450–4, 456–8; *Gervase II*, p. 114; *Oxendes*, p. 152; *Dunstable*, p. 94; Denholm-Young, *Richard of Cornwall*, p. 6.

6. *Rot. Lit. Cl. II*, p. 83; *Wendover*, pp. 460–1, 68–9, 74–6, 80–1; *Dunstable*, pp. 98–101; Denholm-Young, *Richard of Cornwall*, pp. 6–7; Pernoud, *Blanche of Castile*, pp. 122–6. Since Louis's attack on Toulouse was done under the cover of a crusade, Pope Honorius III forbade Henry, whom he considered his ward, to launch any military operations against Louis. In fact, Louis had meant to crusade against Henry's cousin Raymond of Toulouse, who was declared a supporter of heretics, back in 1224, but Honorius called off the crusade at the last moment. Incensed, Louis took his army and conquered Poitou instead. Honorius protested on behalf of Henry, but Louis told him he should be thankful he did not conquer England as well.

7. *CPR 1225-32*, pp. 140–1, 145; *Wendover*, pp. 483, 487–9; *Dunstable*, p. 104; *Waverley*, p. 303; Bower, *Scotichronicon IX*, p. 255; Carpenter, *Henry III*, pp. 68–70; Pollock, *Scotland, England and France After the Loss of Normandy*, pp. 112–3. Richard's first known act after arriving in England was to win a pardon for a certain Roger Wastehouse, who had been ordered to abjure the realm for robbing various Flemish merchants in Kent. It is possible that Roger was in Dover on his way out when Richard landed and he pleaded his case to him. In granting the pardon, Henry calls Richard the count of Poitou (*CPR, 1225-32*, p. 124).

8. *Royal Letters I*, pp. 350–1, 358; *Wendover*, p. 531; Carpenter, *Henry III*, p. 83. A full account of the reasons behind the

expedition can be found in Stacey, *Politics, Policy and Finance*, pp. 160–72.

9. *Royal Letters I*, pp. 364–5, 370; *CPR*, 1216–25, p. 574; *CPR*, 1225–32, pp. 313, 361; *CR*, 1227–31, p. 450; *Wendover*, pp. 534–5, 537–8; *Dunstable*, p. 125; Denholm-Young, *Richard of Cornwall*, p. 15; Carpenter, *Henry III*, pp. 87–96; Wilkinson, *Eleanor de Montfort*, p. 30. The sister is not identified in the letter describing these events, but has long been thought to be Eleanor. She was fourteen and had begun conjugal relations with her husband William Marshal, which Henry hoped would produce an heir in order to keep his huge estate within the royal family. An early pregnancy or miscarriage could have been the reason for the emergency diversion. Eleanor, however, is found in England in July, and in September Henry ordered a 'good boat' to be equipped and readied to ferry her over to Brittany. The other possibility is 16-year-old Isabella. Less than a week after Henry returned to England in late October he told the constable of Marlborough that Isabella was moving in, as if she had just returned from the continent and needed a home. (*CR*, 1227–31, pp. 418, 448, 453.)

10. *CChR*, 1226–57, pp. 126, 129; *History of William Marshal*, p. 183; *Tewkesbury*, p. 78.

11. *CPR*, 1227–31, p. 434; *CR*, 1227–31, pp. 316, 543; *CChR*, 1226–57, p. 139; Carpenter, *Henry III*, pp.100–01, 104; Crouch, 'Countesses', pp. 186–7.

12. *CPR*, 1232–47, pp. 28–30; *Wendover*, pp. 551–5, 557–9, 561–2; *Paris I*, pp. 230–4; *Dunstable*, pp. 128–30; *Tewkesbury*, pp. 81, 84, 86, 88. For details of these events, see Carpenter, *Henry III*, pp.108–21; Vincent, *Peter des Roches*, pp.195–228, 303–20; Soden, *Ranulf de Blondeville*, Loc 1750, 2551, 2988. The Annals of Dunstable (pp. 176,

181, 197) provide a good example of these papal provisions in the parish church of Steppingley. When the English rector of the church was promoted to a vicarate, the priory of Dunstable 'presented' Steppingley to an Italian named Peter Vitelle of Ferentino. He stayed in Italy and farmed the church back to the priory for an annual payment of £5. Every few years Peter came to England to collect missing payments or renew the contract. Officially he was the rector of the church, but the parishioners never saw him or otherwise knew he existed. All services, from baptisms and weddings to mass and funerals, were provided by the priests and deacons hired by Peter.

13. *Wendover*, p. 566–94; *Dunstable*, pp. 136–7; *Tewkesbury*, pp. 89, 90–3; Carpenter, *Henry III*, p.108–21; Vincent, *Peter des Roches*, pp. 334–9, 361–2, 372–440, 455–8.

2 *Rise at Court and Crusade*

1. *CPR*, 1232–47, pp. 67–8, 158; *Paris I*, pp. 30, 34; *Wykes*, p. 81; *Dunstable*, pp. 137, 144; Crouch, 'The Last Adventure of Richard Siward', pp. 23–4. Siward was released within a fortnight thanks to his vow to go on crusade. He was eventually reconciled with Simon de Montfort, who seems to have been his friend and patron when Siward died in 1248.

2. *CPR*, 1232–47, p. 22; *CChR*, 1226–57, p. 191; *CPL*, p. 147; *Wendover*, p. 569; *Tewkesbury*, pp. 89, 92, 93, 98; Baddeley, *A Cotteswold Shrine*, pp. 26-7. The presence of the bishop of Hereford at a baptism so far away from his diocese can be accounted for by his recent return from the continent, where he helped negotiate the marriage contract between Henry III and Eleanor of Provence (*Paris I*, p. 7).

3. *Foedera I*, pp. 219, 223; *Wendover*, pp. 543, 608–09; *Tewkesbury*, pp. 96, 98; Carpenter, *Henry III*, p.106–07;

Vincent, *Peter des Roches*, pp. 277–8. The council, led by Richard Marshal, felt it was degrading for Henry to marry the youngest sister of the king of Scotland while his minister Hubert de Burgh was married to the oldest sister.

4. Burrell, 'The Classification of *Blandin de Cornouailles:* the Romance within and without', pp. 12–15; Rollason, 'From Tintagel to Aachen: Richard of Cornwall and the Power of Place', pp. 1–4; *Geoffrey of Monmouth*, pp. 141–4. The author of the biography of Richard the Lionheart was Jean de Nostradame (1522–76), the younger brother of Nostradamus, *the* Nostradamus.

5. *Foedera I*, p. 232; *Paris I*, pp. 11, 53; *Dunstable*, pp. 145–6.

6. *CPR*, 1232–47, pp. 173, 202; *Foedera I*, p. 203; *Paris I*, pp. 33–4; 42–6, 49, 54–5, 67–8; *Tewkesbury*, pp. 104–05; *Dunstable*, pp. 145–7.

7. *CPR*, 1232–47, pp. 173; 199–200; *Paris I*, pp. 47–8, 117, 130; *Paris II*, p. 442; *Tewkesbury*, pp. 104–05; *Dunstable*, pp. 145–7; Wilkinson, *Eleanor de Montfort*, pp. 44–7.

8. *Paris I*, pp. 120–4; *Tewkesbury*, p. 106; *Dunstable*, p. 146.

9. *CPR*, 1232–47, p. 209; *Foedera I*, p. 235; *Paris I*, pp. 120–4; *Tewkesbury*, p. 106; *Melrose*, p. 181; *Flores I*, pp. 183–5.

10. *CPR*, 1232–47, p. 222; *CR*, 1237–42, p. 149; *CPL I*, p. 167; *Paris I*, pp. 118, 119–20, 124, 125, 129, 130–1, 133–4, 138–9, 155, 279; *Flores I*, pp. 185–6; *Tewkesbury*, pp. 107–08, 113–4; Denholm-Young, *Richard of Cornwall*, p. 39; Rollason, 'From Tintagel to Aachen: Richard of Cornwall and the Power of Place', p. 4; Howell, *Eleanor of Provence*, p. 74.

11. *CPL I*, pp. 177, 184–5; *Paris I*, pp. 132–7, 234–5, 241; Cox, *Eagles of Savoy*, pp. 70–80. The king's main litigation in Rome at this time had to do with the vacant post of bishop of Winchester. Peter des Roches had died in June 1238 and Henry wanted a man very much like Roches to become

the next bishop. In his mind, William of Savoy fit the bill perfectly. He was sharp, industrious, urbane, his continental connections impressive. The monks saw things differently, however. They had had enough of warrior monks like Peter and rejected William as a 'man of blood'. Henry rejected their own candidate, William Raleigh, his former chief justice, thus commencing a bitter standoff that lasted more than six years. Henry was forced to give way by Pope Innocent IV and eventually was reconciled with Raleigh despite his very public insults to the king. Although Winchester was the richest diocese in the land, worth £3,000 per year, Raleigh died in 1250 still indebted from his legal fight with Henry. The nearly £20,000 earned by the diocese while it was vacant went to the crown.

12. *Paris I*, pp. 139, 155, 158–60, 172–3, 194, 239.

13. *Paris I*, pp. 255, 262, 287, 296; *Tewkesbury*, pp. 113–4, 115; *Dunstable*, p. 151. Paris concocts a scene at Reading of wailing prelates pleading with Richard not to leave. '"In your absence, rapacious foreigners will invade us!" they declare. The earl then, in tears, replied to one of them, the archbishop of Canterbury, for all: "My father and lord, of a truth, even had I not assumed the cross, I would still go, and absent myself, so that I might not see the evils of our people and the desolation of the kingdom, which it is believed I am able to prevent, although I cannot really do so."'

14. *Paris I*, pp. 270–1, 288–90.

15. *Paris I*, pp. 272–3, 308–09; *Rothelin Continuator*; pp. 42–4, 45–5; Lower, *Barons' Crusade*, pp. 164–75; Pernoud, *Blanche of Castile*, p. 125. Theobald's co-conspirator in the negotiations with Blanche of Castile was Count Henry of Bar. He went missing at the battle of Gaza and was presumed dead.

16. *Paris I*, pp. 363–8, 373, 385; *Tewkesbury*, p. 118; Lower, *Barons' Crusade*, pp. 175–7.

17. *Paris I*, pp. 259, 391–2; *Chronica Majora IV*, p. 44, n. 4; Turner, 'William De Forz, Count of Aumale: An Early Thirteenth-Century English Baron', p. 248. William Longespee II never succeeded his father as earl of Salisbury because his mother held the title as countess.

18. *Paris I*, pp. 318, 349–56, 367–8, 369–71, 396; *Tewkesbury*, p. 120.

19. *Paris I*, pp. 279, 309–11, 320, 323, 360–1, 381, 394, 397–402; *Joinville*, pp. 38–40; *Waverley*, p. 329. Gilbert's widow Margery, the Scottish princess whom both Richard and Henry had aspired to marry, died in London on 16 November 1244 (*Paris II*, pp. 37).

3 Growing Wealth and Power

1. *Foedera I*, p. 206; *CPR*, 1232–47, p. 274; *Paris I*, pp. 403, 406, 408, 409, 414, 431–3; *Joinville*, pp. 40–3; *Tewkesbury*, p. 124; *Letters of Adam Marsh* (153), pp. 374–5. No meeting between Richard and his mother Isabella was reported in these events, but the French chronicler of St Denis has Isabella kissing Henry sweetly and calling him such a good boy for coming to her rescue. The two of them then talked in private. See Jordan, 'Isabella d'Angoulême, By the Grace of God, Queen', p. 845.

2. *CPR*, 1232–47, pp. 318, 320, 327, 437; *CChR*, 1227–57, p. 276; *CLR*, 1240–5, p. 111; *Paris I*, pp. 434–5; *Paris II*, pp. 489–90; *Tewkesbury*, p. 128; *Wykes*, p. 117. Paris says that the quarrel over Gascony opened a breach between Henry and Richard that was never healed, but it is part of a bogus version that has Henry bribing the people of Bordeaux

to arrest his brother, and Richard escaping at dawn for England.

3. *CPR, 1232–47*, pp. 331, 408; *Paris I*, pp. 404, 445, 455, 459–60, 461; *Tewkesbury*, p. 132; *Dunstable*, p. 161; Carpenter, *Henry III*, pp. 266–72, 416.

4. *Paris II*, pp. 5–6, 23–6, 40–1, 111, 115–6; Carpenter, *Henry III*, pp. 421–31; Mitchell, *Studies in Taxation*, pp. 241–3; Stacey, *Politics*, pp. 247–51.

5. *CPR, 1232–47*, pp. 419, 433, 456–7; *CR, 1234–37*, p. 434; *CR, 1242–47*, pp. 214, 264, 424, 441, 452; *Paris I*, pp. 491, 497–500; *Paris II*, pp. 52–3, 111, 115–6; Denholm-Young, *Richard of Cornwall*, pp. 62–3, 66–7; Maddicott, *Simon de Montfort*, p. 55. The four slain men from Richard's retinue were Alan Buscel, Adam de Moia, Sir Geoffrey Sturmy, and Raymond de Luka, a Gascon crossbowman with whom Henry liked to joke. Money was not the only thing Henry borrowed from Richard. On 23 September 1247, Richard received 35 marks (£23) for seven tuns of wine (6,784 litres) that he delivered to the king out of his own cellar (*CLR, 1245–51*, p. 141).

6. *CPL I*, p. 227; *Paris I*, pp. 392–3; *Paris II*, pp. 43, 52, 144–6, 164.

7. *CPL I*, p. 249; *Paris II*, pp. 45, 49–50, 56–8, 60–1, 72, 133–4, 141–4, 148–57, 170–3, 175–6, 236; *Dunstable*, pp. 166–7, 169–70, 172; *Waverley*, p. 333; Lunt, *Financial Relations*, pp. 226, 432–4. Boniface did not do his due diligence before accepting his appointment as archbishop of Canterbury, otherwise he may have had second thoughts about the massive debts of the diocese that had been accumulating since Stephen Langton put on a grand ceremony for the translation of Thomas Becket to a new shrine in 1220. Boniface's determination to have the other English dioceses help pay the debts off caused great bitterness, but he managed to clear

22,000 marks (£14,667) by 1261, twenty years after his election (*Gervase II*, p. 214, *CPL I*, pp. 273–4).

8. *CR, 1242–47*, p. 279; *CLR, 1245–51*, p. 67; *Paris II*, pp. 129, 175–6, 182, 189, 198; Denholm-Young, *Richard of Cornwall*, p. 162; Baddeley, *Cotteswold Shrine*, p. 27.

9. *CChR, 1227–57*, pp. 288, 294; *CR, 1242–47*, pp. 329, 404; *CR, 1247–51*, p. 22; *CPL I*, p. 240; *Paris I*, pp. 378; *Paris II*, pp. 177, 232–3; Baddeley, *Cotteswold Shrine*, pp. 29–30. Sanchia would have been confined in her last month of pregnancy and so missed the dedication of Beaulieu Abbey. The queen ended up staying at the abbey for another three weeks after Edward, whose seventh birthday passed during the event, fell gravely ill. Her presence on a compound meant for men only created a scandal that cost two of the officials their jobs. See *Waverley*, p. 337.

10. *CPR, 1232–47*, pp. 498, 509; *Paris II*, pp. 177, 229–31, 240–2, 243–4; *Chronica majora IV*, p. 628; *Dunstable*, pp. 171–2; *Annals of Chester*, p. 67. Two other half-brothers, Guy and Geoffrey, were not settled in England, but received money fees, wardships and were often at court. The Lusignan marriages were mirrored by matches arranged by Peter of Savoy to further link the nobles houses of England to their counterparts in Europe (*CPR, 1232–47*, p. 502; *CPR, 1247–58*, p. 3; *Paris II*, p. 230).

11. *CPR, 1232–47*, pp. 503, 505, 508; *CPR, 1247–58*, pp. 21, 94; *Paris II*, pp. 215, 233–4, 262–3, 264–5; *Paris III*, p. 230; *Wykes*, pp. 96–7; *Oxendes*, p. 178; Carpenter, *Henry III*, pp. 264–7; Denholm-Young, *Richard of Cornwall*, pp. 59–62; Cassidy, 'Richard of Cornwall and the Royal Mints', pp. 137–56; Allen, *Mints and Money in Medieval England*, pp. 171–2; Mayhew, *New History of the Royal Mint*, pp. 107–13.

12. *CPR*, 1247–58, p. 38; *Royal Letters II*, pp. 106–07; *Paris II*, pp. 287–8, 308–09.

13. *CPR*, 1247–58, pp. 62, 118; *Paris II*, pp. 324, 326, 329–30, 333–5, 337–9, 377, 538; *Waverley*, p. 342; *Mayors and Sheriffs*, pp. 17, 19; *Oxendes*, pp. 181–2. Paris repeats twice that Louis was captured on the same day that Richard was feasting with the pope in Lyon and informs readers that he got this information from Richard himself.

14. *CPL I*, p. 272; *Paris II*, pp. 351, 366–8, 369–72, 383–6, 402–04, 426, 443–4; *Mayors and Sheriffs*, pp. 17–9.

15. *CPR*, 1247–58, pp. 61, 67, 101, 209; *Paris II*, pp. 424–5, 431–2, 446; *Wykes*, p. 101; Carpenter, *Henry III*, pp. 520–1, 534–6.

16. *CR*, 1247–51, pp. 180, 262, 322, 372, 408 507; *Paris II*, pp. 464–71; Carpenter, *Henry III*, pp. 520–3; Denholm-Young, *Richard of Cornwall*, pp. 75–6; Labarge, *Simon de Montfort*, pp. 117–22.

4 Sicily and the Regency

1. *CLR*, 1245–51, pp. 70, 84; *CLR*, 1251–60, pp. 197, 245; *Paris II*, p. 475.

2. *Foedera I*, p. 284; *Paris II*, pp. 218–9, 413–4, 537–8; *Paris III*, pp. 13; 53–4, 69, 89, 271–2; *Wendover*, p. 610.

3. *CPR*, 1247–58, pp. 204, 209, 236; *CLR* 1251–60, p. 147; *Paris II*, pp. 486–93; *Paris III*, pp. 16, 20, 22–5, 27–8, 29–30; *Dunstable*, p. 184; Bémont, *Simon de Montfort*, pp. 91–111; Mitchell, *Studies in Taxation*, p. 257; Carpenter, *Henry III*, pp. 564–6.

4. *CPR*, 1247–58, pp. 200, 204, 208, 209, 210, 214; *Paris III*, p. 95.

5. *CPR*, 1247–58, pp. 222, 239; *CLR*, 1251–60, pp. 150, 154; *CR*, 1253–54, p. 7; *Paris III*, pp. 29, 30, 40, 56–7, 60; *Dunstable*, p. 191; Baker, *Simon de Montfort*, pp. 74–5, 225–9.

6. CR, *1253–54*, p. 107; *Paris III*, pp. 41–2, 61–3; *Dunstable*, p. 189.

7. *Royal Letters II*, pp. 101–02; CPR, *1247–58*, p. 229; *Paris III*, pp. 439–40; Maddicott, *The Origins of Parliament*, pp. 211–13.

8. CR, *1253–54*, pp. 114–6, 133, 136; CPR, *1247–58*, pp. 223–4, 279–80, 281, 315, 364, 368, 370; CLR, *1251–60*, p. 167; *Paris III*, p. 75, 472–4; *Chronica majora VI*, pp. 286–7; *Dunstable*, p. 190.

9. CR, *1253–54*, pp. 137–8, 143; CPR, *1247–58*, p. 371, 372; CLR, *1251–60*, pp. 172, 175–6; *Paris III*, pp. 80–1.

10. CPR, *1247–58*, p. 371; CR, *1253–54*, p. 114, *Dunstable*, p. 191; *Paris III*, pp. 442–9; *Mayors and Sheriffs*, pp. 22–3. Paris calls Berard de Nympha a 'crafty and wealthy man' who used blank sheets sealed by the papal court to 'fraudulently extort money from the poor as if on the authority of the pope'. He died in 1258 (*Paris III*, p. 295).

11. CLR, *1251–60*, pp. 172, 175–8, 181, 183, 186.

12. *Paris III*, pp. 98, 104–10.

13. CPR, *1247–58*, pp. 390, 392; CLR, *1251–60*, pp. 197, 245, 260, 325; *Dunstable*, p. 194; *Paris III*, p. 115.

14. CPR, *1247–58*, pp. 310, 344; *Paris III*, pp. 82–3, 89–92, 100–01, 122–4; *Dunstable*, p. 197; Carpenter, *Henry III*, pp. 582–5, 594. Paris makes the improbable claim that before his death Conrad wrote Richard a letter of thanks for having the good sense to reject the offer of Sicily. The whole business drove the monk mad to the point of concocting anything to make Henry and Innocent look vile or stupid, even a fantasy dream that arraigns Innocent before the eternal court, accused of inflicting unspeakable misery on the church. 'Then said the Lord, "Go, and receive your reward according to your deserts", and thus (Innocent) was taken away,' i.e. to the fires of hell.

15. *CPR, 1247–58*, pp. 311, 326, 373, 401, 402; *CLR, 1251–60*, pp. 177, 180; *Paris III*, pp. 114–5. An inventory of the treasure drawn up for the loan included 314 rings and Henry's own 'little crown'. One can almost imagine Richard telling his clerk Henry de Wroxhall, who assisted with the inventory, 'Make sure you get the crown.' On 6 February 1253, a foreign merchant received £333 for a crown bought overseas for Henry (*CPR, 1247–58*, p. 400; *CLR, 1251–60*, p. 105).

16. *CR, 1234–37*, p. 46; *CR, 1237–42*, p. 393; *CPR, 1247–58*, pp. 393, 396, 403; *Paris II*, pp. 340–1; *Dunstable*, pp. 192–3, 198; Denholm-Young, *Richard of Cornwall*, p. 69–70; *History of the County of Bedford III*, pp. 288–96, 383–61. The manors in Bedfordshire were Houghton and Hockcliffe.

17. *CPR, 1247–58*, pp. 451, 510; *CR, 1254–56*, p. 241; *Paris III*, pp. 59, 116–7, 122, 138–41, 163, 168; *Burton*, pp. 340–6, 371; *Waverley*, pp. 346–8; Carpenter, *Henry III*, pp. 612, 625–9. Prior to becoming bishop of Lincoln in 1235, Robert Grosseteste was the archdeacon of Leicester and in that capacity became mentor to Simon de Montfort. He was an avid supporter of Richard Marshal, strong opponent of foreign clergy, and often clashed with Henry III over the separation of church and state. He also clashed with his monks, archbishop, pope, and with Richard of Cornwall too, in one case reported by Adam Marsh (*Letters I*, pp. 48–51). He helped officiate at the consecration of Hailes Abbey.

18. *CPR, 1247–58*, pp. 444, 451; *CR, 1254–56*, p. 381; *Paris III*, pp. 133–7, 141–2, 144–7, 151; *Burton*, pp. 349, 360, 371; Carpenter, *Henry III*, pp. 629–36; Carpenter, *Reign of Henry III*, pp. 75–106. Paris says the pope asked Richard to make a secret loan to Henry of £27,000 for the Sicilian business. When that was refused, he tried to get a loan for himself, but Richard again refused, saying, 'I will not lend money to someone

I cannot compel to pay it back' (*Paris III*, pp. 142, 145).

The bishop of Hereford was Peter d'Aigueblanche, a Provencal who arrived in England with William of Savoy. He became bishop in 1240 thanks to Henry, who wanted him to have the income and prestige necessary for the diplomatic missions he was expected to undertake. Paris despised him to high heaven for being the chief architect of the Sicilian business and took comfort in the skin disease that disfigured his face (*Paris III*, pp. 224 244, 270). He died in 1268.

The earl of Warwick was John du Plessis, a Norman who came to England in the 1220s. In 1242, Henry arranged for him to became the earl of Warwick through marriage to Margaret de Beaumont, the countess, who was none too happy about it. She ended up marrying somebody else, but Plessis kept the earldom until his death in 1263. Margaret already being dead by then, the next earl of Warwick was her cousin. See Waugh, *Lordship of England*, pp. 86–7.

By the time of the council meeting at Windsor, they all would have known that Pope Alexander had suffered another defeat at the hands of Manfred and confessed himself to be 'wholly impotent' in the matter. Then, just days after the council's assent, Thomas of Savoy, the queen's uncle who planned to lead an army into Sicily on Edmund's behalf, was captured and imprisoned by his enemies in northern Italy. These back-to-back setbacks doomed the business.

5 A Kingdom Beckons

1. *Paris II*, pp. 227–8, 270–1, 414–5; *Paris III*, pp. 69–74, 118–9, 435–6; Lucas, 'John of Avesnes and Richard of Cornwall', pp. 81–94.
2. *CPR*, 1247–58, p. 481; *Paris III*, pp. 209–10; Bayley, 'The Diplomatic Preliminaries of the Double Election of 1257 in Germany', pp. 474–5.

3. *Mayors and Sheriffs*, p. 26; *Paris III*, pp. 207–09; *Wykes*, pp. 112–4; Huffman, *Social Politics of Medieval Diplomacy*, pp. 284–8; Weiler, 'Image and Reality in Richard of Cornwall's German Career', p. 1114.

4. *CPR, 1247–58*, pp. 373, 528, 532, 591; *CR, 1256–59*, p. 119; *Paris III*, pp. 210, 213, 220; Huffman, *Social Politics of Medieval Diplomacy*, p. 290. Paris did his own calculation and found that Richard could easily spend a hundred marks daily for ten years. That works out to £243,333 (£170 million in modern terms) or ten times Henry's own annual royal revenue. On 4 November 1256, Richard called in 1,207 marks of gold that had been pledged to him for the loans he made to the queen during the regency, but he had enough cash available at the beginning of the month to lend his nephew Edward £2,666 to confront an uprising in his new Welsh lordship.

5. *CPR, 1247–58*, pp. 549, 554, 555–6; *CR, 1256–59*, pp. 65, 70–1; *CLR, 1251–60*, pp. 356–7; *Burton*, pp. 391–2; *Paris III*, pp. 224, 226–7; *Dunstable*, pp. 202–03; Lewis, 'Ottokar II of Bohemia and the Double Election of 1257', pp. 512–5. Paris, who knew Richard well, launches a foamy tirade against him (*III*, p. 230), accusing him of impoverishing an orphan boy and carrying away with him 'never to return, seven hundred thousand pounds, which were bloodstained by many crimes, besides his daily increasing revenues in England, which were daily to be carried off. By such means was England despoiled of these and many other good things, especially money, and reduced to a state of pitiable want, whilst foreigners boasted in the spoils of her.'

6. *CPR, 1247–58*, pp. 542, 589–90; *CPL I*, p. 244; *Mayors and Sheriffs*, pp. 28–30; *Paris III*, pp. 228, 230, 239; *Annals of Chester*, pp. 72–3; *Burton*, pp. 378–81; *Wykes*, pp. 116–7;

Dunstable, pp. 202, 203, 400; *Paris III*, pp. 239; *Flores*, p. 354; *Wendover*, p. 609; *Robert of Gloucester*, p. 359 (415–20); Denholm-Young, *Richard of Cornwall*, p. 92. In one entry (*III*, p. 242) Paris says the bishop of Coventry prior to Roger was succeeded by a 'Master Longespee', leading to the suggestion that Roger was a natural child of William Longespee (d. 1226) and therefore Henry and Richard's cousin. In another entry (*III*, p. 217) Paris identifies Richard as Roger's uncle (*Ricardo, ipsius Rogeri avunculo*). For details, see Richardson, *Plantagenet Ancestry*, pp. 38–40.

7. *CPL I*, p. 346; *Paris III*, pp. 239; Busson, *Die Doppelwahl des Jahres 1257*, p. 36.

8. *CPR, 1247–58*, p. 553; *Paris III*, pp. 209; Weiler, *Henry III of England and the Staufen Empire*, p. 176.

9. *Wykes*, pp. 113–5; *Paris III*, pp. 210–1, 235–6; Martínez, *Alfonso X*, pp. 149–51; Bayley, 'The Diplomatic Preliminaries of the Double Election of 1257 in Germany', pp. 479–80.

10. *Dunstable*, p. 206; Bappert, *Richard von Cornwall*, pp. 12–21; Denholm-Young, *Richard of Cornwall*, p. 93; Roche, *The King of Almayne*, pp. 140–5; Weiler, *Henry III of England and the Staufen Empire*, p. 177.

11. *Paris III*, pp. 207, 212, 249, 256, 258, 265–6, 283, 291, 298–9; *Dunstable*, p. 208; Weiler, *Henry III of England and the Staufen Empire*, p. 180–1; Lucas, 'John of Avesnes and Richard of Cornwall', pp. 95–101. In his 1256 decision, Louis ordered John and his brother to pay homage to Charles of Anjou for Hainault, which was an imperial fief, and Margaret to pay Charles an astounding £40,000 for his military intervention. If she fell behind in her payments, Charles could seize Hainault, thus disinheriting the d'Avesnes brothers entirely. Here Louis's historic reputation for innate justice and fairness boggles the imagination.

12. *Foedera I*, p. 360; *Paris III*, pp. 232, 241, 244, 246, 260, 265; *Dunstable*, pp. 200; *Mayors and Sheriffs*, pp. 31–2; Lunt, *Financial Relations*, pp. 255–90. Around this time, in August 1257, Henry used his gold treasure to mint his own coins, ten years after Richard's highly successful recoinage. The enterprise flopped. All agreed the gold coins were magnificent to behold, but they were useless in an economy where the average wage for unskilled labour was one to two silver pennies per day. Pennies minted by Richard. See Carpenter, *Reign of Henry III*, pp. 107–35.

13. *CPR*, 1247–58, pp. 567, 594; *CR*, 1256–59, pp. 284–5, 326; *Foedera I*, p. 355; *Paris III*, pp. 246, 252–3. Alfonso had a brother named Henry whom he banished from court after a failed uprising. He made his way to England, where Henry III named him to lead his forces in Sicily (*CPR*, 1247–58, p. 567).

14. *CPR*, 1247–58, pp. 626, 628–9, 663; *Paris III*, pp. *Dunstable*, p. 209; Chaplais, 'The Making of the Treaty of Paris (1259) and the Royal Style', pp. 238–42.

15. *CPR*, 1247–58, pp. 645–9; *Paris III*, pp. 233–4, 268, 270, 279–80, 285–6, 301; *Dunstable*, p. 209; *Burton*, pp. 446–7, 501–05; *Tewkesbury*, p. 164. Aymer was implicated in two brawls over church patronage. The first instance occurred on 3 November 1252 when he sent men to rough up a presumptuous official of Archbishop Boniface who infringed one of his appointments in Southwark. Boniface was then out of the country, a regular feature of his, but when he returned it became a huge scandal at court, the 'king's men' (Lusignans) versus the 'queen's men' (Savoyards) . Aymer and Boniface reconciled the following January and it fell to Richard to decide who was in the right or wrong over the appointment. See *Letters of Adam Marsh II*, (186) pp. 450–1.

The second brawl was over a parish church in Shere and resulted in the death of one of Fitz-Geoffrey's men.

16. *DBM*, pp. 91–7; *CPR*, *1247–58*, pp. 633, 637–8, 640, 664; *Paris III*, pp. 287–8, 291–2; *Mayors and Sheriffs*, pp. 40–1; *Tewkesbury*, p. 165; Baker, *Simon de Montfort*, pp. 216–7.

17. *Royal Letters II*, pp. 132–3; *Layettes iii*, nos. 4412, 4423, 4426; *Paris III*, pp. 306–07; Denholm-Young, *Richard of Cornwall*, p. 93–4, 97; Roche, *The King of Almayne*, pp. 146–8.

6 Cool Homecomings

1. *Paris III*, p. 266; Lewis, 'The Election of Richard of Cornwall as Senator of Rome in 1261', pp. 657–8.

2. *CPR*, *1247–58*, pp. 627; *Layettes iii*, nos. 4413, 4423, 4426; *Paris III*, pp. 291, 293–4, 296; *Dunstable*, p. 211. *Tewkesbury* (p. 165) says Clare and his brother William, who died, fell ill after having breakfast with Edward.

3. *CPR*, *1247–58*, pp. 627, 656; *Paris III*, pp. 287, 292, 295, 306–07, 316; *Dunstable*, p. 211. There was a fourth member of the delegation to Cambrai, who was either Roger Bigod (according to Paris) or Richard de Clare (Dunstable).

4. *CPR*, *1259–66*, pp. 10, 14; *Layettes iii*, nos. 4462–3, pp. 443–5; *Wykes*, pp. 121–2; *Paris III*, pp. 313–4, 316–9; *Flores II*, p. 357 says that one of Richard's knights took the oath on his behalf, which was custom for kings.

5. *DBM*, pp. 194–7; *CPR*, *1259–66*, pp. 25–6; *Paris III*, pp. 303–04, 310, 320, 324, 326–7, 329–30, 476–82; Bémont, *Simon de Montfort*, pp. 162–5. Simon's namesake father had won two major battles of the Albigensian Crusade and was recognised count of Toulouse when he was killed in his late forties. His brother Amaury was the constable of France when he died at a similar age, and his cousin Philip was the

lord of Tyre in the crusader states. He was assassinated by Mamluk agents in 1270, aged about sixty-five.

6. *Paris III*, pp. 328, 329; *Flores II*, pp. 362, 364. My thanks to Rich Price for translating Richard's letter to Alexander, contained in the Burton Annals (pp. 466–70), and for pointing out the various subtleties and texture of the composition.

7. *CPR, 1259–66*, pp. 17, 25–6, 34–5, 46, 52–3; *CChR 1257–1300*, pp. 18, 20; *Diplomatic Documents*, no. 209, pp. 204–05 *Flores II*, p. 365.

8. *CPR, 1259–66*, pp. 45, 57; *Flores II*, pp. 371–2, 374; *Dunstable*, p. 135; *Annales Monastici*, iv, xxx, translation in Vincent, 'Richard of Cornwall', *ODNB*; Ray, *Edmund of Cornwall*, pp. 62–3; Page, 'Cornwall, Earl Richard, and the Barons' War', pp. 21–2.

9. *CPR, 1259–66*, pp. 74, 79, 120; *DBM*, pp. 186–8, 202–07; *Flores II*, pp. 375, 378–80, 383; *Dunstable*, pp. 214–5; *Mayors and Sheriffs*, pp. 46–8; *Wykes*, pp. 123–4; Denholm-Young, *Richard of Cornwall*, p. 101. On 18 April, the very day Henry wrote to his brother to guard the coasts of Cornwall, Richard received a payment of £333 for his assignment of the Jewry provided 'it can be established by reasonable account that the earl did not receive from the Jewry as much as he should have done according to the assignment'. Apparently he proved it (*CLR 1251–60*, pp. 500–01).

10. *Flores II*, pp. 386–7; *Gervase II*, p. 211; Denholm-Young, *Richard of Cornwall*, pp. 104–06; Kinkade, *Dawn of a Dynasty*, pp. 82–6.

11. *CPR, 1259–66*, pp. 90, 96, 97; *Mayors and Sheriffs*, p. 48; *Flores*, pp. 380–1; *Dunstable*, p. 215. In an undated letter, Adam Marsh implores Robert of Esthall to take action

against a certain Peter de Esrigge. 'You see, to confide in your discretion, I very much fear the intervention of the lord earl of Cornwall unless you take care to apply an early remedy for the monstrous deeds of this criminal.' Esthall was the vicar of North Stoke, itself a part of Wallingford, and since Marsh calls Esrigge 'the hammer of the whole country', he may have been one of Richard's more zealous bailiffs. See Letter 114, pp. 298–9. Marsh died in 1259 and his letters are usually thought to have been written in the years before and after 1250.

12. *CPR, 1259–66*, pp. 94–5, 113, 126, 128; *Royal Letters II*, pp. 147–8, 150–2; *Flores*, pp. 386, 388–91; *Dunstable*, p. 216; *Osney*, pp. 125–6; Treharne, *Baronial Plan of Reform*, pp. 242–50.

7 Consolidation and Upheaval

1. *CPR, 1259–66*, pp. 141, 148, 149; *CPL II*, p. 619; *Mayors and Sheriffs*, pp. 48–9; Lewis, 'The Election of Richard of Cornwall as Senator of Rome in 1261', pp. 657–62. The pope heard Richard's plea from Laurence of St Martin, the bishop of Rochester, his brother William, the archdeacon, and royal proctor Robert de Barro. All three men are found in Rome during the week of Alexander's death on 25 May 1261 (*CPR, 1259–66*, pp. 150, 155).

2. *Royal Letters II*, pp. 179, 188–94; *Foedera I*, pp. 405, 416; *DBM*, pp. 210–49; *Flores II*, pp. 391–2, 393–5, 397–401; *Gervase II*, pp. 211, 212; *Dunstable*, p. 217; Maddicott, *Simon de Montfort*, pp. 213–4. Edward returned from the continent in April with William de Valence, whose banishment was lifted after an interview with Queen Margaret in France and swearing an oath to the Provisions of Oxford. Having deserted the Montfortians, Edward left

again for another spin on the tournament circuit and was said to have been badly injured in one of them (*CPR, 1258–66*, p. 150; *Flores II*, p. 394; *Dunstable*, pp. 218–9).

3. *Royal Letters II*, pp. 197–8; *Osney*, pp. 128–9; *Gervase II*, p. 213; *Dunstable*, p. 217; Treharne, *Baronial Plan of Reform*, pp. 265–72; Denholm-Young, *Richard of Cornwall*, p. 101–02.

4. *CPR, 1259–66*, pp. 190–1, 193, 195; *Osney*, p. 128; *Flores Historiarum*, p. 471 n. 2; *Letters of Adam Marsh II*, (154) pp. 374–5; Jobson, 'A Queen in the Shadows'; Ray, *Edmund of Cornwall*, p. 60.

5. Bappert, *Richard von Cornwall*, pp. 60–1; Denholm-Young, *Richard of Cornwall*, p. 113–4; Weiler, *Henry III of England and the Staufen Empire*, pp. 183, 186. Falkenstein's family, the Bolanden-Hohenfels, held sway over the Rhineland Palatinate region.

6. *Royal Letters II*, pp. 174–5; *CR, 1261–64*, p. 126; Page, 'Cornwall, Earl Richard, and the Barons' War', pp. 27–30. In his letter, Richard addresses Henry with much flourish and formality. 'To the magnificent prince, lord and dear brother, Henry, by the grace of God, king of England, lord of Ireland, and duke of Aquitaine, Richard, by the same grace, king of the Romans, ever August, greetings and ever increasing brotherly love and devotion.'

7. *Gervase II*, p. 215; *Mayors and Sheriffs*, p. 53; Bappert, *Richard von Cornwall*, pp. 62–4; Rollason, 'From Tintagel to Aachen: Richard of Cornwall and the Power of Place', pp. 13–5. During his third trip to Germany, Richard conferred the regency of young Count Floris V, son of William of Holland, to the boy's aunt, who was Alice d'Avesnes, William's sister and widow of John, the man Richard owed the most for his enthronement.

8. *CR, 1261–64*, pp. 175–6; *Gervase II*, p. 219; Bappert, *Richard von Cornwall*, pp. 64–6, 67–9. *Flores II* (p. 403) says Richard came home because he had 'exhausted all his treasure in Germany', adding the judgement that 'good issues seldom wait on sordid gain'.

9. *Gervase II*, pp. 215–6; *Dunstable*, p. 219; *Tewkesbury*, p. 169; Treharne, *Baronial Plan of Reform*, pp. 285–6.

10. *Royal Letters II*, pp. 242–3; *Foedera I*, p. 416; *Gervase II*, pp. 217, 218, 219; *Mayors and Sheriffs*, pp. 54–5; *Dunstable*, p. 220; Carpenter, *Reign of Henry III*, pp. 253–9; Baker, *Simon de Montfort*, pp. 143–4.

11. *Royal Letters II*, p. 158; *Gervase II*, pp. 219–21; *Dunstable*, pp. 221–2; *Wykes*, pp. 133–34; *Mayors and Sheriffs*, p. 56. In his statement before Queen Margaret at the arbitration in 1262, Simon recalled how Richard intervened for him in 1239. See Baker, *Simon de Montfort*, p. 227. The spiritual leader of the Montfortians, Walter Cantilupe (and his family) had a long history of royal service that he exploited to become the bishop of Worcester in 1236. As a firm believer in pluralism, he opposed papal preferment on economic principle. The more benefices in foreign hands, the less for him, his family and friends. The Montfortian bishops who were later ordered to seek absolution in Rome were Richard Gravesend of Lincoln, Henry Sandwich of London, Stephen Berksted of Chichester, and John Gervais of Winchester. It is notable that all four received their dioceses during the reform period. Three other bishops–Durham, Ely and Salisbury–were indicted for similar transgressions in the king's court.

12. *CPR, 1259–66*, p. 279; *Royal Letters II*, p. 248; *Gervase II*, pp. 221–3; *Dunstable*, pp. 222–4; *Wykes*, pp. 134–36; *Flores II*, pp. 404–08; *Mayors and Sheriffs*, pp. 56–8. Boniface did not return until 1265. The other prelates attacked were Peter

d'Aigueblanche, the bishop of Hereford, and Simon Walton of Norwich, who had helped procure Henry's papal absolution from his oath to the Provisions.

13. *CPR, 1259–66*, pp. 269–70; *Royal Letters II*, p. 247; *CPL I*, p. 402; *Foedera I*, pp. 428–9; *Gervase II*, pp. 222, 231; *Dunstable*, pp. 223–4; *Wykes*, p. 135; *Flores II*, p. 406; *Rishanger*, p. 18; Denholm-Young, *Richard of Cornwall*, p. 122. The existence of these Germans fighting against Henry comes from two papal letters issued on 27 November 1263 (*CPL I*, pp. 397–8). Simon also received his own letter from the pope (*CPL I*, p. 396) naming him among the chief disturbers of the realm and ordering him to work for the restoration of Henry's authority. He too ignored the holy father.

14. *CPR, 1259–66*, pp. 273, 291, 296, 357; *Royal Letters II*, pp. 251–2; *DBM*, pp. 282–7; *Regesta Imperii II*, p. 1014 (5426–8); *Gervase II*, pp. 229–31; *Dunstable*, pp. 225–6; *Wykes*, pp. 137–8; *Flores II*, pp. 409–10; Rishanger, *De Bellis*, p. 17; Denholm-Young, *Richard of Cornwall*, p. 54; Treharne, *Baronial Plan of Reform*, pp. 327–33; Cox, *Eagles of Savoy*, pp. 363–4. The disputed lands in Switzerland were part of the Kyburg inheritance. Hartmann the Young had died in September of 1263, leaving behind an only child, a daughter Anne, whose guardian was Rudolf. Peter was the protector of his sister Marguerite of Savoy, whose husband Hartmann the Old was the uncle of Hartmann the Young and who was content to side with his Savoyard in-laws.

8 War and Imprisonment

1. *DBM*, pp. 252–91; *Dunstable*, p. 227; *Gervase II*, p. 232; *Wykes*, pp. 138–9. The Montfortians have been seen as foolish for accepting arbitration in the first place, knowing

that Louis was under pressure from the sister queens Margaret and Eleanor of Provence, as well as the pope, to rule against them. What they were after, and needed, was breathing space, a way to break up Henry's momentum. They even contrived an escape clause for their oaths, which they expected to break, by arguing that to deny the Provisions of Oxford was to deny Magna Carta. Louis saw the trap and specifically said his ruling had no effect on any charters issued before 1258. The Montfortians freely interpreted that as a validation of Magna Carta, which in their reasoning validated the Provisions of Oxford too.

2. *CPR, 1259–66*, pp. 305–06; *CR, 1261–64*, pp. 334–5; *Gervase II*, pp. 232–3; *Dunstable*, p. 227; *Flores II*, p. 410; Carpenter, 'A Noble in Politics: Roger Mortimer', pp. 183–201; Stewart, 'Simon de Montfort and His Followers, June 1263', pp. 966–7.

3. *CPR, 1259–66*, pp. 307, 308; *Gervase II*, p. 234; *Wykes*, pp. 140–1; *Flores II*, p. 411; *Mayors and Sheriffs*, p. 65; Rishanger, *De Bellis*, p. 22; *Dunstable*, p. 228; *Robert of Gloucester*, pp. 363–6. Henry's nephew (Richard's son?) Roger de Meuland, the bishop of Coventry and Lichfield, still adhered to the king and was one of his proctors in the negotiations with Simon and his bishops.

4. *Gervase II*, pp. 235–6; *Wykes*, pp. 141–7; *Flores II*, p. 411; *Mayors and Sheriffs*, pp. 65–6; Rishanger, *De Bellis*, pp. 23–6; *Dunstable*, pp. 229–31; *Battle*, pp. 200–01. The insurgents included Welsh archers; the number of condemned was reported as high as 315, although ten times less is a more likely figure (*Wykes*, pp. xxx, 147–8).

5. *Gervase II*, p. 236; *Wykes*, pp. 141–7; *Flores II*, p. 414–6; *Mayors and Sheriffs*, pp. 67–9; Rishanger, *De Bellis*, p. 30.

6. *CPR, 1258–66*, p. 317; *Gervase II*, p. 237; *Wykes*, pp. 149–51; *Flores II*, pp. 416–8; *Dunstable*, p. 232; Wright, *Political*

Songs, p. 70; Blaauw, *Barons' War*, p. 353; Carpenter, *Battles of Lewes and Evesham*, pp. 26–34.

7. *Melrose*, pp. 216–9; *Mayors and Sheriffs*, p. 67; *Flores II*, pp. 433–4; *Robert of Gloucester*, p. 368 (824–8, 837).

8. *CPR, 1258–66*, pp. 345, 372, 394; *CR, 1261–64*, p. 396; *Foedera I*, p. 448; *Gervase II*, p. 242; *Melrose*, p. 219; *Wykes*, pp. 152–7; *Flores II*, pp. 420–3; *Dunstable*, pp. 233–4; *Robert of Gloucester*, pp. 368–9 (839–88); *Mayors and Sheriffs*, pp. 71–3; Maddicott, *Simon de Montfort*, p. 324. The bishops put up surety of 20,000 marks (£13,333) for Henry of Almain's return (*Foedera I*, p. 446). He went right back to Kenilworth after the failure of negotiations.

9. *CR, 1264–68*, pp. 84–9; *DBM*, pp. 301–05; *Mayors and Sheriffs*, pp. 76–7; *Flores*, p. 424; Wright, *Political Songs*, pp. 69–71; *Song of Lewes*, p. 41 (387). Powicke, *King Henry III and the Lord Edward*, p. 490; Wilkinson, *Household Roll of Eleanor de Montfort*, pp. 20, 34, 36, 37, 112.

10. *CPR, 1258–66*, pp. 425, 528; *Royal Letters II*, p. 291; *Oxendes*, pp. 227–9; *Flores*, pp. 436–8; *Wykes*, pp. 144, 162–74; *Mayors and Sheriffs*, pp. 78–80; *Dunstable*, p. 239; *Waverley*, pp. 361–5; *Robert of Gloucester*, pp. 371–5 (975–1217), Bémont, *Simon de Montfort*, p. 252; Wilkinson, *Eleanor de Montfort*, pp. 102–3. The negotiations for Richard's release were conducted by the bishops of Worcester and Coventry. Walter Cantilupe had stood by Simon to the bitter end, while Roger de Meuland remained loyal to Henry throughout (*CPR, 1258–66*, p. 307). Since Richard had been deprived of his seal, their seals were used to attest his letter.

11. *CPR, 1258–66*, pp. 450, 453, 454, 470, 495; *Royal Letters II*, pp. 294–6; *CPL II*, pp. 419, 435; *Wykes*, pp. 175, 178–9, 185–6; *Mayors and Sheriffs*, pp. 80–4, 88–9; *Flores II*, pp. 442–3; *Robert of Gloucester*, p. 376 (1226–38); *Oxendes*,

pp. 232–3; Lunt, *Financial Relations*, pp. 294–313; Lewis, 'The Election of Richard of Cornwall as Senator of Rome in 1261', p. 660. The younger Simon had passed through Winchester only two months earlier on his way to his father's aid with troops he raised in London. Lacking money to pay them, he turned the Londoners, who had an ancient rivalry with Winchester, loose on the city and on the Jewish community in particular (*Mayors and Sheriffs*, p. 78).

12. *CPR, 1258–66*, pp. 416, 460, 493–4; *Wykes*, pp. 145, 180–2; *Waverley*, pp. 367–8; *Rishanger*, pp. 41–3; Knowles, *The Disinherited*, pp. (II) 27, (III) 23; Denholm-Young, *Richard of Cornwall*, p. 132. The king's clerk was Thomas Piwelesdone, whose career under Henry included appointment as one of his proctors to the court of Louis IX in 1261 (*CPR, 1258–66*, p. 189). He and the mayor were accused of inciting the mob during the disturbances and were imprisoned by the king and Edward after coming to Windsor under safe-conduct in October of 1265. On 23 December 1269, he and 56 other Londoners were permanently banished from the city (*Mayors and Sheriffs*, pp. 83, 119, 125–6, 155).

13. *CPR, 1258–66*, pp. 530, 582, 613–4; *CChR 1257–1300*, p. 99; *Calendar of Inquisitions Post Mortem*, p. 201 (638); *Royal Letters II*, p. 291; *Mayors and Sheriffs*, pp. 85–7; *Peerage IX*, pp. 546–7; Denholm-Young, *Richard of Cornwall*, p. 134; Roche, *The King of Almayne*, p. 221. Like William de Furnival, Adam Newmarket had been captured at Northampton in April of 1264. Both were imprisoned at Windsor along with Simon the younger and so missed the battle of Lewes. Newmarket was also captured during Edward's raid on Kenilworth and so missed Evesham as well.

14. *CPR, 1258–66*, pp. 517–8; 656, 664; *Flores II*, pp. 411, 444; *Wykes*, pp. 160, 188–9; *Dunstable*, pp. 224, 235, 241;

Mayors and Sheriffs, p. 91; *Robert of Gloucester*, p. 377 (1287–1314).

15. *CPR, 1258–66*, pp. 635, 637, 664, 671–2, 677; *CPR, 1266–72*, p. 257; *CR, 1333–37*, p. 561; *DBM*, pp. 317–37; *Flores II*, pp. 444–5; *Wykes*, pp. 191, 194–5; *Dunstable*, pp. 242–4; *Mayors and Sheriffs*, pp. 93–4; *Waverley*, pp. 371–2; *Robert of Gloucester*, pp. 378–80 (1335–68, 1377–1423); Rishanger, *De Bellis*, p. 56; Knowles, *The Disinherited*, pp. (III) 66, 71; Powicke, *King Henry III*, pp. 552–4. A special class of redemption of seven years was reserved for Ferrers and the leaders in Kenilworth who cut off the hand of one of Henry's messengers. For landless rebels, the redemption applied to their goods. Rebels with neither land nor goods had to find sureties for their good behaviour. To spare those who like Richard, Henry of Almain and Roger Mortimer had a hand in bringing Simon to power the first time around in 1263, the start of the rebellion in legal terms was fixed to the fall of Northampton on 5 April 1264. Gilbert de Clare and others who took up arms against the king after that date were given pardons. Gilbert de Gaunt received a pardon in 1268 and died six years later.

9 Bringing Peace to Two Kingdoms

1. *Wykes*, p. 118; *Robert of Gloucester*, p. 378 (1357–68). The priest was named Philip Porpeis and acted as the surgeon of the garrison, as well as, no doubt, the clown.

2. *CPR, 1266–72*, p. 34; *Regesta Imperii II*, p. 1016 (5435); *Regesta Imperii III*, pp. 1468–9 (9520), 1485 (9680), 1490 (9729); *Regesta Imperii IV*, pp. 1759–60 (11998). Henry of Almain was reimbursed £100 for his travel expenses to Rome (*CLR, 1267–72*, p. 88).

3. *CPR, 1266–72*, pp. 55, 70–3, 87, 143, 144-5, 285; *Dunstable*, pp. 230, 244–7; *Wykes*, pp. 196–206, 219; *Tewkesbury*,

pp. 179–80; *Flores II*, pp. 446–8; *Mayors and Sheriffs*, pp. 94–100; *Osney*, p. 209; *Robert of Gloucester*, p. 380 (1426–54); Ray, *Edmund of Cornwall*, p. 30. The henchman, John Fitz-John, was the son of John Fitz-Geoffrey and the most senior Montfortian to survive Evesham. According to Wykes (p. 141), he personally killed the most distinguished Jew in London, Kok, the son of Abraham, during the slaughter of 9 April 1264.

Pope Clement was furious over the recent disturbance and doubled Gilbert's security to £13,333. He also ordered him to either hand over his daughter to the queen or his castle of Tonbridge to his uncle Henry of Almain to hold, in either case for three years. Henry remitted these two forms of securities on 16 July 1268, but not the money (*CPR, 1266–72*, p. 246).

4. *CPR, 1266–72*, p. 151; *Royal Letters II*, pp. 312–4; *Foedera I*, p. 474; *Wykes*, pp. 210–2; *Flores II*, pp. 446–8; *Mayors and Sheriffs*, p. 100; *Robert of Gloucester*, p. 380 (1426–54).

5. *CPR, 1266–72*, p. 34; *CR, 1264–68*, p. 407; *Regesta Imperii III*, p. 1509 (9907); *Wykes*, pp. 222–3, 225; Denholm-Young, *Richard of Cornwall*, p. 139; Runciman, *Sicilian Vespers*, pp. 99–105; Roche, *King of Almayne*, pp. 204, 214. In promising Richard £1,333 worth of land from the Disinherited, Henry factored in the lands that Richard had already received from Adam Newmarket, suggesting their value was probably not more than £1,000.

6. *CPR, 1266–72*, pp. 187, 243, 244, 246; *Mayors and Sheriffs*, pp. 110, 111; *Wykes*, pp. 217–8, 222–4; *Villani*, pp. 228–32.

7. *Villani*, pp. 232–42; *Wykes*, pp. 223–5; *Osney*, p. 224; *Regesta Imperii II*, pp. 1018–21; Runciman, *Sicilian Vespers*, pp. 107–114; Cox, *Eagles of Savoy*, pp. 367–71; Roche, *King of Almayne*, pp. 203–08; Powicke, *King Henry III*, p. 608; Huffman, *Social Politics of Medieval Diplomacy*,

pp. 295–7; Weiler, *Henry III of England and the Staufen Empire*, pp. 188–9; Vincent, *The Holy Blood*, pp. 140, 149. Conradin's chief supporter among the Ghibellines, Alfonso's estranged brother Henry of Castile, was also captured. He spent the next twenty-three years in prison despite appeals from Henry's sister Eleanor, who was Edward's wife. The most Charles would allow the prisoner was a clean cell.

8. *CPR, 1266–72*, pp. 100, 140–1, 323, 336; *Foedera I*, p. 478; *Wykes*, p. 222; *Oxendes*, p. 236; Knowles, *The Disinherited*, pp. (II) 26, (IV) 98–9; Studd, 'The Marriage of Henry of Almain and Constance of Bearn', pp. 161–75; Powicke, *King Henry III*, pp. 524–6. Esquivat, the present count of Bigorre, signed away the county to his great-uncle Simon in 1256 when he found he could no longer defend it from attacks by Gaston. Three years later he joined forces with Gaston to eject Simon's officials.

   In 1265, prior to vacating Dover, Eleanor de Montfort sent her youngest son Richard, then about fourteen years old, to the court of Theobald II of Navarre with her quitclaim to Bigorre. Theobald attempted to occupy the county, but was repulsed by Anglo-Gascon troops. Richard de Montfort disappears from this time, having likely perished in the fighting. see Arancón, 'Ricardo de Montfort al servicio de Teobaldo II de Navarra (1266)', pp. 411–7.

9. *Mayors and Sheriffs*, pp. 115, 121–2; *Waverley*, p. 376; *Dunstable*, p. 252; *Wykes*, pp. 226–7; *Flores II*, p. 450; *Oxendes*, p. 235; *Paris I*, p. 478; Powicke, *King Henry III*, p. 588.

10 The End of Two Reigns

1. *CPL II*, p. 435; *Mayors and Sheriffs*, pp. 116–9, 127, 128–9; *Oxendes*, p. 236; *Wykes*, pp. 228–33; *Gervase II*, pp. 249–50.

2. *Foedera I*, pp. 484, 485; *Mayors and Sheriffs*, pp. 130, 138; *Flores II*, pp. 450–1; Studd, 'The Marriage of Henry of

Almain and Constance of Béarn', p. 176; If the Flores chronicler can be believed, Louis also wanted to enrich himself on 'the spoils of the barbarians'.

3. *CPR, 1266–72,* pp. 591–2, 613, 700; *Foedera I,* p. 487; *Mayors and Sheriffs,* pp. 132–3, 136–7; *Gervase II,* pp. 250–63.

4. *Foedera I,* p. 501; *CChR, 1257–1300,* p. 146; *Mayors and Sheriffs,* pp. 138–40; *Wykes,* pp. 239–45; *Flores II,* p. 452; *Villani,* p. 254; *Robert of Gloucester,* p. 381 (1477–88); *Oxendes,* p. 239; Powicke, 'Guy de Montfort', pp. 82–6; Baddeley, *Cotteswold Shrine,* pp. 57–8.

5. *CPR, 1266–72,* pp. 531, 533, 543–4, 545, 546, 567, 574, 581; *CLR, 1267–72,* p. 154; *Regesta Imperii II,* p. 1023 (5476, 5480); *Mayors and Sheriffs,* p. 146; *Wykes,* pp. 239–44, 246, 247, 248; *Osney,* p. 247, 248; *Flores II,* pp. 452–3; *Florence of Worcester,* p. 207; Carpenter, *Reign of Henry III,* p. 206.

6. *CPR, 1266–72,* pp. 640, 647; 654–5, 657, 668–9; *CPR, 1282–91,* pp. 248; *CChR, 1257–1300,* pp. 324–5, 349; *Osney,* p. 274; Denholm-Young, *Richard of Cornwall,* pp. 152–3; Runciman, *Sicilian Vespers,* pp. 152–5, 183–4; Baddeley, *Cotteswold Shrine,* pp. 38–9, 118; Vincent, *The Holy Blood,* pp. 138, 151–2. Rudolf of Habsburg also moved to exert his authority over Philip of Savoy, who succeeded his brother Peter as the count in 1268. Philip had helped arrange Richard's marriage to Sanchia in 1243 and attended their wedding in England. It was through a petition by Philip of Savoy to Pope Innocent IV in 1248 that we have our only known existence of Richard's illegitimate son Philip of Cornwall (*CPL II,* p. 244). Bringing the empire's weight to bear, Rudolf won his war with Philip, who died in 1285.

7. See Weiler 'Image and Reality in Richard of Cornwall's German Career' for full elaboration of Richard's legacy in Germany following his death.

8. *Annales Monastici*, iv, xxx, translation in Vincent, 'Richard of Cornwall', *ODNB*; Stubbs, *Constitutional History*, pp. 99–100; Ramsay, *Dawn of the Constitution*, p. 277. The works on Richard are from Gebauer (1744), Koch (1888), Bappert (1905), and Lemcke (1909); on Simon from Pauli (1876), Creighton (1877) Prothero (1877), Bateman (1923), and Bémont (1930).

9. *Paris II*, p. 538; *Paris III*, p. 285; Denholm-Young, *Richard of Cornwall*, p. 155; Roche, *The King of Almayne*, p. 217; Weiler, 'Image and Reality in Richard of Cornwall's German Career', pp. 1116–7. Much is made of Richard's son Henry of Almain serving as Simon's deputy steward in October 1260, but Richard could not have known about it before his return. He did know that his son adhered to Simon during the quasi-rebellion in the spring of that year but Richard felt confident that he could leave the realm after it was over.

Appendix 1

1. *Paris I*, pp. 362–8.
2. *Paris III*, pp. 439–40.
3. *Mayors and Sheriffs*, pp. 28–31.
4. My thanks to Professor David Rollason of Durham University for allowing me to use this excerpt from his article 'From Tintagel to Aachen: Richard of Cornwall and the Power of Place'.
5. *Burton*, pp. 466–8. My thanks to Rich Price for providing the first known translation of this remarkable letter.
6. *Mayors and Sheriffs*, pp. 68–9.

INDEX